The Revival of Buddhist Pilgrimage at Bodh Gaya

The Revival of Buddhist Pilgrimage at Bodh Gaya

(1811-1949)

Anagarika Dharmapala and the Mahabodhi Temple

ALAN TREVITHICK

MOTILAL BANARSIDASS PUBLISHERS
PRIVATE LIMITED • DELHI

First Edition: Delhi, 2006

ISBN: 81-208-3107-1

MOTILAL BANARSIDASS
41 U.A. Bungalow Road, Jawahar Nagar, Delhi 110 007
8 Mahalaxmi Chamber, 22 Bhulabhai Desai Road, Mumbai 400 026
203 Royapettah High Road, Mylapore, Chennai 600 004
236, 9th Main III Block, Jayanagar, Bangalore 560 011
Sanas Plaza, 1302 Baji Rao Road, Pune 411 002
8 Camac Street, Kolkata 700 017
Ashok Rajpath, Patna 800 004
Chowk, Varanasi 221 001

Printed in India
BY JAINENDRA PRAKASH JAIN AT SHRI JAINENDRA PRESS,
A-45 NARAINA, PHASE-I, NEW DELHI 110 028
AND PUBLISHED BY NARENDRA PRAKASH JAIN FOR
MOTILAL BANARSIDASS PUBLISHERS PRIVATE LIMITED,
BUNGALOW ROAD, DELHI 110 007

For My Two Sons

CONTENTS

PREFACE

I know Bodh Gaya from several visits I made there in the early-and-mid-1980's. Twice I went there in order to study the history of the modern development of the temple and its surroundings. These visits were sponsored by grants from Harvard University and from the Fulbright Foundation. On a third visit I came, again, to study the temple's recent history, and also to teach, in a semester-abroad program for Antioch College.

In all these cases I was preoccupied by entirely mundane questions, mundane when one recalls that Bodh Gaya is celebrated as the place where. Gautama achieved enlightenment. I was interested in such questions as how the temple came to have its present well-groomed aspect, how many new temples were springing up around the older site, and how many foreign tourists, many of them religious pilgrims, but many of them not, were converging on what could have been simply another small town in Bihar.

How did all of that come to be? In order to answer that, I had to spend more time *away* from Bodh Gaya than in the town itself, in Delhi, Sarnath, Colombo (as a Fulbright Fellow), London (on a Knox Memorial Fellowship), and also in Cambridge, Massachusetts. where I started this research, as a graduate student in social anthropology, at Harvard University.

For several reasons, including 1) the press of non-academic obligations, and 2) a sense that the manuscript did not fit comfortably within the current stylistic or theoretical parameters of social anthropology, I put the project aside for some years. When I took it up again, though, I realized that my treatment of the subjects involved–colonial construction and reconstruction of antiquities, the intersection of religious, national and global identity-formative processes, the operations of autobiographical narrative, the strategies of ecumenicalism–were of natural interest to many social anthropologists. Having said that, this work was always intended to be of interest to a wider audience, and so I can make no sincere apology for making my points economically and with not much reference to rococo ornamentations of basic social theory.

On another subject, I feel I should make some note, in a general way, of current developments at Bodh Gaya. One sees there today a combination of religious, and secular, and political forces–and globalist, and public, and private, and ritual, and psychological–that, to me at any rate, seem quite natural against the background of the narrative I have provided here.

When this or that official accepts newly discovered relics for placement in Bodh Gaya, or when this or that foreign delegation arrives–a mix of monks and ministers, perhaps–or when this or that congregation of citizens arrives for a convention that will negotiate or define or solidify their common interests–then we see Bodh Gaya functioning as a ritual site that brings together religious and secular impulses in ways that echo back to the town's earliest times.

In all of this sort of activity–and in the biography of Anagarika Dharmapala which is so important a part of the current work–we see interesting phenomena. For instance, in the course of one of the more important Mahabodhi Temple legal proceedings, at the end of the nineteenth century, it came to the lawyers and judges involved in the case that it might be important to judge whether or not Dharmapala was or was not involved in "real" religious behavior.

How would we know? How would we know whether someone was, say, in religious contemplation or not? Meditating or not? Praying or not?

The answer, according to the court at the time–this was a British Indian Court but I do not know that anyone has improved on the thinking–was that we could not *know*, absolutely, but that we could only rely on the "outward and visible" *sign* of religious feeling. If people *look* as though they are meditating we must act as though that is indeed the case. Somehow, this is not entirely satisfying, but at the same time the problem it captures is, for me, much of what this book is really about.

Alan Trevithick
State University of
New York at Stony Brook

ACKNOWLEDGEMENTS

The research on which this volume was based was carried out in London, at the India Office Library and the Public Records Office, in New Delhi, at the Indian National Archives and the Nehru Memorial Museum. As well, a good deal of primary data was collected from Anagarika Dharmapala's unpublished notebooks and diaries in Mahabodhi Society archives at Colombo and Sarnath. I thank the Society for its openness and interest in the project.

I wish also to thank the Ven. H. Saddhatissa Nayaka Mahathera, and the Ven. Dodamgoda Rewatha Thera, for their invaluable criticism and encouragement; and H.L. DeAlwis, of the Mahabodhi Society in Colombo, who kindly guided me through the archives there. As well, I wish to thank Mr. N.P. Jain, at MLBD, for his encouragement and guidance through the mysteries of publication. My thanks to Melkana Brakalova Trevithick Laurie Hart, Michael Rhum, Charles Stewart, Jane Trevithick, Liz and Sandy Huntington; and Tara Doyle, for their encouragement. I also want to thank Stephen Kemper and Michael Roberts for their interest in the project and for their generosity. Others who were at various stages interested in this project are Stanley J. Tambiah, Sally Falk Moore, and Nur Yalman, all of the Harvard Anthropology Department.

NOTE ON THE TRANSCRIPTION OF NON-ENGLISH WORDS

This work makes frequent use of Hindi, Sanskrit and Pali words, primarily place names and proper names. Insofar as most of these have been variously rendered by the source documents employed, which span several hundred years, and also because their precise phonetic transcription is irrelevant to an understanding of the material, I have dispensed with diacritical and other phonetic systems and have employed, in my own prose, the current Romanized forms. Within quotations, of course, I have retained archaic and variant forms (sans diacriticals which, in any case, are usually not employed in the various documents).

ABBREVIATIONS

ADC	The Colombo diaries and notebooks of Anagarika Dharmapala
ADS	The Sarnath diaries and notebooks of Anagarika Dharmapala
ADSU	Unmarked Notebook of Anagarika Dharmapala at Sarnath.
AIHMS	All-India Hindu Mahasabha, Texts of Resolutions passed at 21st Session, Calcutta, Dec. 28-30, 1938
AP	Agni Purana
BAC	Buddhist Annual of Ceylon, Colombo
BG	Bhagavata Purana
BIA	British Indian Association-Annual Reports
BTW	Booker T. Washington Papers, University of Illinois, Volume 13 1914-15. www.historyco-operative. org/btw/Vol.13/ html/507.html
CCIC	Curzon Collection, Indian Correspondence
CCIA	Curzon Collection, Indian Archaeology
CCIP	Curzon Collection, Internal Administration Papers
CCOC	Curzon Collection, Indian Correspondence, Original Letters
CCBG	Curzon Collection, Volume 242, Report and Proceedings of a Commission to Budh Gaya
DIB	Government of India, Political Department, Dispatches to India and Bengal
ECCI	Elgin Collection, Correspondence with persons in India
EDBO	Government of Bihar and Orissa, Proceedings of the Education Department
FDPB	Government of India, Foreign Department, Political Branch, Part A

HDPB	Government of India, Home Department, Political Branch
HMBG	Papers in the Bodh Gaya Temple File of the Hindu Mahasabha
HSIAR	The Indian Annual Register, Calcutta
ILR	The Indian Law Reports, Calcutta Series, 1896, Vol.23
IPC	Indian Penal Code, Act XLV of 1860, 1924 Edition, Bombay, Bombay Law Reporter
LCCI	Lansdowne Collection, Correspondence with Persons in India
MBJ	Mahabodhi Journal
MBS	Rules and Regulations of the Mahabodhi Society
MC	Correspondence with Frederick Max Muller (Oxford)
PHDI	Government of India, Proceedings of the Home Department
PJDB	Government of Bengal, Proceedings of the Judicial Department
PGDB	Government of Bengal, Miscellaneous Proceedings of the General Department
TB	"The Buddhist," Colombo
TT	"The Theosophist," Adyar, Madras

Introduction

APPROACHING BODH GAYA

What follows is an account of a dispute, which spanned the period 1874-1949, over the status of the Mahabodhi Temple at Bodh Gaya, in Bihar.[1] The temple is conventionally thought by Buddhists to mark the place where Buddha first achieved enlightenment, and by Hindus to be a monument to "Buddha Dev," a form of the god Vishnu. Therein lay the conflict: was the temple "authentically" either a Buddhist or a Hindu temple? Complicating this basic difficulty was the fact that the British Government of India (GOI), which held the place in what we might call "archaeological" esteem, was anxious about the possibility of religious discord at the site. British anxiety mounted, in 1891, when a Sinhalese pilgrim named Anagarika Dharmapala arrived on the scene: Dharmapala soon made it his business, through his "Mahabodhi Society," to reclaim the temple for all of the world's Buddhists.

These are the basic elements of the dispute, and the present

[1] The most important primary source documents used in this research have been 1) British colonial records, examined at India Office Library, and Public Records Office, in London, and the Indian National Archives in New Delhi, 2) Anagarika Dharmapala's diaries and letters, examined at the Mahabodhi Society Archives in Sarnath and Colombo, and 3) Indian National Congress and Hindu Mahasabha records examined, primarily, at the Nehru Memorial Museum in New Delhi. One secondary source which deserves mention is Guruge's compilation of letters to and from prominent Sinhalese Buddhists: these have allowed me to follow more closely than I would have been otherwise prepared to do the network of contacts that Dharmapala established with monks and with Theosophists and other westerners.

account details the course of the administrative, legal and legislative activities which attended it. While in the main this is intended as a straight historical account of the events at Bodh Gaya, I will also take up some topics of wider social analytical interest, particularly, the "ecumenical" or "encompassment" language and symbolism which developed as a result of negotiations between the concerned parties.

Overall, the challenge will be to provide a coherent account of events that occurred within a complex, dynamic and shifting series of intercultural frames and spheres of political power. My main goal is to present the relevant actors and the traditions and strategies they used to shape the conflict over the status of Bodh Gaya.

The Bodh Gaya Temple: A Buddhist Shrine in Hindu India

The Mahabodhi Temple at Bodh Gaya dates from the early Gupta period–circa fourth century BCE–but has been rebuilt and modified many times, and the identity of the original builder has not been established. Many of the major Buddhist structures in the immediate area, however, are attributed by authorities to Sinhalese patrons, (Cunningham, 1892:42-47; Roerich 1957:xxviii) and it is clear that, through the seventh century, the site was an important pilgrimage center for Buddhists from not only Ceylon, but from as far away as China, Korea and Central Asia (Beal, 1881). The Burmese were particularly attracted to the site and, during the eleventh century two Burmese missions were sent to attempt temple restoration projects (Cunningham, 1892:75-77). There is also a record of a fifteenth century Burmese mission to the area. (Mitra, 1878: 111-12; Stadtner, 1991:39-40)

When the Tibetan translator Dharmasvamin left for Bodh Gaya in 1234, Muslim invasions had, for thirty years, left their mark on North Indian Buddhist institutions and the

Mahabodhi Temple was not spared. Dharmasvamin found the shrine in great disrepair, attended by only a handful of monks (Roerich, 1957:74). When the Tantric Buddhist Dharmasvamin saw, on the door of the temple, an image of Maheshvara, or Siva, he assumed it to be the sign of a protective deity from the Tibetan Buddhist pantheon, a guardian against the intrusion of non-Buddhists. It was just as likely evidence of an increased level of Hindu activity at the shrine. Dharmasvamin's confusion points, at once, to a close, historical relationship between Hinduism and Buddhism and, to the potential for conflict to arise as a result of different interpretations of commonly held symbolic properties.

We do know that, after Dharmasvamin's visit, the site ceased to be at the center of an active Buddhist cult. I use the phrase "active cult" in order to specify that there had been at Bodh Gaya for some time no Buddhist *institutional* presence. It is unlikely that individual Buddhists have ever ceased completely to visit the Buddhist holy sites in India. One finds occasional evidence of this in the dispatches sent back to England from Bengal. For instance: "Two Buddhist priests who arrived at Darjeeling from Thibet permitted to proceed on a pilgrimage to the Ganges and to visit the temples in Nepaul on their homeward journey." (FDPB, 1878, Oct.1, No. 38) Nevertheless, in time, Buddhist institutions disappeared completely from the site and it became, eventually, a significant Hindu religious property. It is important, in order to understand the course of the modern history of the place, to analyze some features of this "Hinduization."

Elements of a Hindu Mode for the Encompassment of Distinctions

I will discuss in more depth, in chapter one, the Hindu

monastic group that had been resident for centuries at Bodh Gaya, when non-Indian Buddhist began to renew their interest in the site in the nineteenth century, For now, however, I want to point out that the Hindu appropriation of the Mahabodhi Temple depended not only on claims of a purely proprietary sort, but also on an encompassing ideological apparatus. To begin, from a mythological perspective there is a Hindu mythological account of the partial destruction of the Mahabodhi temple which attributes it, not to invading armies, but to the combined efforts of the Hindu godly triumvirate of Vishnu, Brahma and Siva. Bodh Gaya and its environs are further sacralized in some Hindu traditions, as sites of preaching by famous Hindu scholars and sages. (Mitra, 1878:10-14; Vidyarthi, 1961:61)

At a more concrete level, we find that many Hindu shrines in the area are either converted Buddhist temples or constructed with materials, including unmodified statuary and carving, from Buddhist temples. (Beglar, 1887:116) Immediately in front of the Mahabodhi temple, and within the temple compound itself, is a series of small shrines thought by local Hindus to contain images of the five Pandavas, the heroes of Mahabharata. In fact, the images were probably originally created to represent Buddhist figures (Jaques, 1979:13).

One often sees, at Bodh Gaya and elsewhere, the relegation of Buddha to the status of Vishnu's ninth reincarnational form, or avatar. This absorption of the Buddha into the Hindu pantheon has a history, and it seems to mark a shift from an ancient polemics that cast the Buddha into the roles of fraudulent ascetic and heretic.

The Vaishnava reformulation–referring to those Hindus who uphold the primacy of the god Vishnu–accepted the Buddha as an avatar, a form of Vishnu "sent to destroy enemies of the Vaisnavas from within." (Klostermaier, 1979:65; Mitra, 1878:18)

One sees this process of encompassment at work in a number of ritual traditions that feature both Buddhist and Hindu elements (Chakravarti, 1956).

There has been at Bodh Gaya for many years, and still today, for instance, concurrent *Hindu* worship of both Vedic gods and Buddhist Bodhisattvas. The main *Buddhist* view is that a circumambulation of the Bodhi-tree is a sacred commemoration of the Buddha's enlightenment. Hindus visit it to make offerings of rice cakes to their ancestors (Vidyarthi, 1961:24-25).

So, these attitudes, beliefs, and practices are central to what I have dubbed a Hindu mode of encompassment. I employ the term as a convenience, and with no claims for any conceptual innovation. The relevant ground has been well-covered by Dumont and others, who have observed the methods whereby Hinduism has been able to efficiently absorb distinct, even hostile, traditions. It is, however, worth considering how it is that the "differentness" of Buddhism has been articulated by Hindus. "In the hierarchical scheme a group's acknowledged differentness whereby it is contrasted with other groups becomes the very principle whereby it is integrated into society" (Dumont, 1966:191).

It seems apparent that this principle underlies the particular manner of the Hindu mythological absorption of the Buddha figure as an avatar: the Buddhism's assault on Brahmanical theology, its radical "differentness," is not merely accommodated to the Brahmanical system, it is in fact *made necessary* to the maintenance of it.

Clearly, then, the mode of Hindu encompassment of the Bodh Gaya site, and of Buddhism more generally, structured the opportunities for Buddhists to mount a campaign for control of the temple. Throughout this campaign, the Buddhists confronted the curious problem that their tradition, which they were obliged in many instances to represent as opposed to Hinduism, had been transformed, in the general Hindu view, into a subordinate segment of a greater Hindu tradition.

Now, in the nineteenth century, non-Indian Buddhists, and particularly the "Mahabodhi Society," which claimed to represent the interests of this large collection of different Buddhist populations, were determined not only to regain the temple, but also to somehow "re-establish" Buddhism in India.

Not surprisingly, these Buddhists would frequently feel frustrated as they encountered, in India, such statements as the following: 1) "Buddha himself is a follower of the religion of the Hindus," 2) "the Hindus themselves [are] followers of the Buddha, and 3) "The [ancient] Ceylon Bhikshus who lived in the [Mahabodhi] temple were Hindus of the Buddhist (or, more properly, of the Vaishnava) sect" ("Maitreya," 1925: 7,44).

Fundamentally, these statements amount to an assertion that Buddhism was never really established in India, that it cannot, therefore, have disappeared, and, finally, that it cannot, logically, be re-established.

This sort of rhetoric arises as the product of an ideology of encompassment. In the case at hand, the Hindu mode of encompassment shaped many of the strategies and responses of the actors in the Mahabodhi temple dispute, and specific examples of this process will be examined in detail throughout the course of the narrative which follows.

British Archaeologists and Ethnographers at Bodh Gaya

I have discussed the avatar formula whereby the figure of the Buddha is conventionally appropriated by Hinduism. This same formula is a central feature of the first inscription from Bodh Gaya to be translated, in 1788, by a European scholar, Charles Wilkens. The inscription was noticed by an employee of the East India Company, the "Collector of Gaya" Mr. Wilmot, in 1785, and he directed some un-named Pandit to transcribe the passage. The author refers to Buddha as "a portion of Narayan," that is to say, the Buddha avatar of Vishnu (Mitra, 1878:201-202).

Hamilton-Buchanan, during his tour of the area, came to the following conclusion: "I have no doubt...that this inscription is modern, and was composed by some person of the sect of Vishnu." (Hamilton-Buchanan, in Mitra, 1878:203-204). Indeed, the stone from which the inscription was taken has never been seen again, and the only transcript is in Roman transliteration. Also, apparently, a host of internal problems combine to make it, at least thus far, impossible to assign the inscription a solid date.[2]

---

[2] Mitra regarded the inscription as suspect on a number of grounds, including 1) that Amara Sinha, the counselor of Vikramaditya, who was a good Buddhist and a renowned scholar, would not have called Buddha by such names as "Hari, Vishnu, Brahma, the destroyer of the demon Keshi,"etc, 2) that Amara was a Kayastha, a scribe, with the surname Sinha, while the Amara Deva title of the inscription seems to indicate that he was a Brahmin or a Kshatriya, 3) that the putative date of the inscription, Vikramaditya 1005 = AD949, suggests that the script would have been Kutila: "if so, it is difficult to conceive how either Mr. Wilmot or Sir Charles Wilkens could read it, as the key to that alphabet had not then been discovered." (Mitra, 1878:205) As well, the writer/or transcriber had worked in all manner of references to features, such as the "Buddhapad" temple in front of the main shrine, the Panch Pandu Shrine, etc, that post-date the year AD949. In the event, Mitra seems to think that the Pandit who was commissioned to transcribe the inscription either made it all up, or embroidered freely enough so that the composition has no historical value at all:

For now, the primary value of the inscription is to illustrate how, immediately upon their being made aware of the site, the British were confronted with questions that involved competing claims to the sacred space at Bodh Gaya, and competing versions of sacred history. I would like, however, to draw the reader's particular attention to Hamilton-Buchanan's suspicion that "certain persons have imagined the followers of the Buddha to be a branch of the sect of Vishnu." This is an early British reaction to an element of the Hindu mode of encompassment: almost a century later one of Curzon's advisors referred to the Buddh-avatar formula as "one of the most extraordinary perversions of which the Brahmin mind has been capable" (CCIC, Vol 1:76).

If the first epigraphical probe into Bodh Gaya had produced evidence of religious "confusion," the first British ethnographic venture there was consciously undertaken, in part, in order to collect intelligence on precisely this subject. A Scotsman from Edinburgh, Francis Hamilton-Buchanan, on whose reports I have extensively relied, was sent out into Bihar with orders from the Government of Bengal to

---

> While I am writing this I have before me an official letter, in which a pandit is reported to have read the legend of an old Kanouj coin to be Ramarama, of which not a syllable is to be found on the coin, the legend being Srimad Gangeya Deva. At the close of the last century such attempts to impose upon foreigners was greatly more common, and notable instances of it are offered by the forgeries committed by Colonel Wilford's pandits. (Mitra, 1878:206)

Francis Wilford was an officer of engineers, as were so many of the early antiquarians, epigraphers and archaeologists, and had, by over-reliance on his Pandits, committed a number of famous blunders. Cunningham, referring to his "wild speculations," managed, nevertheless, the somewhat ameliorative statement that "his judgement was not equal to his learning." (Cunningham, 1972 [1871]:II)

conduct as complete an ethnographic survey as possible.[3] Certain of the features he was directed to examine are as follows:

> Religion: the number, the progress, and the most remarkable customs of each sect or tribe of which the population consists; together with the emoluments and powers which their priests and chiefs enjoy; and what circumstances exist or may possibly arise that might attach them to the Government, or render them disaffected. (Hamilton-Buchanan,1937:ii)

Hamilton-Buchanan found, as explained, no Buddhist institutional presence, though he did find that the Hindu Giri Mahant "continued to harbour and support one of his Sannyasis," renunciants, who had been converted to Buddhism some years prior by Burmese pilgrims. The new convert "now altogether rejects the doctrines of the orthodoxy." (Hamilton-Buchanan, 1937:140)

This bespeaks a level of Buddhist activity at the site, albeit not much, and a level of Buddhist-Hindu comity, that some later British officials were loathe to accept. One of these, for instance, complained that there is "no complete account" of the place," and that Buchanan had confined himself to

---

[3] Hamilton-Buchanan, originally simply Buchanan, had been assigned, in 1807, with the daunting task of carrying out a "statistical survey of the Bengal Presidency." Such information as I have set forth accredited to Martin (1838) is largely the result of Hamilton-Buchanan's labors. Cunningham was outraged by the Martin's manner of appropriating another man's work. To Martin "we certainly owe the publication of this valuable work; but I must confess that the warmth of my gratitude for this welcome service is absolutely frozen by the coolness of appropriation displayed on the title page, where the name of Buchanan is entirely omitted." (Cunningham, 1972 [1871]:IV)

"what he had heard of its history from a pervert."[4] (FDPB, Feb.1878, no.135) This is but one example among many of the British Indian anxiety that religious groups be kept separate, definable, bounded, and easily managed.

Hamilton-Buchanan further found no evidence, at Bodh Gaya, of anything immediately liable to render folk there disaffected. He did, however, relay the information that certain priests—Gayawal Brahmins—at the larger town of Gaya, seemed unusually conservative and xenophobic. This contributed, no doubt, to the British belief that Gaya District was a center of stubborn orthodoxy.

Hamilton-Buchanan had not been sent out with any archaeological warrant—as yet there was no developed Company policy on the subject—but he did broadly characterize the state of the ancient and modern structures in the area. Gaya rather reminded the Scotsman of his home town: "The streets are narrow, crooked and dirty," he wrote, and, "in walking through the town, precautions are necessary as formerly in Edinburgh. The passenger must call out to prevent inundation from above."

Contemporary experience in Gaya recalled an experience "formerly in Edinburgh," and helped to place Gaya within a familiar and comfortable developmental sequence. The larger town of Gaya, to Hamilton-Buchanan, seemed have been built up out of an ancient rubble. Of the structures there, he wrote that "in a great measure they are composed evidently of ruins." (Hamilton-Buchanan, 1925:40-41)

Of the Mahabodhi temple at Bodh Gaya, Hamilton-

[4] Hamilton-Buchanan's 1811 report on a conversation with "Sorujugiri, a learned Dasnami of Buddh Gya" is interesting. Soruju claimed that "none ought to be admitted as Sannyasis but Brahmans, Kshatriyas and Vaisyas," that is to say, those from the "twice-born castes," and, "in this district no Sudras are admitted." On the other hand, Soruju also testified that the Dasnamis "give Upades [ordination] to all castes. (Hamilton-Buchanan, 1925:38-39)

Buchanan wrote that "almost every part of the Mondir [Mandir-temple] is rapidly hastening to decay, except the northern and western sides of the terrace, which have [been] very recently repaired by a Maratah chief." This was the terrace of the Bodhi-tree, which was said by the Hindus with whom Hamilton-Buchanan talked to have been "planted by Brahma." In 1811, the pipal itself was "a fine tree in full vigour." (Hamilton-Buchanan, 58-59)

A decade later, Mackenzie, the first Surveyor-General of India,[5] received a report from one of his staff of Pandits that "much of this temple is still standing," which is, of course, to say that much of it had fallen. At least one of the Buddha figures from the shrine had been "carried away by the Bairagis [Shaivites] of this place, who keep it in their convent." The Pandit was told that, in the upper stories of the temple there had been perhaps "a lakh of small, elegant images and vases," but that they had either been "destroyed by time," or "removed by the Bairagis, and some carried off by English gentlemen." (Mackenzie, 1820:74)

Bits and pieces of the temple had been carried off, no doubt, by a variety of persons for a very long time, but it was not until 1847 that "English gentlemen" began to consider organizing the removal of antiquities in the manner we think of as early modern archaeology. In fact, until this time, when Captain Markham Kittoe[6] was appointed to the part-time

[5] Mackenzie (1753-1821), another surveyor for Bengal, was, like Cunningham, a great collector, specializing in coins, manuscripts, and inscriptions. He is said to have moved about "with a host of Pandits." (Imam, 1966: 17) The Jain Pandit who gave him the report on Gaya was a South Indian, and, indeed, most of Mackenzie's work had been in the south.

[6] Kittoe was made "Archaeological Enquirer" in 1847, "in accordance with detailed suggestions from Lord Hardinge...the Court of Directors gave a liberal sanction to certain arrangements for examining, delineating, and recording some of the chief antiquities of India." In fact, the sanction could not have been very liberal: Kittoe's various other duties, which included

post of "Archaeological Inquirer," (Imam, 1968:48) archaeology was the poor cousin of the more well-nourished and established orientalism of the Asiatic Society. As the following indicates, the Mahabodhi temple was a central property in the new concern for Indian antiquities.

> We have recently had presented to us, by Captain Kittoe...drawings of sculptures at Boodh Gaya, of considerable interest. He has offered to collect for our museum, remains of such as may throw light on the ancient history of the Country. (GOIPDD, Vol.54, item 731, #25 of Dec. 29, 1847)

Kittoe, however, overworked and in poor health, was unable to complete either his archaeological research or to undertake any collections. In 1848, Alexander Cunningham, a military man but one with deep interests in Indian antiquities, proposed the establishment of a more thorough survey. (Cunningham, 1848:535-36)

Major-General Sir Alexander Cunningham (1814-1893) began his Indian career as a 2nd Lt. in the Bengal Engineers, retiring in 1846. (Imam, 1966:3) He was a close associate of James Prinsep (1799-1840), who in many ways might more

---

designing the Sanskrit College at Benares, in combination with a manic devotion to duty, kept Kittoe so constantly occupied that he soon lost his health. He was, according to Cunningham, rather like James Prinsep, the pioneering epigrapher, often "off kedgeree," and overly devoted to both work and avocational pursuits. Of Kittoe, a friend observed that, on his final trip back to England, in 1853, "he went straight to his home and died."

"Like Prinsep he sank from overwork, and at about the same age." (Cunningham, 1972 [1871]: XVI,XXVI-II) Mitra says that Kittoe only contributed one paper for us, again on the sculpture, but that "on his death his papers were dispersed and no use could be made of them. (Mitra 1878:2) Tantalizingly, Cunningham mentions a letter from Prinsep in which the latter claims to have in his possession "a beautifully illustrated journal from poor Kittoe."(1837) (Cunningham, 1972[1871]:xxiv-xxvi)

properly than Alexander be called the "father" of Indian Archaeology. Cunningham's activities, and the intersection of these with the Burmese Mission of 1874, is addressed in detail in chapter two.

Bodh Gaya was a key property in the development of Indian archaeology: the ideological weight of this became salient in the form of a British conviction that, if much of India was an ancient rubble, much of that rubble had been the material of a Buddhist golden age from which contemporary India had declined. This was the sort of thing that provided for British imperialists—be they viceroys or collectors—a morally compelling rationale for being in India in the first place.

Anagarika Dharmapala, A "Buddhist" Pilgrim at Bodh Gaya

Modern Bodh Gaya can be regarded as a latent ground for action based on pan-Buddhist sensitivities: it is one of four places mentioned in the *Mahaparinibbana Sutta*, one of the most ancient of Buddhist texts, that a faithful practitioner should regard, and is encouraged to visit, with "feelings of awe and reverence." (MPNS, 5.16-20) Yet it must also be said that, for at least six hundred years, Bodh Gaya was a Buddhist site in an area of Hindu India where no Buddhists were resident and where very few Buddhists ever visited. It was only after the Sinhalese religious activist Anagarika Dharmapala arrived on the scene that the place began to enjoy any great modern popularity in the imagination of any Buddhist population. Thus, Dharmapala will be an important figure in this narrative, as the individual who more than anyone else amplified the temple conflict to a degree never previously achieved, and in the process brought the temple fully into modernity.

Much of Dharmapala's story will unfold in the course of the main narrative, and I have also provided an appendix, detailing aspects of his life not covered on the main text, but, for now, one crucial point: Dharmapala seems to have began his adult life not as a conventional Sinhalese Buddhist, but as an adherent of that interesting and peculiar western import called "Theosophy." This robustly occult movement was central in shaping Dharmapala's mission and its outcome.

Briefly, the Theosophical Society—examined in some detail at a later point—was founded in order to develop an intercultural and ecumenical network of believers in the existence of "perfected masters," spiritual adepts who operated in an unbounded "esoteric" manner beyond the boundaries of named and "exoteric" traditions.

I myself cannot see that there is anything very Buddhist about Theosophy, but Dharmapala for some time, and perhaps until the end of his life, thought there might be. He was not always sure. At any rate, Theosophical sympathizers in Asia, Europe and North America were important to Dharmapala, and this network—very eclectic it was—provided him with a number of significant supporters and benefactors.

Pilgrimage and the Pilgrim: New memories

As the anthropologist Victor Turner put it, early pilgrimage sites and circuits "in all the major religions were highly consonant with both the social and religious systems which in some measure they served to maintain." That is to say, they were exemplary of the bounded sociocultural domains that produced them. They functioned, in particular systems, to replicate and strengthen those very same systems. On the other hand, claimed Turner, *modern* pilgrimage is "increasingly, not integrated into a wider sociocultural system." (Turner, 1978:39; Turner, 1974:171-72)

This insight may work well even for the Islamic world which has, in recent times for instance, given us some ideologues who might happily use the *Haj*—and with regard to *Haj*, of course, pilgrimage is far more a duty of every able-bodied individual believer than it is elsewhere, and therefore arguably a more reliable pillar for consensus-building—to construct a totalizing Islamic sociocultural system. But this does not seem to work: no matter how many Muslims go on pilgrimage, they mostly do not, afterwards, go home to *actively* work on Pan-Islamic communitarian schemes. Some do, of course, but most do not.

Pilgrims of whatever ideological stripe may experience, to use another of Turner's concepts, a deep feeling of communion—"communitas," something that is "anti-structural" in the sense of creating an openness to new forms of human connection (Turner, 1969, 1974, 1982)—between Arab and Arab believer, and/or between Arab and Indonesian and Malay and Albanian believer and whomever. But this does not in itself reflect or maintain or create an integrated "Islamic world."

Witness, for instance, the relative satisfaction or even extreme jealousy with which modern Islamic states, like other states, regard their national sovereignty, this in spite of all talk, much of it quite persuasive and plausible, about the artificial and arbitrary divisions created by colonialism.

Not to put too fine a point on it, but if Muslims cannot do it, who can? No doubt people would *like* to feel communitas, but it is hard to move, emotionally, beyond local boundaries, and harder still to move beyond regional boundaries. Perhaps the Islamic word, or some other religiously defined set of populations, will someday successfully institute a pilgrimage that maintains and integrates a very extensive sociocultural domain, but I myself think that this idea, like all such—homogenization or globalization theories notwithstanding—is not terribly persuasive.

At any rate, the wider integrative pilgrimage model certainly does not pertain today at Bodh Gaya, because so many Buddhist pilgrims—and tourists, we might say, some of whom are probably thinking about whether or not they are truly pilgrims in a religious sense—are drawn from so many disparate places throughout the world, without, on the other hand, regarding each other—again, we should allow for the emotional pleasure of *communitas*—as members of the same sociocultural system.

This is just part of modernity, this detachment of religion from a total social universe and its transformation into a more private journey, and in the case at hand it is all the more interesting, I think, because, as I shall show, Dharmapala himself was not integrated into any bounded sociocultural "system." In chapters three and four and elsewhere throughout the course of this history, I will have much to say about how Dharmapala, by undertaking the recovery of Buddhist sacred ground, also initiated a personal project, a private project, of constructing an authentic Buddhist identity.

My point now is that, as he did this, he did not have the premodern socially integrative model available to him—in the Buddhist case, of finding a good strong king to feed, house, protect and discipline a community of helpless, non-productive and celibate monks This model, and it is important to underline that it is a *model* and not some uncomplicated and simple sociohistorical fact, is, I think, best explored by Tambiah, in his 1976 work, *World Conqueror, World Renouncer.* In reference to Tambiah's work, Amunagama nicely summarizes the issues, for the colonial period, in the form of a question:

> How did Buddhists, under colonial rule and deprived of the traditional "protector" of the

> religion, transform their ideology and practice of a Buddhist polity? (Amunugama 1985: 699)

Actually, although I recognize that Dharmapala is an important figure in Sinhalese political thinking, I believe his mission in regard to Buddhism was in large part to legitimate its *separation* from "polity" and to bring it into modernity, by using methods of volunteeristic organization, marketing, and public relations. I will explore some of these subjects and also continue to document the nature of British official interest in the site, in chapters three and four.

When Dharmapala first arrived in Bihar, he could see "lying scattered here and there" on the dirt road that led south from Gaya toward the site of Gautama's enlightenment, "broken statues of our Blessed Lord." This was part of the great Buddhist rubble that Hamilton-Buchanan had seen in 1811, and it clearly moved Dharmapala deeply, but, on the other hand, at that time, and for a long time thereafter, he was religiously immersed in Theosophical speculations as much or more than he was in any conventional Buddhist traditions. And, as far as organization went, he had to be innovative, again on the Theosophical model, a modern model, of lecture circuits, private donations, and public relations initiatives: this is not Dharma on the royal patronage model at all, but religion as it tends to appear in the free-market cafeteria.

Confrontations, Negotiations, Accommodations

The remainder of the narrative is, in large part, an examination of how, in legal, executive, and legislative spheres, Hindus, British authorities, and Buddhists pursued their preferred solutions to the problem of how to allocate the sacred space at Bodh Gaya. In chapter five, for instance,

I take up the subject of the long legal proceedings that were initiated by Dharmapala in 1894, and which tested, one against the other many of the interests and claims I have described thus far.

In chapters six and seven, I review another form of intervention into the situation at Bodh Gaya, this an executive thrust from the Government of India under the direction of Lord Curzon, another of the several remarkable persons who were instrumental in shaping the conflict. In the course of this narrative it becomes clear, I think, how difficult a task it was for either the British or for Dharmapala's Mahabodhi Society to engage usefully in any direct confrontation with the Hindu apparatus of encompassment.

Chapters eight and nine document a period, from 1910 until shortly after independence, when government had for a time withdrawn from the conflict, and during which the Mahabodhi Society, particularly after Dharmapala's death, largely abandoned its confrontational tactics in favor of a strategy that emphasized the close historical relations or "inheritors of one great Aryan tradition." between the two traditions. "Buddhists" and "Hindus" thereby became "Aryans".

Chapter One

HINDU BODH GAYA

In the Winter of 1874, the Government of India received a communication from the King of Burma, Mindon Min. The Burmese wanted to send a mission to Bodh Gaya because "it is His Majesty's wish to repair the enclosures of the Great Bodi Tree, which from a long state of existence must have fallen into decay" (FDPB, Nov. 27, 1874, Nos.124-25).[1]

The Bodhi-tree, beneath which the Buddha attained enlightenment, is the physical marker of the Buddhist sacrality of Bodh Gaya, and the original monument there, a throne platform erected in front of the tree, is attributed to the great emperor Asoka (Cunningham, 1892: 56). But by the nineteenth century, of course, Britain was the Imperial power in India, and in South Asia generally, and Britain brought to Bodh Gaya their own imperial values and concerns.

The values and concerns of the British authorities, who decided to facilitate the Burmese request, included the desire that nothing be done that would "offend the prejudices of the Hindoos," who now, and for hundreds of years, had overwhelmingly populated an area that had once been the heartland of Buddhist India. Also, the British, who had come to value the shrine as an important archaeological site, were concerned about the "authenticity" of the restoration ef-

[1] Some parts of this chapter, and parts of the next, appeared in *Modern Asian Studies*, Cambridge University Press, in 1999. (Trevithick 1999)

fort, and wished to insure that nothing would be done to damage or disfigure a temple which recalled what they regarded as a great and ancient civilization. They believed it was an important purpose of responsible government to defend such sites against the negligence of decadent and ignorant subjects.

The Bodh Gaya Giris

With regard to the "prejudices of the Hindoos," the most salient group at Bodh Gaya was the Giri sect, and, interestingly, it seems clear that the Giri Mahant (Abbot), who was recognized by the British as the proprietor of the place, was not offended by the Burmese visit. In fact, the Mahant's Shaivite sect was for awhile the beneficiary of both Burmese largesse and British technical assistance in the reconstruction of the main Mahabodhi Temple. Yet the Giris were fated to become bitter opponents of the later Mahabodhi Society campaign to reclaim the building.

At the most general cultural-constitutive level, the Giris were established as a Hindu monastic order by the Hindu philosopher Sankara in the ninth century CE. The Giris are one of ten such orders, collectively referred to as the Dasanami orders. Most of the Dasanami names correspond easily, and the remainder with a little imagination, to geographical categories. Thus, the Giris and Parvatas are mountain-dwellers; Vanas and Aranyas, forest-dwellers; Puris, town-dwellers; Sagaras, those who dwell near the ocean, and so on. It is certain that these titles reflect Sankara's intention, and the intentions of his followers, that the Hindu monastic system comprehensively blanket the sub-continent.

It is equally certain that the sects have long been so distributed as to make hash of the geographical system. The significance of the list of dasanami names in respect to geography is that the sects are theoretically specialized only by region, and therefore are co-equal (Olivelle, 1977:187).

Therefore, at least at a formal level, the ten classes of Shaivite ascetics are constitutive of a whole, and each section is regarded as co-equal. As one might expect, however, and particularly in a Hindu context, it becomes clear at another level that this quality of wholeness presides over an internal ranking of the classes. For instance, Wilson claimed that the Giri ascetic was generally regarded, by Tirtha [or Indra], Asrama, Saraswati and Bharati classes of the Dasnamis, as having fallen from the "purity of practice" that is required in order to be a real "dandi," that is to say a staff-carrying renunciant. The Giris were said, although to be religious, to have abandoned the staff, and to use clothes and ornaments forbidden to orthodox Dasanamis, and to make cash transactions.

Giris were, as well, known to prepare their own food, not relying solely on contributions. Finally, they seemed to be unusually open about, and accepted ascetics from, "any order of Hindus." (Wilson, 1980 [1832]:181) Farquhar reported the same basic information. (Farquhar, 1925: 13) This is validated in a recent work, by a Giri ascetic, Swami Sarananda Giri, who writes that so-called "orthodox" Dandin Brahmin Sannyasins tend to treat the Giris, as well as several other Dasanami sects, as relatively impure. (Giri, 1976:20)

What perhaps most distinguishes the Bodh Gaya Giris from the more "orthodox" dasanami orders is the method they employ in electing their Mahants. Among the more "pure" sects, a new Mahant is chosen by a nominating board, theoretically answerable to the entire body of monks. The head of this board is chosen at the Kumbh Mela—a great gathering of ascetics held every six years at the North Indian pilgrimage towns of Hardwar or Prayag. The Mahants of Bodh Gaya are not elected in this manner, nor is there a requirement that the process be initiated at the Kumbh Mela.

Hamilton-Buchanan recounts that the Mahant appointed his own successor. After the Mahant's death, the abbot-designate was confirmed in his new position at Bodh Gaya by the ascetics when they gathered in assembly, "marking the successor's forehead and giving him a present." (Martin, 1838:197)

Seventy years after Hamilton-Buchanan's visit, the Collector of Gaya, G.A. Grierson reported a somewhat different method. At the death of a Mahant, the "general body of disciples" nominated, at Bodh Gaya, five electors known as the Sri Panch, or "Holy Five." These were charged with "selecting the most learned, pious and capable disciple to sit on the Gaddi, or throne, of the monastery (Grierson, 1893:17-18). A more recent account seems to confirm Grierson. (Giri, 1979:49)

Thus far, I have focused on the position of the Bodh Gaya Math within the wider context of Shaivite Dasanami organization. The portrait that emerges is of a Hindu monastic sect in some ways idiosyncratic, and held by more orthodox groups to be somewhat "impure."

It must immediately be said, however, that throughout the period when the Giris sought public support against the claims of the Buddhists, general Hindu opinion, as indexed by newspaper articles and by public statements from religious leaders, was that the Giris were unambiguously "sanatan," or orthodox. This simply makes the point that in a graded Hindu hierarchy, "impurity," relative to other high ranking groups, in nowise implied unacceptability.

The impurity of the Bodh Gaya Giris might possibly have become an issue had they attempted to "rise above themselves," say, in an arena, the Kumbh Mela, for instance, where their claims might have conflicted with other groups. This, as I have indicated, they seem never to have done. At any rate, in a graded hierarchy, most things are either more or less pure, not absolutely one way or another. So, whatever their relative "impurity," it was not at that extreme where they were counted out of the "orthodox."

The Giris as Legitimate Landowners: Landgrants and Custom

The Math at Bodh Gaya has been, for possibly four hundred years, corporate headquarters for the Giri sect, a sect that has had since its establishment no strong institutional or administrative links with any other ascetic organization. The date of the actual foundation of the Bodh Gaya Math is in some doubt, but the accounts all point to a date between 1590 and 1690. Giri control of the sacred area around Bodh Gaya, including the Mahabodhi Temple, was primarily validated by reference to Mughul grants of land and rent obtained by the sect during the seventeenth century. The Giris have, however, on several occasions, offered brief mythological accounts to bolster their status at the site, and these are of some interest.

Such little special Giri mythology I have been able to discover is reviewed in a letter written in 1860 from the Collector of Gaya to his District Commissioner at Patna. This concerns a Giri Mahant, or "Abbot," in connection with a question of exempting religious institutions from taxation.

In the course of pursuing this matter the Mahant, Bhaipat Giri, had supplied the Collector with his "Kursee Namah" or roll of descent, and according to this document, which has not been preserved, the Mahant counted himself the 63rd representative of his sect at the site. This, if it were true, would have projected the Giris back to a deeply ancient time in the area and, as the account goes on to link the Giri presence in the area to the wandering of a Vedic Rishi, it would seem to mark an attempt through mythology to establish the oldest of Giri connections.

The Mahant Bhaipat Giri was apparently the source of another legitimating device, this one constructed from recent historical events. The assertion—I have never encountered any extended narrative form of the claim—is that the Giris had been of aid to British forces during the Mutiny.

(Grierson, 1893:17) In fact, there is no evidence that the Giris rendered "valuable aid" during the Mutiny, and some indication that they were not involved in any way. Nevertheless, the Mahants on several occasions, while negotiating with local authorities, returned to this story, and it was accepted by the British, on the basis of no other evidence, as the truth. (Roy Chaudhury, 1958:117-18)

These two fragments largely exhaust the subject of a special mythology of entitlement for the Giri sect at Bodh Gaya. This appears quite in contrast to the Gayawal mythology: the Giris posit with mythological specificity *no* basic connection between their social status and the proper functioning of the universe, or the commands and wishes of the gods. Instead, the Giris, throughout the period of negotiations with British officials and Buddhist groups, linked their jurisdictional rights to land grants awarded prior to the British era, and to the weight of customary practice at the shrine complex. Let me now, therefore, examine what is known about the Giri sect at Bodh Gaya in the late medieval period.

The settlement, at Bodh Gaya, of the Shaivite Giris, is generally credited to one Gosain Ghamandi Gir, who arrived in the area about the year 1590, found the place deserted and, thus, a suitable site for an ascetic's abode. Most sources agree that Ghamandi was followed by his disciple Chaitanya. In addition to Hamilton-Buchanan's information cited earlier, Colonel Mackenzie's Jain Pandit, in 1820, was told that the area, prior to Ghamandi's arrival, and even for some time afterward, was deserted and overgrown. His followers "cut down the woods," and, after the succession of the third abbot, "built up the place." (Mackenzie, 1902:75)

Hamilton-Buchanan's informant also told him that Chaitanya had received the right to collect revenue from the village of Buddha Gaya. (Hamilton-Buchanan, 1937:139) Grierson's dates for the period of Chaitanya's abbotship are 1615-1642, and he records no major expansion of the sect's presence in Buddha Gaya until the next abbot, Mahadeva Giri, came into office. Mahadeva is said to have built the actual Math structure that houses the sannyasins (renunciants) today, and therefore Grierson dated the building of the monastery itself at some point between 1642 and 1682. (Grierson, 1893:17)

Rajendralal Mitra, an important figure in the Bengal Renaissance, and a figure associated strongly with the Asiatic Society and the development of early modern Indian archaeology, in 1876 found that, according to a "memorandum" prepared for him by the Mahant, Mahadeva Giri received a "Royal Firman from Shah Alum"—a grant from the Mughal Emperor—but no date was supplied. (Mitra, 1878:4) This probably refers to Bahadur Shah I, who acceded in 1707, though it might refer instead to Shah Alam II, who reigned more than fifty years later and into the first years of the nineteenth century. Also, it appears that the Giris received land, and the rights to rent from land, from a variety of sources. Mackenzie's Pandit, for instance, was told that when the "third Bhairagi [Shaivite] of the order succeeded to the abbotship," certain un-named zamindars (either actual landowners or Mughal officials with rights to tax revenues from land) granted him four villages in jaghir, that is to say not subject to taxes or fees. (Mackenzie, 1902:75)

In all of this discussion concerning grants, strict documentation is not possible, and the sources, while recording the claim that a grant was received, fail to identify the benefactor. The problem of documentation was recognized by British authorities as well. Mitra, writing for Government of Bengal, wrote, after extensive research into the subject, that "the old records of the Gya Collectorate having been destroyed by the mutiny, I could not find out the terms on which the permanent lease had been granted."

For present purposes, it is sufficient to have demonstrated

that, since the late medieval period, the Giris at Bodh Gaya had managed to establish themselves in a manner that satisfied both Government of Bengal and Government of India, in spite of the limited documentation, that "possession and control" of the temple and its surrounding were legitimately held by the Math. (Ronaldshay, 1928: 337)

In the next chapter, then, I would like to describe how, initially, the British attempted to balance this legitimate Giri possession and control against what were considered equally legitimate, if limited, claims by non- Indian Buddhists for access to the temple. The British reaction to events at Bodh Gaya generally fell into one of two patterns.

The first pattern, unsurprisingly, revealed a concern for the establishment and maintenance of the public peace. When operating in this mode, officials exhibited an anxiety that Buddhist claims to the area might trigger serious local and regional opposition. The second bears testimony to a British concern for the preservation of Indian antiquities and, as well, a sympathy for the Buddhists that was rooted in a valorization of what was regarded as the authentic past.

Chapter Two

A BUDDHIST TEMPLE IN BRITISH INDIA

Indian archaeology was established during a time of great interest, on the part of European scholars in the largely unexplored field of Indian Buddhist studies. Major-General Alexander Cunningham shared this interest, and early projects undertaken by the Archaeological Survey in large part reflect this. Quite early in his archaeological career, while still an amateur, "he was leaning more and more towards the study of Buddhism, its archaeology and history in India." (Imam, 1966:33-34)

This tendency had ripened by 1861 when, newly retired from the Bengal Engineers, he sent a memorandum to the Viceroy, Lord Canning. I take the following excerpt from Volume I of Cunningham's *Archaeological Survey of India*, published ten years later.

> In describing the ancient geography of India, the elder Pliny, for the sake of clearness, follows the footsteps of Alexander the Great. For a similar reason, in the present proposed investigation, I would follow the footsteps of the Chinese Pilgrim Hwen Thsang, who, in the seventh century of our era, traversed India from west to east and back again for the purpose of visiting all the famous sites of Buddhist history and tradition. In the account of

> his travels, although the Buddhist remains are described in most detail with all their attendant legends and traditions, yet the numbers and appearance of the Brahmanical temples are also noted, and the travels of the Chinese pilgrim thus hold the same place in the history of India, which those of Pausanias hold in the history of Greece. (Cunningham, 1972 [1871] :iv)

Lord Canning responded that "it would not be to our credit, as an enlightened ruling power," to allow the neglect of Indian antiquity to continue, and sanctioned the establishment of the Archaeological Survey. Cunningham was appointed its first director, and terms were drawn up to recompense him for his labors, which put the matter, in the context of the history of archaeology, on a professional basis. (Cunningham, 1972 [1871]:ii-iii)[1]

Cunningham's entry into this field also inspired a renewed interest in Indian Buddhist sites in Ceylon. Cunningham corresponded, for instance, with the great Sinhalese Pali scholar Waskaduwe Sri Subhuti Nayaka Maha Thera, who

---

[1] Lord Canning had this to say about Cunningham's remuneration:

> Colonel Cunningham should receive Rs.450 a month, with Rs.250 when in the field to defray the cost of making surveys and measurements, and of other mechanical assistance If something more should be necessary to obtain the services of a native subordinate of the Medical or Public Works Department, competent to take photographic views, it should be given. It would be premature to determine how the results of Colonel Cunningham's labors should be dealt with; but whilst the Government would of course retain a proprietary right in them for its own purposes, I recommend that the interests of Colonel Cunningham should be considered in the terms upon which they may be furnished to the Public. (from Cunningham, 1972 [1871]:iii)

answered many questions about Buddhist texts, and was, in turn, periodically given progress reports on Cunningham's labors. Significantly, Subhuti was most intrigued by the possibility that relics of the Buddha's disciples might have been unearthed.

Subhuti not only wanted these relics to be sent to Ceylon, he also put forth a personal claim for them: "these are not only invaluable to us, but I am persuaded by a strong desire to have them compared with those that are in this island." So then, the beginnings of Buddhist archaeology in India are not only political in the British Indian sense, but in the Sinhalese world as well. Cunningham's first project, undertaken by the new survey, in the winter of 1861, was a fieldtrip to the Hindu pilgrimage town of Gaya and to its more famous if smaller satellite, Bodh Gaya. (Imam, 1966:56)

Buddhist Stupas and Hindu Lingams: "No Conversion is Required"

At Bodh Gaya, Cunningham found that "the celebrated Bodhi tree still exists, but is very much decayed." He also noted that, inside the main temple, there was a stone lingam, the phallic emblem of Mahadeva—the god Siva—which possibly dated from the time of the Hindu King Sasangka, a sixth century ruler who had attempted to convert the shrine to Shaivite worship. (Cunningham, 1972[1871]:5-10; 1966 [1873]:83-84)

This first trip to Bodh Gaya was only one phase of what was in effect an elaborated inventory of Indian antiquities, and involved no excavation. Excavation was, however, undertaken two years later when one Major Mead, under Cunningham's direction, submitted a report that casts light on the processes whereby Hindus had literally incorporated the material of Buddhist imagery.

The cutting of a trench along the eastern face of the temple had "yielded a considerable quantity of masonry in situ, and large numbers of handsomely carved model stupas [reliquary mounds], of which *hundreds* of specimens have been disinterred by our excavations." Not long thereafter, we read this:

> Not a single specimen of these *hundreds* is now to be seen. I suppose they have been carried off to Gaya, and are now doing duty as lingams, or symbols of Mahadeva. *No conversion is required, as the people accept one of these votive stupas of the Buddhists as a ready-made lingam.* When I was digging round the Buddhapad [part of a famous Hindu shrine at Gaya] the workmen lighted on the top of one of these stupas. Several times they tried to move it, but in vain. "Mahadeo [Siva] won't move," said one, at which there was a general laugh. "How strong Mahadeo is," said another, which was followed by another laugh (Cunningham, 1966[1873]Vol.III: 87) (My emphasis).

Mitra, writing fifteen years after Mead, again noted the ease with which the Buddhist stupa could be substituted for a Shaivite lingam. A lingam is commonly placed atop the graves of Shaivite ascetics who are, as is usual with all classes of Hindu ascetics, not cremated. During a tour of the graveyard at the Bodh Gaya Math, Mitra found the following.

> For Mahants the [funerary] temple is large and elaborately ornamented. It would seem that even for neophytes a lingam was held essential; but in the majority of cases its place was supplied by a miniature votive stupa picked up from the Buddhist ruins in the neighborhood. Half-buried on the top on the mound, it passes very well for a lingam. (Mitra, 1878:4)

At a very concrete level, then, important symbols of the two faiths were interchanged with great facility: the historical relations between the two traditions are here experienced as material fact.

Describing, Looting or Preserving? Modes of "Collecting" at an Archaeological Site

Returning to Mead's excavation, it should be noted that his task did not involve any questions of actual preservation. "What is aimed at," as Canning specified to be the goal of the survey, "is an accurate description...of such remains as deserve notice, with a history of them so far as it may be traceable, and a record of the traditions that are retained regarding them." (Cunningham, 1972 [1871:ii-iii)

What happened to artifacts and antiquities beyond this was of relatively little concern to government. Cunningham's terms of employment, in fact, stipulated that he be allowed to take for himself a goodly portion of such artifacts as might be unearthed during the course of the survey.

He did quite well for himself and, on the disbanding of the first survey, in 1865, he returned to England, for five years, to become the Director of the Delhi and London Bank. (Imam, 1966:191) In England, he "carried on a profitable business in coin selling—particularly to the British Museum." As well, he had "amassed a unique and unrivalled collection of coins, seals, stone implements and other objects including smaller statues and relic caskets." (Imam, 1966:232)[2]

So then, images and other artifacts continued to be "carried off by European gentlemen," and by others, even after the establishment of the Archaeological Survey and, in real-

[2] Cunningham claimed in 1874 to have had some relics in his possession: "But it has been my bad luck to lose everything that I left behind in England by the great fire at the Pantechnicon, including all my Buddhist antiquities and relics." (Guruge, 1984:158-60)

ity, one might say that such a practice was designed into the survey. The haphazard looting of the past had achieved some degree of organization, no doubt, but the destruction of the archaeological value of sites, as we currently recognize such value, continued apace. The Mahabodhi temple at Bodh Gaya, evermore denuded of its ornamentation, its grounds and foundations quarried for building materials, continued its decline into an unreadable rubble of the past.

The British often seemed genuinely unaware of their *own* role in this process of decay, and Cunningham, on several occasions, placed all the blame on the negligent and unmindful, or devious and cunning, practices of the Brahmins. Upon discovering that an inscribed plaque had been utilized in the construction of a gate at the Giri Math, Cunningham—the collector of antiquities—pronounced that "Brahman malignancy has sadly mutilated this inscription." (Cunningham, 1966 [1873]:126)

Meanwhile, the temple slipped away, bit by bit, into new structures and new histories. The Deputy Magistrate of Shergatty, on holiday at Bodh Gaya in 1866, recorded the temple's condition. "Taking photographs of old Boodhist temple 'til 11:00AM. The temple apparently falling fast into ruin. It is a great pity that such a fine, old and picturesque looking building could not be preserved." (Roy Chaudary 1958:87-89)

At this point, however, there was no question that the building could be, in any case, simply "preserved." It needed, first, to be restored. This was a project not considered to be within the scope of the first survey: Canning had specifically noted that to restore ancient monuments, "or even to arrest their decay," would require an expenditure far beyond what government was prepared to accept. (Cunningham, 1972 [1871]:i) In 1871, the survey was reactivated and Cunningham was recalled from London to take its directorship. A pronounced shift was apparent.

In giving directions to his subordinates, Cunningham now specifically made mention of those buildings that "are worth preserving." These were, in general, those monuments that, either by their association with significant events, or by virtue of their "beauty and grandeur" alone, were "worth preserving either wholly or in part, as historical specimens." (Cunningham, 1966, 1873:v) Bodh Gaya was to be judged as such a monument, and the government came to take up much of the responsibility for its repair and preservation. Government commitment to this project, however, did not arise simply out of a shift in archaeological policy, but was triggered by the intervention of the Burmese mission alluded to earlier, which was charged by King Mindon Min with the task of restoring the temple.

"Nothing to Offend the Prejudices of the Hindoos"

Burmese Kings had on a number of prior occasions, from the twelfth century onward, sent missions to Bodh Gaya. Two of these missions, dated rather uncertainly at 1100 and 1296, were dispatched with the intent of restoring the temple, and both succeeded in significantly altering the original design. Hamilton-Buchanan, upon his arrival at Bodh Gaya in 1811, was told that Burmese Buddhists "again" were inquiring about the condition of the site. As well, having traveled, for the Company, in both Thailand and Burma, he recalled that, in 1795, "the priests of Buddha were seriously alarmed at the influence the Brahmans had then acquired." (Hamilton-Buchanan, 1925: 139; Barua, 1934:44)

Mindon's was to be the last mission to Bodh Gaya initiated by a Theravadin Buddhist kingdom and undertaken in that mode of kingly benefaction that traditionally sought to express the integration of sacred accomplishment with legitimate secular rule. (again, see Tambiah, 1976)

In response to the Burmese inquiries, a reply was drafted to Mandalay that, although approval could be reasonably anticipated, "it should be clearly understood that nothing was to be done in that respect [repairs, improvements, etc.] which could offend the prejudices of the Hindoos, who also possess shrines near the temple." (FDPB, Jan. 1876, Nos.50-56, enclosure)

For its part, Government of Bengal was initially of the opinion that the proposed repairs would be "gladly accepted by the Mahant." However, the Magistrate of Gaya, F.M. Halliday, delivered a report that indicates not only that the Burmese had made inquiries about the condition of the site on several occasions since Hamilton-Buchanan's time, but also that the Giris had some reservations about the Burmese plans.

"There has been, undoubtedly, for many years past, a disinclination on the part of the resident Hindoos to yield even a foot of ground to the Burmese or to give them any encouragement." Nevertheless, upon receiving Halliday's assurances that his interests would be protected, the Mahant agreed to examine the plan in more detail.

Bengal then recommended that approval be granted the Burmese, with the following limitations to apply:

> Under the tree there are altars and gods belonging to the Hindoo religion where hindu rajahs and rich men resort to and offer Pindas [riceballs] and perform sacrificial ceremonies. Near the tree and within the enclosure round it there is at present a place of worship of the Hindoos. I therefore submit that if anything other than that allowed by the Hindus be offered to the tree, the Hindus will have objection to it. If the King of Burmah send anything to be offered to the tree that is prescribed by the Hindoo religion, there will be no objection to it. (FDPB, May 1878, Nos.10-28)

Government of India then asked for clarification from the

Burmese as to their intentions, and, in August of 1875, Mindon's negotiators drew up and sent a list of specifications. The King wished 1) to repair the Bodhi-tree enclosure itself, its walls and terraces, as well as all the structures within, 2) to repair the cehtiya of Asoka over the site of the Apara-jita (throne), 3) to prop up with masonry the weakened right limb of the tree, 4) to build near the Bodhi Tree a monastery that might house up to twenty monks, 5) to enclose this monastery within a masonry wall, 6) to erect a storage place (paribhoga) for the deposition of royal gifts to the Bodhi-tree.

The Burmese list of improvements and additions was then passed on again, in October of 1875, to Government of Bengal with the request that "if there is no objection on the part of the Hindoos, cause every reasonable facility" to be given to the Burmese scribe dispatched to draw up plans at Bodh Gaya. (FDPB, Oct. 1878, Nos. 277-79) That December, Halliday informed the Commissioner of the Patna Division that the Mahant "raises no objections to the proposals of the King of Burmah." The Mahant nevertheless pointed to three areas that were of concern to his sect, and asked that these be made clear to the Burmese.

To begin with, the Giris demanded that no Hindu images be displaced by the reconstruction work. Then, they wished to lease, but not to sell, the land necessary for the construction of the Burmese resthouse, and stipulated that the land would be provided rent-free by the Mahant. Finally, the Mahant asked that the Burmese monks not be permitted in any way to interfere with the Hindu religious rites of pilgrims, particularly those associated with the Bodhi-tree. (MBJ,Vol.VI, No.2, May 1897:6)

The "royal scribe" arrived in Bodh Gaya in January of 1876 and apparently drew up plans satisfactory to both Mindon and the Mahant. Actual work at the site began the following year, when, in January, "the late King of Burmah deputed three of his officers to superintend the repairs." (Mitra, 1878: i) The work, under solely Burmese direction with the approval of the Mahant, continued for about six months until it came to the attention of the Government of Bengal that, at least from an archaeological point of view, "Burmese workmen were making a mess of the old temple at Buddha Gaya." (FDPB, Feb. 1878, Nos. 129-51)

The Burmese are "Ignorant of the True History of Their Faith"

Rajendralala Mitra, of the Archaeological Survey of India, was then deputed by Bengal to report on the situation. His instructions, in part, were as follows.

> It is not desired to interfere with the Burmese gentlemen beyond giving them such guidance as may prevent any serious damage being done to the temple, of which it seemed at one time [in] some danger from their laying bare a portion of the foundation; and to arrange for such of the antiquities as are worth preserving being properly taken care of. They are at present building them into walls, and sticking foolish heads onto ancient torsos & c. Mr. Eden [Lt. Governor of Bengal] wishes to know if you can make it convenient to pay a visit to Buddha Gaya to inspect the work and the remains collected, and to give advice as to their value and to their disposition, and whether there are any that should go to the Asiatic Society; and generally to advise the Government in regard to the manner in which the operations of the Burmese excavators should be controlled. (Mitra, 1878, ii)

Mitra was not pleased with what he saw. He found that the Burmese were working "energetically and piously," but according to no "systematic or traditional plan."

> They are ignorant of the true history of their faith and perfectly innocent of archeology and history, and the mischief they have done by their misdirected zeal has been serious. The demolitions and excavations already completed by them have swept away most of the old landmarks, and nothing of ancient times can now be traced on the area they have worked upon. (FDPB, Feb. 1878, Nos. 129-51)

Part of the stone railing around the temple, as well as a number of other structures, had been "entirely swept away" by the Burmese. Thirty-two pillars from the railing were located by Mitra in the veranda of the Mahant's residence.

Virtually all of the buildings within the courtyard had been in ruins, but in situ, when Mitra had visited the area in 1864. Now, "the foundations of these have been dug out by the Burmese gentlemen for bricks," and the resulting debris raked out to level the ground. Mitra was thrown into an archaeological melancholy: "nothing can now be done in the way of identifying any of the old buildings, or the site of the old wall."

The Burmese had also undertaken certain restorations inside the temple itself and had plastered smooth and flat many of the inside walls which once had been carved and niched for the placement of images. Mitra was glum with regard to one platform in the first floor chamber, which he felt had some interesting and as yet unmolested carving. "It is likely that the Burmese gentlemen will place a statue on it, and this cannot be objected to, though I feel pretty certain that it will be an execrably ugly one." (FDPB, Feb. 1878, Nos. 128-51)

"All Such Monuments Belong to Government"

Apparently nothing of Mitra's archaeological horror had been experienced by the Mahant, or by Hindu pilgrims, as there are no recorded grievances against the Burmese. Possibly, the Burmese had been, as agreed, solicitous of Hindu "sentiment."

Mitra did note that there were a number of Hindu images, such as the Savitri figure on the eastern side of the temple, that had not been disturbed. On the other hand, the Theravadin Burmese might or might not have known that the figure was, at least by original design, one of the a Tantric Buddhist version of the Bodhisattva, Padmapani. At any rate, whether because the plan to preserve Hindu images had been carried out successfully, or because the images of the two (or more) religions were so easily confused by members of either religion, there appears to have been no friction caused by the Burmese operation.

This absence of Hindu-Buddhist conflict is at odds with certain of Mitra's attitudes, which typified an over-sensitivity, on the part of the Governments of India and Bengal, to the possibility of inadvertently offending some ill-defined segment of orthodox zealots. For instance, Mitra recommended that, in any future restoration, the stairs leading up to the bodhi tree terrace, although recently installed by the Maratha benefactor to whom I referred earlier, be left in place as they were "of great use to Hindu Pilgrims who would feel greatly offended" if they had to use the steps employed by Buddhists.

I do not wish to underestimate the degree to which Hindu feeling in the region, and throughout India, might have been bruised by certain of the developments at Bodh Gaya. Indeed, as I shall show, many Hindus did come to feel that foreign Buddhists were acting in an arrogant manner in demanding exclusive control of the temple, and some felt that no accommodation to Buddhist desires was necessary or desirable. Nevertheless, over the next thirty years, British officials would often exhibit what seems, in retrospect, to have been an exaggerated anxiety with regard to the possibility of offending religious sensitivities.

At this very early point in the modern re-development of Bodh Gaya as a Buddhist pilgrimage site, Hindus and Buddhists appear to have had no serious conflicts. Indeed, in April of 1878, after the Burmese had completed their restoration efforts, the Magistrate of Gaya reported that two monks had been left behind and that "they have quarters in the Mahant's residence." (FDPB, Feb. 1878, No. 159)

Mindon's mission to "restore" the sacred structures at Bodh Gaya was an archaeological disaster, but perhaps no more so than any of the several previous missions of "restoration" undertaken centuries earlier. Neglect and abuse had for years worn away at the structure. More recently, it had been treated as a source of information about a Buddhist Indian past that had been, in the eyes of government, erased by an unmindful and heedless Hindu populace. Having served that function well enough, within the context of an infant archaeology, the temple became a store of artifacts from which to fill up “”collections" in Calcutta and London, and to pay the salaries of the new archaeological inquirers.

Nevertheless, although rather too late in the interests of archaeology, and with only the most tentatively established legal warrant, Mitra voiced an emergent official attitude that shifted the concept of preservation to a different level.

> It is impossible to suppose that an ancient building, belonging to a sect which has long disappeared from this country, can have been given away as an appurtenance to a village. All such monuments belong to Government, and Government has every right to see to their

Here I refer to an "attitude" because, thus far, there was no actual policy or legislation, or legal precedent, or contractual agreement, that had established any of the sorts of rights that Mitra seemed to imagine were naturally enjoyed by the government. At this point, however, no conflict arose. The British, the Burmese, and the Giris, by cooperating so well to complete the task of either obliterating or recovering the past at Bodh Gaya, had created a complex new reality into which Dharmapala and his Mahabodhi Society would soon enter. Dharmapala, in turn, brought with him new ideas about what it was that had been destroyed and what it was that should be recovered.

Chapter Three

ANGARIKA DHARMAPALA AT BODH GAYA

The title of this chapter is perhaps somewhat misleading, as it involves, not only Dharmapala, but also Colonel Olcott and Madame Blavatsky, the founders of the Theosophical Society, and Sir Edwin Arnold, the British journalist, poet and, it must be added, avid British imperialist. All, in fact, had a significant impact on the shaping of the debate of the Bodh Gaya problem. Blavatsky, though, as far as I can tell, never said or did anything directly regarding the Mahabodhi Temple, and while Olcott and Arnold did, they also were most effective, and very dramatically so, when they inspired Dharmapala to take direct action.

Broken Statues of Our Blessed Lord

On the dirt road that led south from Gaya toward the site of Gautama's enlightenment, "you could see lying scattered here and there broken statues of our Blessed Lord." So reads an entry in the diary of a Sinhalese Buddhist pilgrim, who at the time went by the name "Dharmapala Hewavitarne." He had arrived in Bodh Gaya on January 22, 1891 and, in spite of the recent Burmese restoration project, his first impression was that the place had been neglected and allowed to decay. That afternoon, at the temple itself, Dharmapala experienced a sense of mission that would structure the remainder of his life.

> As soon as I touched with my forehead the

> Vajrasana [the "diamond throne" of Gautama] a sudden impulse came to my mind to stop here and take care of this sacred spot, so sacred that nothing in the world is equal to this place where Prince Sakya Sinha attained enlightenment under the bodhi tree. (ACD, Jan. 22, 1891)

Within the week, Dharmapala discovered that the temple was in the custody of the Giri sect, and angrily recorded that "a powerful Buddhist's eloquent voice is needed to show the knavery of the selfish bigoted Brahman priests." (ACD, Jan. 28, 1891) With this entry he inaugurated a campaign for Buddhist control of the temple that lasted for the next forty years. I have called Dharmapala a Buddhist pilgrim. In fact, by undertaking the project for the recovery of Buddhist sacred ground, he was continuing with a personal project of constructing what he considered an authentic Buddhist identity.

Mother-Tongues and Father-Figures

Dharmapala was born, in 1864, to a very wealthy Buddhist family in Colombo, and given the name Don David Hewavitarne. He grew up in a household where English was spoken and he almost exclusively attended, as far as I can tell, English-medium Christian schools. I am putting this strongly because I wish to address a long-running problem in studies of Dharmapala's career: his Sinhala language (not to mention his Pali) facility, as opposed to his great facility in English, and the fact that he wrote his private diaries exclusively in English.

A fairly typical approach to Dharmapala has been to assume, as for instance Amunugama does, that he was from an early age at ease in Sinhalese, and that he "absorbed himself in the study of Pali which meant also a study of the Buddhist doctrine." I think that this was probably *not* the case, or, at least, that it was probably not *exactly* the case. For instance, with regard only to Sinhala language, Amunugama also quotes Dharmapala, in English, from a 1918 *Diary*—I believe from the attribution that this is a compilation from Mahabodhi Society sources—the following extraordinary statement: "I *began to learn* Sinhalese when I was eight years old." (my emphasis)

Now, the rest of the *Diary* section may well indicate that Dharmapala was referring to the writing and not the speaking of Sinhalese: "and I finished the preliminary course in two years. That knowledge helped me to be of use as a vigorous writer of Sinhalese articles." (Amunugama 1985: 706, 709) And, indeed, no one would dispute that he later *did* become a vigorous writer of Sinhalese articles. However, it certainly seems peculiar for a speaker of "the mother tongue" to write, in the colonial language that he very fluently controls, that he began to "learn Sinhalese" only when eight years old.

Now then, I will augment one of my earlier statements: it seems reasonable to assume that Dharmapala grew up in a household where English was certainly spoken very often, and probably was the prestige language, and where no doubt some Sinhalese was spoken as well, though how much is open to question. I am myself very open to correction on this, but I think that it has too often been assumed, without much evidence, that the situation was the reverse of what I am suggesting.

This is an important issue, among others, because it has a direct bearing on Dharmapala's openness, or vulnerability, to a variety of outside influences, where "outside" means figures such as the English-speaking Theosophists, who became for Dharmapala important proxy-parental figures. Of Dharmapala's natural parents we learn, in fact, remarkably little from his own writings.

I concur with Obeyesekere that Dharmapala idealized his moth-er, and to a significant extent identified with her, and that his father was a somewhat distant figure. (Obeyesekere 1975:247-48; 1976: 230) He seems (see appendix, this volume) to have felt that his father did not find for him the sort of education he might have wanted, and that he was discouraged from entering into the family business.

It is really, though, his proxy parents who are more interesting The Theosophists were the most important of these, but there were earlier models as well. For instance, as a boy, Dharmapala had dutifully participated in both Catholic and Buddhist rituals, and, in Dharmapala's writings, published and unpublished— particularly the latter—there is considerable ambiguity expressed about both classes of authority figures, priests and monks, he knew from childhood.

He often tried to remember things in a sunny way, so that, of the Sinhalese monks he once wrote, and published, "I loved their company and would sit quietly, in a corner, and listen to their wise discourse," and of the Catholics padres that "they gave us bonbons and stroked our hair to show us that they loved us." (Dharmapala 1927: 721-23) But not much later, in his private diary, we read "The Sinhalese Catholics are idiots. The Catholic Padres are like vampires. The Bhikkhus are drones." (ADC Oct. 3, 1930)

He also remembered his own psychological profile from childhood in a conflicted way, wring that "I had an unbending will," but also that, when a Catholic Bishop came to his school to visit, he kissed his ring because "I was too young to refuse and to reason 'why should I kiss his ring'?" (Dharmapala 1927:721-23)

Dharmapala and His Theosophical "Foster-Parents"

So, well educated and well provided for, he was a thoughtful and rather confused boy of sixteen when, in 1880, two exotic westerners entered his life. These were Madame Helena Petrovna Blavatsky and Colonel Henry Steel Olcott, founders of an occult organization, the Theosophical Society. The two Theosophists effectively adopted the young Dharmapala, and he often referred to them later as his "foster-parents." Had he not met them, Don David might never have left Ceylon.

He learned from Madame Blavatsky, a chain-smoking Ukrainian mystic, of the existence of "The Masters," ethereal adepts normally resident in the deep Himalayas who made their desires known through raps on window panes or through "precipitated" letters.

Don David read widely in the "Theosophical literature," and was particularly impressed with Mrs. Blavatsky's *Isis Unveiled,* and Sinnett's *Occult World.* As well, he developed a passion for the English romantics, and particularly for the work of Shelley, whose "Queen Mab" became his favorite poem.

All three works present the reader with portraits of a limitless ethereal domain through which worthy beings are favored to pass. The fairy "Queen Mab," for instance, awakens the spirit of a slumbering girl, Ianthe, in order to conduct her beyond the boundaries of the mundane world. This, in order that the spirit, in its "changeless purity, may know soonest how to accomplish the great goal for which it has its being."

The spirit journey of Queen Mab and Ianthe seemed to parallel the trajectory of the Theosophical "Master," Koot-Hoomi, who was capable of projecting his soul into the astral plane. The master had "found the key of his prison"—the body—and could "emerge from it at will." Dharmapala, in truth, often did complain that his body was a prison, and from an early age suffered from progressively debilitating illness, including rheumatism, ulcers and sciatica. Nevertheless, throughout his life, he was a fearless and indefatigable traveler.

Olcott and Blavatsky were responsible for initiating Dharmapala's long career of travel and exploration. The Theosophists transported him across many boundaries, and, with Colonel Olcott, a veteran of the U.S. Civil War and a one-time lawyer from Red Bank, New Jersey, Dharmapala traveled extensively throughout India and the Far East. The Colonel taught Dharmapala the principles of "mesmerism" and "animal magnetism," and, as well, introduced him, directly or not, to a global network of mystical confederates.

When Dharmapala first arrived in Bodh Gaya, he considered himself a "chela"—a student—of "Master Koot Hoomi." Thus, much in Dharmapala's religious odyssey had little to do with Sinhalese Buddhism and a great deal to do with the Theosophical Society and its "Occult Science."

Spiritual Pluralism and the Common Enemy

When the Theosophical Society was founded, only two years prior to this, in New York City, the stated goal was to investigate "those laws of Nature which were so familiar to the Chaldeans and Egyptians," but which had been lost to "the modern world of science." (For a good recent introduction to these matters, particularly with regard to Colonel Olcott's point of view, see Prothero 1996) Put most simply, we can say that the "occult science" of the Theosophists was to be found in those "laws of Nature" that had been forgotten by contemporary scientists: forgotten they were, but they could be recovered by competent psychics.

Now, aside from these rather confident aspirations, the society appears to have had two other purposes. These were to swell with new recruits the ranks of the society's constituent cells, and to sell the books written by Madame Blavatsky and her associates, books which contained the lost wisdom of the ages, or at least a great deal of it such as would suffice for a general readership until the next revelation.

In 1878, when Blavatsky and Olcott first sought to recruit

Sinhalese monks to their movement, they styled as their aim the achievement of "a true Brotherhood of Humanity." (Guruge, 1980: 338) In a letter to Ven. Piyaratna Tissa Mahathera,[1] Olcott, in a typical formula, 1) awarded that scholar-monk, "by order of Council," the "Diploma" of the Theosophical Society, 2) regretted that "it is not in my power to send you a copy of *Isis Unveiled,* the great work from the pen of H.P. Blavatsky, the Corresponding Secretary of our Society," but noted the address of a Bombay bookseller from whom the occult bestseller was readily available, and 3) ventured the assumption that "you will have guessed that we, the leaders of the Theosophical Society believe in the Incomprehensible Principle and the Divine Philosophy taught by Sakya Muni."

This rather nicely sums up, I think, several aspects of the Theosophical society. First, they were truly adept—with a devastatingly deadpan technique—at the invention of new organizational structures (the "Council"), and the confetti of serious scholarship ("Diploma"). Second, they certainly *did* sell books—today Priyaratna would have been directed to Amazon.com where, indeed, he would find *Isis Unveiled* robustly alive as a classic occult commodity. Third, they were always willing, in a pinch, and in order to avoid unnecessary specification or discussion of a particular principle, to invoke the problem of "incomprehensibility."

To all of this, Olcott added that the Society was formed "on the basis of a Brotherhood of Humanity," The brotherhood was specialized, however, in a way that was naturally appealing to those who had experienced the aggressive evangelizing that typically accompanied western imperialism: "I might admit that it also is a league of religions against the common

[1] Piyaratana, of Sailabimbarama, Dodanduwa, in South Ceylon, was one of a number of scholar-monks who corresponded regularly with western Orientalists during the latter half of the nineteenth century. He was a close associate of both Hekkuduwe and Gunananda. (Guruge, 1984:335)

enemy —Christianity." (Guruge, 1984:339-340).

In a subsequent letter to Piyaratana Tissa, Olcott urged him to be in contact with "Our Brothers," Sumangala and Gunananda. The first named Monk was Sri Hekkuduwe Sumangala Mahathera, the principal of the Vidyodaya Pirivena, an "Oriental College" in Colombo that had been founded with the financial aid of Dharmapala's maternal grandfather. The second, Mohotiwatte Gunananda, was "a golden tongued orator," and the chief monk at the Dipaduttaramaya Temple at Kotehena, the temple most favored by the Hewavitarne family. (Malalgoda, 1976:188) Sumangala had supplied scholarly support for a series of debates, held throughout Ceylon, between Christians and Buddhists on the merits of their respective religions. Mohotiwatte had contributed the rhetoric. "His words were like sweet honey to me," wrote Dharmapala of one such debate, "where the Christians on the one side, and Gunananda on the other argued out the truth of their respective religions." (MBJ, Vol.41, July/Sept, 7,8,9; Dharmapala, 1927:721-23)

Sumangala and Gunananda were offered, apparently, appointment as "Councilors of our Society," with "full representative authority in Ceylon," and the Theosophists' communications with them, and with Piyaratana, and other renowned Sinhalese monks, became the subject of much popular excitement in Ceylon. They were received, as had been intended, as an invitation to form an alliance against a common Christian foe, and, of course, in the British colonial context, Christianity had become a reliable symbol of imperialism, so that opposition to Christianity began to function as a form of early modern Sinhalese nationalism.

The combination was seductive, and, as the Theosophical correspondence was printed and widely distributed, in English and Sinhalese, many Sinhalese responded warmly, as did Dharmapala, who wrote "My heart warmed towards these two strangers, and I made up my mind that, when they came to Ceylon, I would join them." (Dharmapala, 1927:723)

They arrived in Ceylon, in 1880, attended by "a committee of Hindu and Parsi Theosophists from Bombay." Their express purpose was to organize "the Buddhist Branch of our Theosophical Society, the more effectually to spread throughout the world of Christendom the holy teachings of the Lord Buddha." (Guruge, 1984:349)

In the Theosophical understanding of things, the teachings of Buddha were fundamentally identical with those of, say, Zoroaster and Ramanuja, or Shankara, or Madhva: their constructions of Buddhist philosophy benefited from a most generous exegetical standpoint. This included, of course, those interpretations gleaned from the messages of the "Masters."

As well, while they were clearly on record as preferring ancient to modern science, they were not averse to sometimes employing some of the less well-known findings of the latter, as when, in an explanation of Buddha's teachings on the "atman," Colonel Olcott pressed into service the conclusions of one Dr. Jager, to the effect that "the soul is an odoriferous principle capable of solution in glycerine." (Olcott, 1880:26)

In Colombo itself, on June 3, 1880, the Theosophists arranged, with Sumangala's cooperation, a public lecture, and it was here that Don David first had an opportunity to see and hear the exotic strangers. The Colonel explained to his audience that the purpose of the Society, a non-sectarian group, was to discover "natural laws." On this occasion the "laws" flowed from a vastly expanded list: they were known to the "priests of ancient Persian, Indian, Egyptian, Hebrew, Chaldean, Grecian, Roman, Keltic, Scandinavian, Peruvian, Mexican, and other religions," and were used by those priests to produce "weird and occult phenomena." (Olcott, 1880:26)

The immediate goal being the establishment of a "Buddhist Branch" of the Society, the Colonel found it appropriate to make reference to the career of Gautama. Gautama, said the Colonel, had been the embodiment of Universal Love, stainless, most pure, most gentle, zealous, wise, tolerant, charitable, heroic, and noble.

Very little in Olcott's address could be described as distinctively Buddhistic, except perhaps that "as man creates his own destiny, so he must be his own Saviour and Redeemer, and can have no other." The Colonel thought it expedient also to note that no western Theosophist "holds to his or her ancestral sect, nor has any belief in, or connection with, Christianity in any form whatsoever." (Olcott, 1880:37)

One can easily imagine the attractive novelty, in colonial Ceylon, of a westerner disowning Christianity, and championing the "natives" and their religion. It is in that context that Olcott's address was widely popular in Ceylon, and Don David shared in the general enthusiasm:

> I remember going up to greet them. The moment I touched their hands, I felt overjoyed. The desire for universal brotherhood, for all the things they wanted for humanity, struck a responsive chord in me. (Dharmapala, 1927:723)

It is, though, difficult to specify more exactly what it was that Don David found so attractive. The Theosophists held generally anti-Christian sentiments, no doubt, but, as the Colonel explained, there was nevertheless room in the society for "Christian free-thinkers." They had no distinctly Buddhist message, and what Buddhist elements they did adopt were interwoven with ideas from a dozen different religions, and from Blavatsky's interpretations of communications with various unseen beings who were, so to say, under exclusive contract to her.

Perhaps they had room for everyone, and that was enough for Don David, who decided soon after their first visit that he would devote himself "to the welfare of others." He had no idea how this resolve might be translated into action, and yet "felt sure that somehow the way would be found in the writings of Madame Blavatsky." (Dharmapala, 1927:723) When, therefore, the Theosophists again visited Ceylon, Don David was prepared to follow wherever they might lead.

The Theosophical Contribution to Dharmapala's "Buddhism"

Olcott and Blavatsky returned to Colombo in 1884, and Don David was "initiated" by the Colonel as a candidate for "adeptship" a status invented by the Theosophists and loosely modeled, as were most Theosophical concepts, on interpretations of older traditions. This required, among other things, that the aspiring adept remain "perfectly chaste, perfectly abstemious, and indifferent to luxury of any kind." (Sinnett,1969 [1880]:21-23)

Celibacy, anyway, was a natural role for Dharmapala. At the age of nine, he had made the brahmachariya vow—of celibacy—as a conventional and temporary act associated with the lay observance of the Buddhist Poya—full-moon—holy days. Dharmapala, however, came to regard the vow as permanently binding; "In my case it had made a permanent impression on my mind." (Dharmapala, 1927: 721) Later, at the age of sixteen, after the death of his infant sister, he had reaffirmed his boyish vow, resolving "never to be the cause of sorrow to a woman."

It is a measure of his experimental religious attitudes that Don David did not seek to institutionalize his celibate aspirations within the most culturally available role, Buddhist monkhood. Nevertheless, as Theosophist or Buddhist, throughout his life Dharmapala tied his sense of mission to the denial of sexuality.

He was now an initiate of the Theosophical Society and, in December of 1919, on the eve of their return to the Adyar Theosophical headquarters near Madras, Blavatsky and Olcott invited the young man to accompany them. His family, and the Hekkuduwe Sumangala, were initially opposed. At the point when they had nearly "dissuaded Col. Olcott to take me to Madras," the flamboyant Blavatsky burst into the room declaring "if you don't let him go he will die!" Don David was permitted to take leave of his family. (ADS, Vol. 3, May 1919)

> It was my first voyage in a steamer outside of Ceylon. The voyage was a stormy one and I was sick all the way. The steamer entered the harbour and the Madras Theosophists came on board and received HPB with divine honours. Brahmans prostrated before her. (ADS, Vol. 3 May, 1918)

At the Adyar headquarters, which was in his memory of the times, "saturated with the aroma of the devotion of the Himalayan Masters to the Lord Buddha," (Sangharakshita, 1980: 47) David was given a mission.

> HPB studied the philosophy of Buddhism and became a Buddhist and paved the way for Buddhism by her writings. She did not advise me to study Theosophy but advised me to study Pali, and to work for humanity. (ADS Vol. 38, 1923)

This construction of Blavatsky's influence is typical of Dharmapala's attitude towards her. Indeed, he maintained, even after she had fled India to escape the publicity that had attended a fraudulent demonstration of "occult powers" at Adyar,[2] that she had never been anything less than a

---

[2] A cabinet in the "shrine room" at Adyar, the scene of many a supernatural phenomenon, was discovered to have been fitted out with hidden trap-doors. The natural suspicions arose. (Campbell, 1980:88-91) In the few references

devout and orthodox Buddhist. Also, the passage demonstrates Dharmapala's mature attempts to represent his life as an unbroken commitment to the propagation of Buddhism. Actually, Blavatsky's advice to Don David was simply the normal Theosophical procedure for the expansion of the society's influence.

The Theosophical movement was, in effect, a franchise operation. The first society established in Asia was "The Theosophical Society of the Arya Samaj." The Arya Samaj was a Hindu reform movement of the time with which Blavatsky and Olcott were briefly associated.[3] There then came to be such units as "The Parsi Section of the Theosophical Society," "The Anglo-Indian Theosophical Society," the Rangoon, Singapore, and other local societies, and dozens of other sub-societies organized either by region or by the predominant religion of the membership. The organization of societies by region and religion was what the Theosophists might have called a reflection of the "exoteric" diversity that masked, necessarily, a unified "esoteric" philosophy, the "ancient wisdom-religion," that could be approached only by perfected adepts. (Sinnett, 1969[1880]:143)

Don David had been chosen to establish and maintain one more "exoteric" branch society and, in his diaries, it is apparent that his commitment to conventional Buddhism was weak and undefined.

> Had I remained in the TS I don't know what
> I would have become. I would have studied

---

he makes to the matter, Dharmapala exonerates Blavatsky and indicts the Coulombs, the couple who had first discovered and reported the fraud. This particular scandal made no impression on Dharmapala's attitude. For inatnce: "As long as H.P.B. was alive there was only Buddhism." (ADC, July 15, 1902)

[3] Farquhar writes that the "Theosophical Twins" enjoyed only the briefest of associations with the Arya Samaj, whose members soon began to question their commitment to Hindu reform. (Farquhar, 1915:226)

> Theosophical literature and become a half-Vedantin, half Buddhist, or I would have become a chela and worked in the Theosophical Society, carrying out the orders of Theosophical leaders, or become General Secretary of the Buddhist section. (Dharmapala, SUMN, 1919)

He did, following Blavatsky's advice, take up the study of Pali, and his earliest available diaries frequently contain exegetical passages on key passages of Theravada philosophy. Again, however, he showed no inclination to take up a Buddhist monkly vocation and still aspired, as a "chela," to attain the status of a Theosophical "Master."

"In 1886 I Severed from the Bustling World": "Renunciation"

In the several years after his brief trip to Adyar, Dharmapala worked closely with Olcott, and with the Theosophist C.W. Leadbeater (Tillet, 1982), on a variety of Theosophical and Buddhist projects. As well, he held a post as a clerk in the Department of Public Instruction. At one time he was notified by the department that, based on his examination performance, he would be offered a better post. His father counseled him to take the job, and to further his Theosophical interests by contributing his salary to the society. By this time, however, Don David was beginning to take decisions for himself, and he declined the post. He recalls, "In 1886, I severed from the bustling world." (ADC, March 1, 1891)

This is a strange memory of those times, that he "severed from the bustling world," for, while his religious aspirations had sharpened, and had found an expression that precluded the pursuit of a conventional career, he was increasingly involved in "the bustling world" in the sense of becoming an organizer for the Theosophists, which involved considerable strategizing and organization.

The social anthropologist Gananath Obeyesekere, in considering Dharmapala, has called this decision "this-worldly asceticism," following the sociologist Max Weber, who first called attention to the phenomenon of those who employed a terminology of the traditional ascetic but pursued, in fact. a specific kind of highly active and public religious career, (Obeyesekere, 1976:236; 1972:68). I think it is probably not so that Dharmapala is a good example of this, but Dharmapala's various decisions about himself are certainly interesting to sociologists and historians of religion.

"To Follow the Aryan Customs"

Dharmapala did, at this time, begin to make decisions for himself. At some time prior to Feb. 3, 1889, he had came to a decision to change his name and, in a letter to Weligama Sumangala, we find the first instance of his signature as "Dharmapala Hewavitarne." In an attempt to enlist the support of the Nayaka Thera, he explained his decision.

> I have renounced the foreign name, which I had used hitherto, and have added to my surname "Dharmapala." This letter is written to your reverence so as to obtain a list of Sanskrit and Pali names. Please send a list suitable for both males and females. It is not befitting for Sinhala Buddhists to bear Christian foreign names. Please help us, therefore, to achieve our objective. (Guruge, 1980: xxxix)

Obeyesekere makes the reasonable suggestion that Dharmapala's renunciation of his birth name represents, not only a rejection of some colonial and Christian elements of his identity, but furthermore functions as a recovery of a Sinhalese Buddhist heritage. (Obeyesekere, 1975:252) Much of Dharmapala's life can be read as following out this general pattern. Nevertheless, it is also clear that other issues of identity, not at all clearly encompassed by Sinhalese nationalism or Buddhism, continued to be of concern to Dharmapala.

True, Dharmapala developed, in later years, an attitude that can only be described as an aggressive Sinhala chauvinism. On the other hand, this attitude, even when fully developed, was not at all continuously held, but interrupted at frequent intervals by contempt for the Sinhalese, and particularly for Sinhalese monks. This contempt was often accompanied by a despair about the ability of the Sinhalese ever to meet what he saw as the challenges of the modern world.

This sort of ambivalence is certainly not unparalleled in nationalist leaders—witness Herzl's not infrequently rude comments about his fellow Jews—but I nevertheless think that it is worthwhile to explore ideas other than nascent Sinhalese nationalism in regard to Dharmapala's particular identity struggle. Consider, for instance, that, writing in 1923, Dharmapala, proudly specifying that it was his own idea, explained his reasons for his change of name:

> My visit to Adyar and the sight of the Brahmans made an impression as to make me follow the Aryan customs. Then I had a Christian name. Nobody suggested that I cast it off. It was in 1887 that the idea came to me to take on an Aryan name, and I myself selected the name Dharmapala. (ADS, 20/10/23)

Here there is no Sinhalese nationalism at all but rather the rejection of a western, and specifically, of a Christian, association. Furthermore, however it may have later come to seem but a step in his ultimate commitment to his "native religion," it is here a bid to take on not a *Buddhist* but a pan-Asian, or "Aryan," identity.

Finally, only very much later, when as an old man he was ordained a Theravadin Bhikku with the name Sri Devamitta

Dhammapala, was a name used that could clearly represent an indisputably Sinhalese Buddhist identity. Here, *contra* Obeyesekere, some four decades after the change of name to "Dharmapala," is a better place to locate, if indeed we can, his embrace of a Sinhalese Buddhist identity. For some time to come, in Dharmapala's life, the concept of "Aryan," as processed by Theosophy, would continue to operate.

The notion of an "Aryan," tradition, much favored by the Theosophists, marked an attempt to portray a great Asian stream of tradition, ancient and multi-civilizational in character, that could be powerfully opposed to the idea of "the West," and/or Christianity. In Dharmapala's life considered as a whole, it had a bi-polar character, capable, on the one hand, of pulling together diverse traditions under the rubric of a very general project, such as a search for "Universal Brotherhood," and capable on the other hand of being *eventually* recovered in a chauvinistic Sinhala form, by viewing Sinhalese Theravada as the most "authentic" form of "Aryan tradition."

Either way, interestingly, this sort of thinking could encompass diversity, in a very broadly ecumenical manner, or in a hierarchical mode.

The Buddhist Catechism

One project with which the Theosophists and Dharmapala were involved was the editing, translation and distribution of a so-called "Buddhist Catechism." This has very much the form of a Christian catechism and represented, for the Sinhalese, a genuine innovation. Olcott himself puts the matter quite well, in his 1903 preface to the fortieth edition of the work, he wrote:

> It has always seemed to me incongruous that an American, making no claims at all to scholarship, should be locked up to by the Sinha-

> lese to help them teach the dharma to their children; and as I believe I said in an earlier edition, I only consented to write the Buddhist Catechism after I had found that no Bhikkhu [monk] would undertake it. (Olcott, 1903,viii)

The work was largely compiled from English translations, many of them the work of the Pali Text Society, then vetted by Don David, and translated by him into Sinhalese.

The catechism received a recommendation from Sumangala Sri Hikkuduwe, who wrote that "the same is in agreement with the Canon of the Southern Buddhist Church." It has, in fact, on two separate occasions, received formal approval from authoritative monks of virtually every Buddhist community in the world, and not just from the "Southern Church," which here means Sinhalese Theravadins. Here, then, is one project that to some extent validates Dharmapala's later recollection of his life's work as having been fundamentally Buddhistic.

Having said that, the idea of the catechism was originally Olcott's, and the idea that is most famously attached to Dharmapala's himself, the "recovery" of Bodh Gaya, was also attributed, by Dharmapala himself, to someone else, Sir Edwin Arnold. So, if the Theosophists first introduced Dharmapala to India and the "Aryan" tradition, Arnold first introduced him to Bodh Gaya.

Sir Edwin Arnold and *The Light of Asia*

The success of the Buddhist Catechism made available to the Theosophists a wider audience in the Buddhist world, as was evident in 1884 when Dharmapala accompanied Colonel Olcott on a trip to Japan. This was intended, naturally, to establish new Theosophical outposts, and to further popularize the Catechism. Dharmapala seems to have been ill for most of his stay in Japan, and while laid up, in a hotel room in Kyoto, he read Sir Edwin Arnold's *Light of Asia.*[4]

> The idea of restoring the Buddhist Jerusalem into Buddhist hands originated with Sir Edwin Arnold after having visited the sacred spot in 1886. It was he who gave me the impulse to visit the shrine, and since 1891 I have done all I could to make the Buddhists of all lands interested in the scheme of restoration. (Guruge, 1984:366)

Arnold was born, to comfortable Kentish gentry, in Gravesend, on July 10, 1832. Five years old when Victoria came to the throne, he outlived that monarch by almost three years, dying, in London, on March 24, 1904.

This close Victorian tracking seems appropriate, given Arnold's travels throughout the empire, and given his enthusiastic though by no means always uncritical support of the British imperial mission. Arnold was responsible, for instance, for much of the arrangements for Stanley's Congo adventure, and is said to have coined the phrase "Cape to Cairo Railway," a concept championed by Cecil Rhodes.

Early on, though, nothing would have predicted the role he would come to play in the revival of a Buddhist pilgrimage site in Bihar. I cannot, though, resist the following vaguely karmic observation: Arnold's entry into the great stream of Buddhist history dates from his matriculation, in 1851, at University College, Oxford, when he moved into quarters once occupied by Dharmapala's favorite poet, Percy Bysshe Shelley.

[4] Elsewhere, Dharmapala notes that he was aware of *The Light of Asia* immediately after it appeared in print. In 1879, Gunananda received from Olcott, who was then in Bombay, a copy of the first edition of " The Theosophist," in which appeared "an admirable review of *The Light of Asia.* Evidently, Gunananda must have shown this to the young Don David, who wrote that "I thought it was light from heaven." (MBJ, Vol. 41, July/Sept 7,8,9.

In the year of the Mutiny, 1857, the young classicist was offered the principalship of Government College at Poona, in Bombay Presidency, and it was there that he began to interest himself in Indian religious and literary matters.

Arnold returned to London in 1860, to take up a position at the "Daily Telegraph," and thereafter traveled widely, coming to know many parts of the British empire, but also Japan and other parts of Asia, During the period when Dharmapala came to know him, Arnold's life was devoted to both journalism and poetry. (Wright, 1957:passim)

In 1879, Arnold's biblicized Buddhist epic, *The Light of Asia,* the work that so impressed Dharmapala, was published. This was a poetic account, drawn from English translations, that chronicled the career of Gautama Buddha.

The general flavor of the work is perhaps adequately suggested by the following evocation of the Bodhi-tree at Bodh Gaya:

> The Bodhi-tree (thenceforward for all years
> Never to fade and ever to be kept
> In homage of the world), beneath whose leaves
> It was ordained that truth should come to Buddh,
> Which now the Master knew, wherefore he went,
> With measured pace, steadfast, majestical
> Unto the Tree of Wisdom, Oh ye worlds
> Rejoice! Our Lord wended unto the tree!
> (Arnold, 1879:155-56)

I am not a literary critic, but I have to say I do not like this very much. In fact, in one draft of the current work (never published), I had characterized Arnold's *Light of Asia* as a "wretched production," and one of my anonymous reviewers sternly inquired as to my authority for so writing. At the time, I had nothing to offer but my own untutored taste, and taste in these matters is notoriously idiosyncratic. I have lately, however, come across this passage, from *The Cambridge History of English and American Literature*, in the section "Lesser Poets of the Middle and Later Nineteenth Century":

> Whether Edwin, later Sir Edwin, Arnold can be called a more popular poet than lord Lytton is a question which might occasion logomachy; but he certainly escaped the unfavourable criticism which, in this way and that, " Owen Meredith" attracted. Although we do not now write *Arts of Preserving Health* or discussions of the sugar cane in verse, there has never failed a public for poetry which, as the naive phrase goes, " tells you something" ; and The Light of Asia, Sir Edwin's best known poem, gained vogue as an easy version of what some said was a very exoteric Buddhism. Despite active employment, first in educational matters and then in journalism, he produced a good deal of verse on many different subjects and in many different forms. Some of it obtained considerable praise, while, on the other hand, there are critics who are seldom able to perceive true poetry in anything that Sir Edwin wrote—his blank verse appearing to them fluently insignificant and his lyrics, with one remarkable exception, lacking life, wanting in intensity and in anything but rather commonplace

music.

Perhaps there is more to be said about this aspect of things, but I cannot think of anything. The "remarkable exception," by the way, is a poem called *He and She*, which has nothing to do with the present topic: *The Light of Asia* was Arnold's one and only Buddhistical production.

More substantively, it might be noted that the idea that "it was ordained" that truth should "come" to Gautama under the Bodhi-tree is problematic in general Buddhist context: it is by one's aspirations and exertions that one is said to achieve enlightenment. Such difficulties aside, in a short time, Arnold's poem became the most widely read English work ever published on Buddhism.

By 1885, Trubner had issued thirty editions of *the Light of Asia*, in England, and pirated editions were selling briskly in the United States. It was soon translated into the major European languages, and its popularity earned for Arnold "the Order of the White Elephant" from the Thai government, for making some version of Buddhist doctrine widely available in the west. (Peiris, 1970:30-34)

While Wright, Arnold's biographer, was unable to arrive at a firm figure for sales of the *Light of Asia*, such information as he collected suggests that it did as well as, say, *Huckleberry Finn*, during the same period. (Wright, 1957:70-73) Arnold's poem was well-known and well-received in Ceylon very shortly after publication and this served as an opening for the friendships that Arnold subsequently cultivated with influential Sinhalese monks.

Arnold Returns to "Forgotten" Bodh Gaya

In 1886, Arnold, now retired from the editorship of "The Telegraph," returned to India for an extensive tour and, from Calcutta, he wrote the monk Weligama Sri Sumangala, a great Sanskritist, to announce his intention to visit Ceylon.

"I have lately passed very happy days at Sarnath, Buddha Gaya and other places made famous by the feet of the great Tathagatho about which I hope to tell you."

Arnold had formulated a proposal that Bodh Gaya and other sacred sites be transferred to Buddhist guardians and this excited great interest during discussions he held with Sumangala at the western coastal town of Panadure. On his departure, Arnold told Sumangala "I shall try to see if anything can be done in this direction and if my efforts be at all successful I will communicate with you." (Guruge, 1984:363-66)

Arnold's initial efforts took the form of letters written to the Governor of Ceylon, and to the Lieutenant-Governors of Bengal and Madras. It was, however, Arnold's several articles in the Telegraph that served most effectively to advertise the cause. As these point to virtually the full range of attitudes, obstacles and opportunities that would influence the Bodh Gaya campaign for the next half-century, it will be convenient to reproduce the following somewhat lengthy passage.

> The Buddhist world had, indeed, well-nigh forgotten this hallowed and most interesting centre of their faith—the Mecca, the Jerusalem, of a million Oriental congregations—when I sojourned in Buddha Gaya a few years ago. I was grieved to see Mahratta peasants performing "Shraddh" in such a place and thousands of precious ancient relics of carved stone inscribed with Sanskrit lying in piles around. I asked the priest if I might have a leaf from the sacred tree.
>
> "Pluck as many as ever you like, sahib," was his reply, "it is as nought to us."
>
> Ashamed of his indifference, I took silently

> the three or four dark shining leaves which he pulled from the bough over his head, and carried them with me to Ceylon, having written upon each the holy Sanskrit formula. There I found them prized by the Sinhalese Buddhists with eager and passionate emotion. The leaf presented by me to the Temple at Kandy, for example, was placed in a casket of precious metal and made the centre of a weekly service, and there and then it befell that, talking to the wise and learned priests at Pandure —particularly to my dear and wise friend, Sri Weligama—I gave utterance to the suggestion that the temple and its appurtenances ought to be, and might be, by amicable arrangements with the Hindoo College and by the favour of the Queen's Government, placed in the hands of a representative committee of the Buddhist Nations. (Arnold, 1896:310-11)

Arnold's editorial may be fruitfully examined in some detail. Let me begin with his notion that the site had been "forgotten" by Buddhists.

Bodh Gaya: "Sacred Peripherality"?

Narratives of the Buddha's career, and thus some sense of Indian sacred geography, were an element of each textual package by means of which the formal doctrine had diffused throughout the Buddhist world. As well, due to the peculiar portability of the Bodhi-tree's sacrality, the prestige of Bodh Gaya had botanically diffused, as layered cuttings, to Thailand and Ceylon.

Even the Mahabodhi Temple itself had been reproduced, mainly in miniature but sometimes full-scale, in Burma, Thailand, Nepal, Tibet and China. (Bharati,1970: 115;

Griswold, 1965: passim) So, there was no danger, at the time Arnold was writing, that Bodh Gaya would somehow slip away from the Buddhist memory.

Yet, how salient was the prestige of Bodh Gaya, even to the Sinhalese Buddhists with whom Arnold consulted? It is quite inconceivable that a scholar-monk such as Weligama Sumangala could have been unfamiliar with the Pali texts that detail Gautama's experiences at Bodh Gaya. On the other hand, it is possible to overestimate the degree to which such apparently basic texts were known throughout the lay community.

For instance, one would have expected a well-educated Buddhist layman, like Dharmapala, to have been familiar with these. Yet, Dharmapala routinely credited Arnold, and not any canonical source, with having introduced him to the Buddhist geography of India.

There is obviously a gap between a memory, erased in some Buddhist collective unconsciousness, and the "eager and passionate emotion with which the leaves of the Bodhi tree were received in Ceylon. On one level this can be characterized as the latency of Bodh Gaya as a ground for action based on Buddhist sensitivities. Arnold, I assume, meant to suggest, not that Buddhists had literally forgotten Bodh Gaya, although many no doubt had never heard of the place, but that the site was no longer host to an active Buddhist cult. In this, he was correct, for, in spite of the recent Burmese reconstruction effort, Burmese Bhikkhus were not regularly resident at the shrine, there were no other monks resident there, and Buddhist folk from any country only rarely, and in small numbers, made pilgrimage to Bodh Gaya.

Let me refer briefly, from a comparative perspective, to the latent quality of the sacrality of Buddha Gaya. The site has operated as a magnet, of historically fluctuating strength to draw religious folk from throughout the Buddhist world. It has, on the other hand, never been doctrinally stipulated by any Buddhist tradition that Buddhists are *obliged* to visit what Arnold called "this hallowed and most interesting centre of their faith."

Islam, of course, is the religion that has most clearly and doctrinally established an obligatory pilgrimage. Now Bodh Gaya is not central as Mecca is central but, oddly, both sites have acquired a similar *formal* peripheral quality. To take up Victor Turner's influential ideas about pilgrimage, consider the following:

> Despite its centrality for the religious domain, however, Mecca is certainly peripheral to each and all of the many social and political systems into which Muslims have become secularly organized. It is almost as though Islam by a kind of paradox had made sacred peripherality itself central to man's authentic existence, at least in terms of the ideal model it presents to the world. (Turner, 1974:195)

The comparison is invited. The obvious distinction, at the outset, is that, unlike Bodh Gaya, Mecca is doctrinally placed at the center of the ideal religious life. Certainly, however, Bodh Gaya is peripheral to all those systems into which Buddhists had become secularly, and, moreover, ecclesiastically, organized. Insofar as Bodh Gaya had become an empty point, marking the founding inspiration of Buddhism yet entirely encompassed by Hindu India, its peripheral character was far more complete than Mecca's. Actually, it is not clear that the peripherality of Bodh Gaya has somehow functioned to amplify its sacrality except for, very importantly, peripheral *people*, such as Arnold and Dharmapala. To conclude, Bodh Gaya had not been entirely forgotten by the Buddhist world, but it had not either, by Arnold's time, been widely elevated to a sacrality marked as distinctive by virtue of its peripheral position.

Tibetan Buddhists at Bodh Gaya

I have discussed the early Burmese mission, and also Dharmapala, whose attitude, though in a complicated way, illustrates a Sinhalese and Theravada point of view. Looking northward, one finds for Tibet a distinctive view of Indian Buddhist sites. India was neither forgotten by Tibetans, nor was it highly salient. Tibetans largely confined their travels to an impressively extensive pilgrimage circuit within Tibet itself. It is intriguing to note that one Tibetan place of pilgrimage, Garsha, near Ladakh, is held to be "equal in sanctity to Bodh Gaya." (SC: item 5) Here, then, it is a question not of forgetting, but of replicating the Indian Bodh Gaya.

India was conventionally revered by Tibetans as the Buddhist homeland, but, even when they turned their attention to India, they tended to do so with no special regard for Bodh Gaya. In fact, Tibetans tended to conceptually organize Indian geography, not so much according to the career of Gautama, but rather with reference to an elaborate Tantric cosmology.

Certainly, from the time Buddhism was first introduced into Tibet, many scholars and translators traveled to India to obtain sacred texts, and, upon their return, were able to wear the badge of pilgrimage as a marker of religious prestige. Nevertheless, such travels were quite rare, not least of all because the climate of the Gangetic plain seemed almost impossibly inhospitable to the high-altitude Tibetans. In the eighteenth century, the unusually adventurous third Panchen Lama did send a number of missions to Indian Holy places.

Yet, during trade negotiations with the British, the Panchen evinced a great interest, not in Bodh Gaya, but in the possibility that "Shambul," [sham-ba-la], a Vajrayana paradise, might be located near Calcutta. In short, that which might have been considered more central, by the text-based standards of Theravada orthodoxy, was secondary to the interests of Tibetan Buddhists. (Markham, 1879:168-69; Petech, 1950:335)

Thinking about Sinhalese (and Burmese) and Tibetan approaches to Bodh Gaya leads to a further consideration: the ecumenical thrust of Arnold's proposal. Arnold styled Bodh Gaya the center for the faith of "a million oriental congregations." His plans for Bodh Gaya, and the Mahabodhi society campaign that followed, were predicated on the assumption that these congregations, however diverse and scattered they might be, would respond in a unified fashion to a call for the recovery of a common center.

"Buddhist" and "Hindu" Ritual at Bodh Gaya

I have demonstrated that this center was not unproblematically "central," but, beyond these considerations, to exacerbate an already complicated situation, the "center" in question was encompassed by Hindu India. Arnold had expressed his distaste at seeing Hindu peasants performing ceremonies for their ancestors at the site. There is the notion, amplified later by Dharmapala, that such behavior was fundamentally inappropriate.

In the same passage, Arnold manages to associate this ritual performance of shraddh with the general neglect of the area and the scattered debris of the Buddhist past. What should be especially noted here is the idea that a great divide between Hindus and Buddhists can be easily marked by making the appropriate distinctions in ritual behavior: this is something that both Government of India and Government of Bengal believed, and, as I shall later demonstrate, the idea heavily shaped official attitudes. At first glance, of course, it would appear to be unexceptionable.

After all, Hindus visit the Bodhi tree, as one tree among several in the Gaya area, and one among countless trees in Hindu India, in order to offer pindas to the ancestors, while

Buddhists, at least according to Theravada orthodoxy, are to merely circumambulate the temple and the tree, and to view the latter, not as an object of special ritual efficacy, but as a commemoration of the Buddha's enlightenment.

These are real distinctions, but they can be misleading. A major feature in the development of disputes between Hindus and Buddhists at the shrine would be, as I shall show in the next chapter, the varied characterizations, by all concerned parties, of the ritual behavior that was considered natural, appropriate and "orthodox" for each community.

Is the daubing of the Buddha's forehead a "Hinduization" of a Buddhist image? Or is it also properly a feature of Tantric Buddhist ceremony? Is it "orthodox" Hindu behavior to worship at an image of the Buddha, or is it anathema? Or does the distinction depend on a mental operation of the worshipper, who may, with the greatest of ease, transform Gautama Buddha into Buddha Avatar? Even with regard to the Bodhi tree itself, the reliability of the ritual divide between Buddhists and Hindus, in one intriguing case, fails dramatically.

Among small communities of Bengali (Magh) Buddhists, ancestor offerings are routinely made at "bodhi-trees" of village viharas. At the death of a pregnant woman, such offerings must be made at the tree in Bodh Gaya itself. (Chaudhuri, 1982: 76-77, 103) These practices very much recall the ancestral offerings (shraddh) made by Hindus at Gaya and elsewhere.

This overlap of ritual behavior, and, in the case of the worship of Buddhist images, the avatar formula that conventionally expresses Hindu attitudes to Gautama, were to become major sources of confusion in the events that molded the modern outcome of the interfaith configuration at Bodh Gaya. As well, the charge, implicitly in Arnold's writing and voiced later with some belligerence by Dharmapala and the

Mahabodhi Society, that Hindus were guilty of a distinctive misuse of the sacred properties of Bodh Gaya, became a staple in the conflict.

With regard to the possibility of conflict, it is intriguing to note that Arnold, and Dharmapala initially, anticipated facing few obstacles in their project to recover the temple. As Arnold put it, the whole thing could be managed through "amicable arrangements," between the various concerned groups and the Giris of the "Hindoo College." Neither Arnold nor Dharmapala understood the extent to which the temple was embedded in a system of longstanding local and regional relationships, at a concrete social level, and neither did they appreciate the extent to which the Buddha, and Buddhism itself, were encompassed, culturally and ideologically, by Hindu practices and ideas.

The Buddhists and their allies initially found the social difficulty trivial: the Mahant could be bought out and no objection was anticipated. How could Hindus object to the sale of a Buddhist temple to Buddhists? When, in fact, the Mahant refused, as I shall shortly document, Dharmapala responded first with disbelief and then with outrage.

The Theosophists had introduced Dharmapala to a notion of legitimate religious pluralism, and he had not, upon his arrival at Bodh Gaya, developed any anti-Hindu sentiments at all. However, Dharmapala's pluralism admitted only that distinct religious persons and groups performed worship appropriate to their distinct traditions. Buddhists worshipped in Buddhist temples, regardless of whether or not they were also Theosophists, and Hindus did not.

That was, for Dharmapala, the natural and appropriate arrangement and, in a sense, it was not at all contrary to the Theosophical principle that "exoteric" distinctions between sects should be maintained except, perhaps, for the elect. This was, however, not the arrangement Dharmapala found in place at Bodh Gaya.

Chapter Four

BUDDHIST FLAG AT BODH GAYA

"The Bengalees love Lord Buddh," wrote Dharmapala in his diary for January 21, 1891. "His blessed life has been dramatized and he therefore became popular among them. They call him Buddha Deva." (ADC, Jan.21,1891) Buddha Deva, of course, is the Budh Avatara, and it is noteworthy that this formulation, which shortly became such an irritant to Dharmapala, now seemed acceptable: from the "high Theosophical" point of view, such ecumenicalism could even seem attractive.

He was on his way to Bodh Gaya, in the company of several Bengali Hindus he had befriended through his Theosophical contacts in Calcutta. Also with him was Kozen Gunaratna, a Japanese Shingon priest[1] he had recently met at an Adyar Theosophical conference. (TT, Vol.XII, #5, Feb, 1981:xxi)

On the afternoon of his arrival, Dharmapala visited the Bodhi-tree, accompanied by Gunaratna. "I gathered some leaves of the tree and one was very peculiar in its formation. The tissues of the leaf were like veritable roots." He saw in this an affirmation of the notion that he should take up a project for "saving the place," and asked Gunaratna if he would help.

---

[1] The Shingon is a tantric sect, whose priests marry and whose temples are generally passed on in patrilineal succession to the eldest son. An irony of Dharmapala's life, one of many for an individual who is generally regarded as a pillar of Theravadin orthodoxy, is that his first Buddhist associate in the Mahabodhi temple campaign was from such an exuberantly Mahayana tradition.

> He joyously assented and, more than that, he had been thinking the same thing. We both solemnly promised that we would stop here until some Buddhist priests come and take charge of the place.

The possibility that someone might already be in charge of the shrine does not seem to have occurred to either of the pair. Of the Mahant, Dharmapala noted only that "he lives in a splendid place," and "is a chief of the vedanta school." (ADC, Jan. 22, 1891) This latter characterization of the Giris bears testimony to Dharmapala's less than expert knowledge of Hindu religion: the phrase "the vedanta school" is not terribly specific with regard to any actual sect.

Two days later, Dharmapala found himself in conversation with Durga Shankar Bhattachariya, a local zamindar and the Vice-Chairman of the Municipal Board of Gaya Township. He spoke to Durga Babu of his hope of "doing all we can to re-establish the sasana [Buddhist doctrine] in India."

This is surely a grandiose project and one that, in later years, Dharmapala would advocate with great energy, often with a studied disregard for Hindu sensitivities. Now, it was a pure enthusiasm, it appeared natural to Dharmapala, it had no very immediate or concrete expression, and it involved no sense of opposition. Such enthusiasm, earnestly expressed and joined to no clear plan of action, probably seemed either attractive or harmless, or both, to Durga Babu, whom Dharmapala describes as "extremely obliging and kind." (ADC, Jan. 24, 1891)

Yet, the seed of a more concrete project had been planted during his experience at the vajrasana and, soon, Dharmapala's weightless vision came to have more force and substance. Several events mark the transition.

Dharmapala as Religious Revitalizationist

One of the aforementioned events was a dream, one that triggered an amplification of Dharmapala's sense of mission.

> Nasty nocturnal sights. Dream. Bad friend who taught me bad things. One night father comes to the room then finds that something bad is done. He inquires. A plea is given. He goes and I am left alone. He asks the friend to go out. He goes and I am left alone. My mother comes. Takes care of me. The scene opens with a new tableau. Saw area with a new title. Beautiful illuminations of a company of men preaching. (ADC, Jan 24, 1891)

This is a dream about sexual temptation: his diaries document a long struggle with both hetero-and homo-sexual feelings, which left him feeling shamed and weak. Consider, for instance, the following 1889 diary entry, of a kind that appeared very frequently for decades thereafter:

> Bad dreams. Why should it be so is a thing I cannot understand. I am trying to lead a celibate life yet, why should there be these nocturnal emissions? (ADC, Nov. 10, 1889)

Much of this—the search for new parents, the anxiety about his destiny, the cultural confusions of his childhood and early adulthood, and sexual anxiety and guilt—is well contextualized by reference to Wallace's classic essay (1956) about religious revitalization.

Wallace's ideas, though they seem in some way dated—particularly, his characterization of a society as a "system" that gets perturbed and then corrected by this or that social-mechanical process seems now heavy-handed—are applicable in the present case. Consider, for instance, the various conditions for the sociocultural "production," so to say, of a revitalization movement. I paraphrase, and comment where appropriate:

1) Steady State—at this moment a society has reliable techniques for dealing with reliable levels of "stress."
2) Increased Individual Stress—individuals may experience various degrees of novel stress due to a variety of causes, including climate or ecological change, military or political defeat, epidemic disease, and so-forth. For our purposes particularly we should note the colonial subjugation of Ceylon and the active proselytizing by foreign Christian missionaries: this represents, in Wallace's terms, "extreme pressure toward acculturation resulting in internal cultural conflict."
3) Cultural Distortion—this is a sort of internalized feeling that the culture has gone wrong, cannot cope, is inadequate. This feeling, according to Wallace, can lead to a variety of "psychodynamically regressive" responses, including alcoholism, disregard of kinship and sexual mores, and extreme passivity and indolence—which Dharmapala seemed not to experience—and/or also the development of "highly ambivalent dependency relationships" and "states of depression and self-reproach," which he *did* experience with great frequency.
4) Mazeway Reformulation—"mazeway" being Wallace's term for a sort of cultural cognitive-emotional map that one carries around, that normally serves to internally explain, justify, and predict life. Some individuals, under conditions of considerable ongoing stress, seek to reformulate their mazeways, and when they do so successfully, they sometimes produce what we call a revitalization movements which Wallace defines as "a deliberate, organized effort by members of a society to reconstruct a more satisfying culture."

Dharmapala's "mazeway" reformulation follows, not perfectly, but very closely, Wallace's steps. "Every religious revitalization movement," he writes, "has been originally conceived in one or more hallucinatory visions by a single individual." The language of his next sentence makes it clear that "dream" and "vision" are interchangeable, and these dreams contain clear themes:

> 1. The wish for a satisfying parental figure (supernatural, guardian-spirit content).
> 2. World destruction fantasies (the apocalyptic, millennial content).
> 3. Feelings of guilt and anxiety (the moral content).
> 4. Longings for the establishment of an ideal state of stable and satisfying human and supernatural relations (the restitution fantasy or Utopian content). (Wallace 1956: 264-281)

With reference only to the dream mentioned above, three of four elements are obviously apparent. With regard to the second idea, about world destruction, I admit that the fit is not perfect, as Dharmapala seemed to have few or no anxieties in this regard. On the other hand, he did frequently give way to despair that, if not the world, his idealized Sinhalese world, might be destroyed by imperialism, by Christianity, or by the "indolence" of his countrymen and co-religionists.

So, three out of four fit quite robustly, and the fourth arguably also applies, which yields an excellent concordance between Wallace's detailed description of religious revitalization and some intimate details of Dharmapala's career.

Certainly the longing for parental figures is obvious, as are the guilt-feelings, and the "longings for the establishment," in this case, of a "company of men preaching."

That company may also stand for the brotherhood of "perfected masters." In short, the dream expresses an intensification of an aspiration to pursue a mission within a "purified" community.

Dharmapala's Mission

Now, Dharmapala's aspirations, however they may have been at least in part driven by a psychosexual struggle, had acquired a central and public object, the recovery of the Mahabodhi temple. The means whereby he might attain this object were still quite unclear, but the "impulse of recovery" had given Dharmapala's mission a content quite distinct in character from his previous unfocused desires to "work for humanity," or for "the brotherhood of man."

In turn, the acquisition of such an object entailed the arising of new forms of conflict. In Dharmapala's construction of the terms of this conflict, a second shift of vision is apparent.

The primary difficulty, from Dharmapala's point of view, was that people did not seem to be acting appropriately. A week into his first pilgrimage to Bodh Gaya, he noticed that Hindu folk were offering, at the Bodhi-tree, "pindas to Bhagavan Budh." (ADC, Jan. 28, 1891) Of course, his Bengali friends routinely referred to Gautama as Buddha Deva or Bhagavan Budh, but their attitudes were not conjoined to any particular practice.

In contrast to merely amiable interfaith rhetoric, the Hindu offerings of pindas at a Buddhist site seemed to be of a different order. Even more distressing to Dharmapala was his discovery that the Giris claimed the temple as their own. This he saw as simple duplicity. "The Brahmans worship Buddha," he wrote, "but under different names," and they use the temple "for their own selfish purposes." (ADC, Jan. 29, 1891)

In reaction to what he saw as such Hindu "selfishness," Dharmapala took up a new tactic in the construction of Buddhist solidarity. In this construction, a vital element of any genuine Buddhist identity had to be outrage at Hindu control of the Mahabodhi Temple.

Working with this outrage, Dharmapala attempted to recruit a small party of Arakan Buddhist pilgrims, from the Chittagong hill tracts area of what is now Bangladesh. To the monk accompanying them, he had strong words to say:

> I impressed on the Arakanese the absolute necessity of taking the Maha Bodhi under our control and asked him to use all influence in his own country. How shocking it is to see the noble and majestic statue of our Lord descrated and lowered in the eyes of the lingam worshipping Hindu! (ADC, Jan. 29, 1891)

Thus, in addressing his fellow pilgrims, Dharmapala committed one of his first acts of Buddhist unity, using speech that deprecated Hindu rights and beliefs. His next ecumenical act was directed at the disruption of the long-standing relationship between Burmese Buddhists and the Giris.

During the second week of his pilgrimage, a contingent of Burmese Monks visited Bodh Gaya, as they had seasonally done, and for short periods, since the agreement of 1874. Although, by the terms of that agreement, there was a resthouse available for them, where Dharmapala himself was lodged, they settled into apartments at the Giri Math. This had been their custom, but it seemed intolerable to Dharmapala, and he refused to allow the situation to remain undisturbed. "First they took up lodging at the Mahant's bungalow, but I made them take up quarters with us." (ADC, Jan. 31, 1891)

"The Sinhalese Alone are Competent"

At the same time, Dharmapala was writing to Colonel Olcott, "to get him to use his influence with the Tathanabaing [the chief Burmese Buddhist abbot] of Mandalay, to get Bodh Gaya from the English under our control." (ADC, Jan 39, 1891) As is evident from this passage, Dharmapala was not clear about the jurisdictional situation at the temple.

He was not entirely to blame for this: in spite of Mitra's wishful pronouncement noted earlier—that "all such monuments belong to Government. . ." —the situation was not quite clear to any of the interested parties. He was aware of the Giri claims, of course, but dismissed them out of hand.

The superintendent of the temple grounds, an employee of the public works department, had told him "the temple is under the control of the government but the Mahant has the right of the management thereof." (ADC, Jan. 28, 1891) Armed thus only with the vaguest notion of how interests at the site had been allocated,

Dharmapala nonetheless acted on an urgent need to mobilize support for his evolving project, and fired off letters not only to his father, to ask for money, but also Olcott, the Tathanabaing, Edwin Arnold, the Governor of Ceylon, the Kings of Bhutan and Thailand, and the Lieutenant-Governor of Bengal.

In his diary for March 1, 1891, there appears the first example of an intriguing practice to which Dharmapala became addicted. This was a sort of personal history, often presented in the form of a list. The first such list reads: "In February 1884 I joined the T.S., in 1885 Feb. I was in office but my soul yearned for peace; in 1887 working for humanity, in 1880 ditto, 1889 in Japan, in 1890 working for humanity, 1891 in Buddha Gaya." Subsequent chronologies include similar personal events, but place them in ever grander and more significant historical structures. For now, it is interesting to see that the first list contains several clearly Theosophical elements. The phrase "working for humanity" for instance is one associated with his early Theosophical aspirations, and, particularly striking is the casual use of the concept "soul," a thoroughly non-Buddhistic feature.

Other writings from the same period also reveal the blend

of influences to which Dharmapala had been exposed. In the following passage it is clear that Dharmapala was struggling with a variety of approaches to the religious life, and was beginning to formulate a more Buddhistic outlook.

> Prayer to a god won't relieve man from the miseries of existence. Rites and ceremonies won't do. Purity of life is needed. This night at 12 for the first time I experienced that "peace which passeth all understanding." The life of our Lord is a lofty and elevating subject for meditation. The four truths and the Noble Eightfold Path alone can make the devoted pupil of nature happy. I take refuge in Buddha, Dharma and Sangha. (ADC, March 1, 1891)

It should be noted that Dharmapala never entirely lost the tendency to ornament his English rhetoric with biblical language: here I would understand that the phrase "the peace which passeth all understanding" (Philippians IV:7) is made to mark some mental state achieved through meditation. Nevertheless, the direction of the change is plain, even though the quote signals only a partial transition to a more clearly Buddhist stance.

That the shift was, at this stage, partial is also apparent in his continued devotion to his Theosophical mentors. Several months after his arrival in Bodh Gaya, for instance, Dharmapala received his "Certificate of Admission to the Esoteric School of Theosophy." For instance, we find Dharmapala writing, in March of 1891, "May the T.S. prosper and H.S.O and H.P.B. and all their colleagues live long to carry on the work which they have begun. I shall listen to the voice that speaks to me in silence." (ADC, March 4, March 9, 1891)

This "voice" is probably that of the Master Koot-Hoomi, and

is extremely important and interesting in Dharmapala's life—I have dealt with it more extensively in the appendix to this work. For now, I will note that the voice was not always able to provide Dharmapala with the confidence that his project would succeed and, in a number of entries he expressed his doubts that he was capable of "the work." "Indescribable anguishing of heart. Why should this be so? The Priest [Gunaratna] is in the same state. Was it a case of mental suggestion?"

Then too, Kozen Gunaratna "consulted the oracles," and found that "just at present everything seems against us but we shall wait and see. The last thing is death." (ADC, March 9, 1891)

Conjoined to this inaction and anxiety was a growing sense of urgency. "The Buddhist Flag must again be hoisted here on the Full Moon Day of Wesak this year and the Budhist [sic] Mission established here before that time." That is to say within three months. (ADC, March 12, 1891)

As yet, Dharmapala had developed no very specific plan for the implementation of his vision, but at the least, it appeared to require some purchase or lease of land in Bodh Gaya. The Collector, G.A. Grierson (this was the brilliant George Abraham Grierson, who later directed the Linguistic Survey of India) had intimated that property might be available from the Mahant, but Dharmapala seems to have decided that the temple itself belonged to the government and might be for sale.

Grierson, again departing from Mitra's assertion that all such monuments belong to government, attempted to make plain to Dharmapala that the Temple "belongs to the Mahant, not to Government," and, furthermore, that the Mahant, claiming that the temple was sacred to him, declined to discuss its sale. Dharmapala, unimpressed, wrote that "certainly Mr. Grierson ought to know better," and he preferred to believe what he had heard previously from the custodian, that the place was government property, and that the "Mahant has no rights." (ADC, March 9, 1891) However, the question of an actual purchase had not at this time come up as Dharmapala, despite his various pleas, had not amassed sufficient funds.

By the beginning of April, Dharmapala began to seriously worry about the absence of a significant response to his proposals. The "natural" response had not been forthcoming, and the latent sacrality of Bodh Gaya had to be coaxed into revealing itself. Dharmapala was particularly disappointed in the Sinhalese who he characterized as "callous and indifferent." The date he had set himself was fast approaching. "Why won't they reply? There are only twenty days until the Wesak." (ADC, April 13, 1891)

On the other hand, he also soon came to the conclusion—he did this frequently—that the Sinhalese were the only people who could undertake the task of recovery he had envisioned, and, in the first real sign of the Sinhala chauvinism with which he would later be identified, he wrote that "with all their backwardness, the Sinhalese alone are competent to carry out the work of propaganda. " (ADC, May 11, 1891)

The Founding of the Mahabodhi Society and Journal

When it became apparent that the Wesak would pass without his goal being accomplished, he decided to return to Ceylon. On the day of his arrival in Colombo, "I went in the evening with my father to see the H.P. ["High Priest"—Sumangala Hekkuduwe] to arrange about Buddha Gaya Mission." (ADC, May 18, 1891) Two weeks later, Dharmapala called an inaugural meeting, at Vidyodaya College, for the establishment of a "Maha Bodhi Society."

Hekkuduwe Sumangala was elected President, Olcott, Director, and Dharmapala himself became the General Secretary. Sumangala was delegated to inform Edwin Arnold about the formation of the Society, and to ask for his support. (Guruge, 1984: xxxix)

The aims of the society were "to make known to all nations the sublime teachings of the Arya Dharma of Buddha Sakya Muni, and to rescue, restore and re-establish as the religious centre of this movement, the holy place Buddha Gaya, where our Lord attained supreme wisdom." From the outset, Dharmapala made explicit his ecumenical ambitions:

> The society representing Buddhism in general, and not any single aspect of it, shall preserve absolute neutrality with respect to doctrines and dogmas taught by sections and sects among Buddhists. It is not lawful for anybody, whether a member or not, to attempt to make it responsible, as a body, for his own views.(MBS1:1-2)

Membership was open to all non-Buddhists who were sympathetic to the goals of the society.

Although he hoped to assemble and consolidate a very diverse group of supporters, at the very least he felt that his new organization would galvanize Sinhalese interest. Yet, a month later, he wrote that Hekkuduwe was "still shilly shallying about sending Priests to B. Gaya." (ADC, July 3, 1891)

Shortly thereafter, though, in early July, he had managed to receive permission to send four monks, of Hekkuduwe's Ramannya Nikaya, to Bodh Gaya, and these were sent on ahead of Dharmapala.

When he arrived in Bodh Gaya a week after the monks, he found, again, that local conditions presented special difficulties. "Found to my astonishment Priests not in the Burmese Rest House. Found Priests in the baradari [upper story of the building] of the Mahant," Hem Narayan Gir. As he had done earlier with the Burmese, Dharmapala prevailed on the Sinhalese monks to move out immediately. (ADC, July 19, 1891)

The following night, Dharmapala arranged a celebration. His recollection of the event again illustrates the extent to which he was concerned to place himself within a significant history. "The Burmese illuminated the temple, and the Buddhist flag was hoisted again after seven centuries. Buddhism was absent from India for nearly seven centuries and after seven months of hard work I have succeeded in establishing a Bud. Mission." (ADC, July 21, 1891) On the other hand, Dharmapala had not yet succeeded in obtaining any land at the site, and neither had he established any special rights of access to the temple. This is a task he now began to pursue.

There is a loose note in the Colombo Mahabodhi Society collection of Dharmapala's papers, without details, dated July 25, 1891, concerning a "quarrel with Mahant about size of land to be leased." Apparently, thereafter, Dharmapala asked the Collector to intervene and, on July 31, Grierson met with the Mahant and "recommended our Society highly." However this might have been, it seems somewhat unlikely that the cautious Grierson would have then, in Dharmapala's words, "told the Mahant" to lease to the society a parcel of land to the north-west of the temple.

As will shortly become evident, the Government of Bengal was not at the time inclined to coerce the Mahant in any way. At any rate, nothing came of the proposal: "The Mahant digs his feet in," saying only "come another time." (ADC, July 31, 1891)

These happenings—the establishment of the Mahabodhi Society, the negotiations for the purchase of land, and Edwin

Arnold's private lobbying efforts—were the subjects of routine dispatches from Grierson to his commissioner at Patna, and through the latter, to the Lieutenant-Governor of Bengal. By August of 1891, the situation had grown sufficiently complicated that C.A. Elliott, the Lieutenant Governor, felt obliged to notify the Viceroy, Lord Lansdowne.

Elliott informed Lansdowne of "a Ceylonese offer to buy up the place," and noted that he had given a "temporizing reply," and now wished to review for the Viceroy the interests that appeared salient to Bengal. The government had in the past expended considerable energy in assuring that the temple be properly restored, and maintained an interest in "keeping it up."

The Mahant had been willing to deal with Bengal on this basis but government had not thereby established any rights of proprietorship, nor did it envisage seeking to do so. Therefore, with regard to the purchase offer, the policy had to be "that if the Buddhists want to put in a priest of their own, they must buy the Mahant out, with the goodwill of the Hindu community." (LCCI, Vol. 21, Aug. 26, 1891)

"We Ought to Treat it as a National Monument"

To Elliott's formula the Viceroy offered no objection and, at the local level, the policy appeared to have been exactly that as had been represented by Grierson. Dharmapala, however, was still unwilling to accept the situation, and continued to maintain that the government could, and should, intervene to assure the sale, not only of property near the temple, but of the temple itself. This attitude prompted Grierson, in late October, to visit Dharmapala in order to make plain that the temple "is not under the control of the British Government and that, if the Buddhists want it, it must be purchased from the Mahant." (ADC, October 27, 1891)

At a symbolic level, and although he had still obtained no property at Bodh Gaya, Dharmapala chose to act as though his mission was a fait accompli. Three days after his meeting with Grierson, he staged a "memorable Buddhist Convention." This celebration, which Dharmapala styled later in his journal an "International Buddhist Conference," was attended by a handful of Buddhists, some of them pursuing their own private pilgrimages, and some recruited through the Indian Theosophical network. "After 691 years the Buddhists of all countries met together at the Central Shrine. After 8 or 9 years Buddhism will be accepted by the Bengalees." (ADC, Oct. 30, 1891) That night, "again Buddhist and Japanese flags [were] hoisted near the Bo-tree, the place illuminated by the Chittagong and Burmese Buddhists."

The Mahant, naturally enough, found this activity somewhat disturbing and his complaints to the Collector, as well as the unsettling claims being broadcast by the Mahabodhi Society, brought Bengal's Lieutenant Governor Elliott to the site. His opinions, as expressed to the Viceroy, were as follows:

> I have been to Budh Gya, and find that there is not the slightest probability of the Mohunt's consenting to sell or give up his connection with the place. He is proud of it, and took so much to heart the reports in paper about its possible session to a Buddhist committee that he was seriously ill for a time, and only revived when he heard that I refused to give some representatives of that party an interview. The Mahant is a fine old fellow, with a grand following of yellow robed monks, a magnificent castle of a house in which he and they live, and a grand landed estate, which he administers with liberality. We could not possibly put any pressure on him.

On the other hand, the collector of Gaya, "who loves the place with a passion," now expressed his opinion that "we ought to treat it as a national monument, acquire it on behalf of government, and not allow it to fall into private hands."

Elliott, while not impressed with the idea of formal government jurisdiction, agreed about the latter danger. "I would scrutinize very closely the nature of any committee or society that desires to acquire it." He added that, in his opinion, it was most likely that the "Hindu community would object if any definite project were started for making it over to unknown strangers from Ceylon or Burma." (LCCI, Vol.21, #261b, Nov. 6, 1891)

A Clash with Colonel Olcott

It was precisely such a project that Dharmapala now had in mind, but he had yet to devise a realistic plan for its implementation. The progress of a second, inner project, however, proceeded unchecked. In late November 1891, Dharmapala, on board a train to Calcutta, received encouragement from some ethereal source. "Go on my son, I will help you, says the voice." (ADC, Nov. 23, 1891)

Although his diary for 1892 has not, I believe, survived, it is possible to reconstruct many of his activities during that year. Most of these were undertaken, often in association with Olcott, to publicize the goals of Dharmapala's new society, and, especially, to mobilize support for the temple campaign. As a first step in facilitating this, he opened a Mahabodhi Society headquarters in Calcutta, where it has since remained.

In May of 1892, he inaugurated the Mahabodhi Journal and, beginning with the first issues of the journal, Dharmapala's editorials utilized a formulaic code, clearly borrowed from Arnold, which compared Bodh Gaya to the religious centers of other faiths. Bodh Gaya was to Buddhist what Mecca was to Muslims, what Jerusalem was to Christians and Jews.

At the same time, he continued to badger important Buddhist figures throughout Asia, and particularly the Sinhalese. To Hekkuduwe Sumangala he wrote "I do not know why the Buddhists of Ceylon do not put in a greater effort even though Sir Edwin Arnold is exerting himself immensely." (Guruge, 1984:xl)

I have already mentioned the problem of whether this sort of formula expressed widely-held Buddhist sentiments, or, on the other hand, functioned more to re-awaken, or perhaps to invent, such sentiments. Certainly, however, it was through Dharmapala's tireless editorializing, and through his active proselytizing, in Ceylon, Japan, Burma, and throughout India, in Bengal, Chittagong and Darjeeling, that the site became a salient concern for a small but significant number of Buddhists.

And yet, on one such early tour, to Arakan, it was Olcott and not Dharmapala who was billed as the main attraction, being named in the local press "European High Priest of Buddhism."(Olcott, 1931:502) No doubt the Colonel was comfortable with this designation. He had just prior to his voyage written the Sanskritist Max Muller that "the Arakanese Buddhists have urgently called me to Akyub to explain Buddhism to them, and I sail this week." (MC, Oct 6, 1892) On the occasion of a second tour, however, to Darjeeling, Dharmapala took the lead, arranging for a procession of monks and layfolk from the residence of the scholar- adventurer (and British agent) S.C. Das, to a local temple. Once there, the Tibetan Lamas were given relics, and leaves from the Bodhi-trees. Along the way they had sung a Tibetan song, Gya-gar-rdo-je-dan, "Flourish Bodh Gaya." At the close of the ceremony, Dharmapala gave a talk on the decline of the Indian holy places.

"The homeless one" evidently impressed the Lamas as sincere and sympathetic as, in spite of the chauvinistic Sinhalese and Theravada tone of his later writings, Darjeeling Buddhists—of Tibetan traditions—from this time on were included in the ceremonial events Dharmapala staged at periodic intervals in Bodh Gaya and Calcutta. Olcott, on the other hand, was singularly unimpressed by Dharmapala's handling of the event and wrote sourly that "the Darjeeling affair came to naught through lack of an organized plan for carrying it out into practical results." (Olcott, 1931: 487)

Indeed, it is true that this affair led to no immediate gains in the temple campaign, but much of Olcott's attitude is best attributed to jealousy. Olcott tended to regard the Mahabodhi Society as one more Theosophical branch organization, and he was increasingly irritated by signs of his protÈgÈ's independence. As well, Olcott was disturbed by Dharmapala's evident disregard for Hindu feeling. "There was, at the time spoken of, a growing feeling of hostility among the Bengal Hindus (Calcutta) which had been stirred up by the activities of the Maha-Bodhi Society."(Olcott, 1931:509)

Theosophical and Buddhist Ecumenicalism

Dharmapala was now dedicated to sharpening the distinctions between Buddhist and Hindu traditions, and this indicates that he was shifting away from certain features of what we might call Theosophical piety. The following is a typically inflammatory passage from the Mahabodhi Journal:

> The point at issue is: is the temple held sacred by the Hindus? Old Hindu residents at Gaya will tell you that the temple was looked upon by the orthodox Hindus as a place associated with heterodoxy, who use [sic] to scowl and spit upon the images of the BUDDHA and throw stones at the temple. (MBJ, Vol. VIII, Dec. 1892)

Now, aside from the fact that I am aware of no other sources that bear testimony to this sort of practice, Dharmapala's rhetoric is quite out of keeping with Theosophical policy. The senior officers of the occultist organization viewed their mission as the promotion of an esoteric message within an evangelical field that was, properly, religiously plural at the exoteric level. That is to say, they had their own ideology of religious encompassment, regardless of what may have been, in certain cases, their less savory motivations, and this ideology precluded, with the sole exception being Christianity, the abuse of other faiths.

Olcott, for instance, had put Theosophical principles to work in his own religious behavior. Having, in 1884, taken the "triple refuge," in Buddha, Dharma and Sangha, and having thereby declared himself a Buddhist, he had in 1891 been "invested with a sacred thread by the Pandits of Benares," thus declaring himself a "twice-born" Hindu. This latter information comes from an appreciative letter written by one A. Sankariah, an official of the orthodox reform organization, the Hindu Sabha (Benares). Olcott's symbolic incorporation into the orthodox Hindu fold was not accompanied by any renunciation of previous "conversions," and he continued to represent himself as a Buddhist in front of Buddhist audiences in Colombo and elsewhere. After all, these trivial distinctions were dissolved in the ether which pervaded the esoteric realm.

Yet Olcott's version of the interfaith dialogue only thinly veiled the conflicts that lay beneath. Sankariah's attitude towards religious pluralism, for instance, typified the Hindu Sabha view that all people should be re-admitted to the Hindu fold who are now "apostates," including Buddhists, from the Hindu sastric (text) and srauta (oral) traditions, that is to say from Hindu orthodoxy. (TT, Vol, 12, #7, April 1891:442) Clearly, with this sort of support a major pillar of his Indian movement, Olcott was concerned to ameliorate any potential for "exoteric" conflict to arise. He noted with approval that Annie Besant, who was eventually to succeed Blavatsky in the organization, had done much to "remove the uneasy feelings which had prevailed that H.P.B. and I were hoping to convert the Hindus to Buddhism." (Olcott, 1931:502)

The Mahant "Refuses the Most Generous Offers"

In February of 1893, the uneasy feelings that were beginning to prevail at Bodh Gaya took a new form. "Startling news," wrote Dharmapala, "Sumangala Bhikkhu assaulted by the Mahant's people." The assault was apparently serious, with blood being spilled on the floor of the Burmese Resthouse. (ADC, Feb. 4-5, 1893) Olcott, who was at Bodh Gaya in order to negotiate for the sale of the temple, was also told that "one of the poor and inoffensive monks had been brutally beaten." The monk was Sumangala Malatte, one of the four that Dharmapala brought over from Ceylon.

It was not, in fact, ever established that the "Mahant's people" were responsible, and neither Sumangala nor the police were able to identify the assailants. However, as suspicion was being cast on the Giris, Olcott and Dharmapala thought that under the circumstances the Mahant might be inclined to accept a new proposal for the transfer of the temple.

In this attempt they were disappointed and, in Olcott's words, the Mahant "refused the most generous offers." (Olcott, 1931:12) In this increasingly confrontational context, during a period when, after all, the Giris were prime suspects in an assault case, even the most liberal offers of the Mahabodhi Society might well have been regarded by Hem Narayan Gir as a form of attempted blackmail. However, there was very little possibility that, even in the best of circumstances, the Mahant could have been convinced to sell.

As the sect had already demonstrated, and it was often forgotten in negotiations that the Mahant was answerable to a community of monks, they were on principle opposed to the outright alienation of Math lands. The Mahant continued to maintain, as he had in the past, that while the shrine was open to all, it was particularly sacred to him as a commemoration of the Budh Avatar of Vishnu. (MBJ, Vol. XI, March 1893:7-8)

Olcott and Dharmapala realized that, at least for the moment, outright purchase of the temple was not possible, and began to search for land nearby. On separate trips to Burma, they had each received promises of financial backing from wealthy Burmese. Both potential patrons, however, had tied their backing to the condition that the temple be included within the proposed plot. Nevertheless, apparently Olcott and Dharmapala, after the breakdown of negotiations with the Mahant, were quite prepared to acquire any land available near Bodh Gaya, on the strength of their patrons' offers. At the time, a parcel of land, in the Tekari Raj estate, was on the market and it would no doubt have been interesting to trace out the response of the Burmese had their agents obtained a plot of land with no temple on it. In the event, however, the sale was blocked.

"All was proceeding well until the Government of Bengal, or in other words, Mr. Cotton—whose son was engaged as counsel for the stubborn Mahant of Bodh Gaya—came to know of it." (Olcott, 1931:31) Olcott was mistaken here: the Tekari Raj heir was a minor and Cotton senior was, indeed the manager of the estate by appointment of the Court of Wards. He was not, however, an official of the Government of Bengal. Although Cotton junior was the Mahant's counsel, it was unintentionally ironic that Olcott identified him as representing the interests of Bengal. Within the decade, the younger Cotton, Joseph, became a major source of frustration to Government of Bengal and to the Government of

India, both of which had in the meantime come to desire a significant change in the jurisdictional status of the Mahabodhi Temple. I shall return to this at a later point. As to the blocked sale, it is easily explained as due to the well-grounded fear of the Mahant that Dharmapala and his Society intended, eventually, to displace him.

Arnold and Dharmapala Petition Government

The Cottons had, no doubt, brought to the Mahant's attention Edwin Arnold's March 1893 editorial, "East and West, A Splendid Opportunity," which was reprinted, from the "Daily Telegraph, in the Indian newspapers, and in the Mahabodhi Journal. In the course of expounding on this opportunity, Arnold explained that, in 1889, he had expected the temple matter to be amicably arranged in line with his suggestions to Indian and Ceylonese officials. However, "the letters I received from the East showed that the old Brahman had memorialized the Government, in his alarm or avarice, and that the local authorities had for quiet's sake reported adversely to the negotiation." Government had not acted with sufficient resolve.

> If the Home Government had seen its way to make the Mahant well-disposed, I could have recommended any sum which might have seemed fair and necessary. But the idea was too intelligent for the official grasp, and the golden moment went by.
>
> Nevertheless, Asia did not abandon its new desire, and I received so many and such pressing communications that I went at last to the new Indian Secretary of State, Lord Cross, always intelligent, kindly and receptive, and once more pleaded for the Great Restoration.

> "Do you wish, Lord Cross," I asked, "to have 400 millions of Eastern peoples bless your name night and day, and to be forever remembered in Asia, like Alexander, or Asoka, or Akbar the Great?"
>
> "God bless my soul, yes," answered the Minister, "how is that to be done?"
>
> Then I repeated all of the above facts, and produced so happy an effect on the Indian Minister's mind that he promised to consult the Council, and to write—if the idea were approved—to Lord Lansdowne. (Daily Telegraph, March 25, 1893, reprinted in Arnold, 1896:314)

To this proposal, Lansdowne replied in agreement with Government of Bengal: Government had no absolute objection to the transfer of property, provided it were accomplished with private funds and without alienating the feelings of the Hindu community. In truth, as I have shown, Government had expressed reservations about any plan that might transfer the temple to private, and particularly, to non-Indian hands, but these reservations had not as yet translated into a firm policy. Arnold, however, now urged executive action to implement precisely that arrangement about which government was growing nervous.

> The Mahant and his college will, no doubt, have to be bought out, and rather expensively, now that delays have made him master of the bargaining. But if an enlightened Minister and Viceroy will—as they may—facilitate the arrangement, all must end well, and grateful Buddhists would furnish whatever cash is requisite. No orthodox Hindu will be wounded in sentiment, because by strict truth

> the Mahant, as Brahman and follower of Sankarachaya, goes against his shastras by keeping control of a Buddhist temple. However, it brings him much personal dignity and so much money that these things must be compounded for, no doubt; yet a well-disposed collector and a far-seeing Government could find a score of pleasant ways to make him willing to give up his tenure. (Arnold, 1896:321)

The Mahant, of course, regarded the temple as a Temple of the Buddha, but for him it was a shrine for the Buddha avatar of Vishnu and not Gautama Buddha. Arnold's notions of how "orthodoxy" might or might not be offended are therefore really quite off the mark. As well, Dharmapala's actions showed little concern for avoiding the possibility that Hindus "not be wounded in sentiment," and this could not encourage the government to intervene in the manner suggested.

Dharmapala had alienated much Hindu opinion without, on the other hand, having gained any support from the Government. Government was quite prepared, given its sensitivity to the "authentic," to recognize Buddhist claims in the abstract, and was unembarrassed in undertaking archaeological projects to recover a past that had been forgotten by Hindu India. If, however, such recoveries appeared to involve the reawakening of old conflicts, government was generally not inclined to be enthusiastic.

Dharmapala had also strained relations between his new organization and the Theosophical Society, which Olcott persisted in viewing as the parent organization. Dharmapala received, in February, 1893, an invitation to attend the World Parliament of Religions in Chicago. "Colonel strongly disapproves my going to Chicago." (ADC, Feb. 27, 1893) What disturbed Olcott was that Dharmapala had been invited, and had accepted, as "a representative of the Southern Buddhist Church," that is to say as a Theravada Buddhist and not as a Theosophist. The Colonel, having failed to dissuade his younger colleague from attending the congress, exacted a promise that he would at least keep in touch with Annie Besant, the Theosophical delegate from London.

Enroute to Chicago, Dharmapala stopped at London, for the first time, and was received there by a party of eager and solicitous Theosophists, including Arnold, Annie Besant, and the infamous Rev. C.W. Leadbeater, who was accompanied by a Sinhalese boy he had abducted from Colombo. (Tillett 1982: 84-88; ADC Nov.10, 16, 1889)

Dharmapala was put up at Arnold's residence and, on August 15, the pair called on the new Secretary of State for India, Lord Kimberly, to whom they presented their by now familiar case. Kimberly, as Lord Cross had done before him, dispatched the proposal to India where it was now received with some alarm.

In light of the conflict that had recently attended the temple negotiations in Bodh Gaya, both Government of India and Government of Bengal now took a very firm stand against Arnold's program. In a letter to A.P. MacDonnell, the new Lieutenant-Governor of Bengal, Government of India expressed the new position:

> The permission which Sir Edwin suggests should be given by Lord Lansdowne to the Collector of Gaya would be so obvious a departure from the usual course of procedure that the idea cannot for a moment be entertained.

As well, the Mahabodhi Society was viewed with some suspicion.

> I am unable to inform you whether the Mahabodhi Society is a corporate body, where it has its domicile, whether its financial position is a sound one, or whether it may be accepted as the exponent of the aspirations of the Buddhist communities. (LCCI, Vol. 25, #125)

Notice that the government did not reject the notion that there might be some body capable of expressing "the aspirations of the Buddhist communities," but only questioned whether or not the Mahabodhi Society was the genuine voice for such expressions.

MacDonnell, in his response. supplied no further information on the Mahabodhi Society, but was concerned that the activities of "outsiders" might accelerate existing religious tensions. Here he introduced a consideration that seemed to have no bearing whatsoever on the specific difficulty at Bodh Gaya. He informed the Viceroy of an episode of Hindu rioting over Muslim cow-killing in Sarun District, which abutted Gaya.

> In this province there is much trouble caused, I fear, from Gya. This will be traced out. It would be a terrible thing to come into conflict with Brahmanism. (LCCI, Vol.25, #264)

I have found nothing that indicates a connection between the events in Bodh Gaya and Hindu cow-rioting, which in many districts of Bihar had been a perennial concomitant of the Muslim sacrifices and feastings associated with Id-ul-fitr. Nevertheless, the anti-bovicidal disturbances that so frequently disrupted public order in Bihar, in combination with the as yet localized hostilities in Bodh Gaya, seem to have recommended to MacDonnell that the status quo there be maintained.

Dharmapala, by the way, was well aware of the cow problem, and, indeed, one of the first entries in Dharmapala's early diaries reads "wrote letter to Sawai about the prevention of cow-killing asking him to get up a movement for [its] prevention. (ADC, March 13, 1889)

MacDonnell felt that there was precedent for his caution. "I understand from Mr. Cotton, however, that Sir C. Elliott," MacDonnell's predecessor, "was not favorably disposed towards Sir Edwin Arnold's proposals." MacDonnell was equally opposed, and went on to note that "the Hindus have had the place under Royal Firman for two and a half centuries," and seemed to have been in actual possession "since the thirteenth century."

> There is no knowing what might be, in the present temper of peoples' minds in Behar, the effect of the transfer of the shrine from the Hindus to strangers. If the place were to change hands, it should go to the Government and not to the Mahabodhi Society which is only two years old, I believe.
>
> So far as I understand, the Society appeals greatly for support to Siam, Anam, Cambodia, and countries in that direction over which French influence is being established. I should greatly deprecate the establishment of a society affected by such influences at Budh-Gya, to which not only millions of our own subjects turn with religious fervour, but also the Nepaulese, the Thibetans, Chinese, Cingalese and others.

Parenthetically, I might say that this passage illustrates the strong and specific loyalty that British India seemed capable of extracting from its colonial servants: note that the phrase "our subjects" appears to refer to Indians only, with the people of British Ceylon being lumped in with all those other strange populations "outside," in the French Empire, in

Nepal, Tibet, China, and in other exotic and dangerous quarters. Indeed, whatever these greater imperial considerations might have meant to the Lieutenant-Governor, their importance was dwarfed by the pressing demands of the Indian situation.

No proposal for transfer should be considered necessary or desirable, he concluded, until the present crisis is over. At the moment, "when considerable agitation of a religious character possesses peoples' minds' in Behar," the greatest care was called for. (LCC, Vol. 25, #333)

Dharmapala: an International Figure

While the two governments thus fretted over the possibility that religious agitation might break out over the Bodh Gaya affair, Dharmapala had proceeded on to Chicago, in the company of Besant, who "was a mother to me." (ADC, Aug., 15, 1893) Yet, although Olcott had hoped that this proxy parenthood might slow his disciple's move towards independence, Dharmapala's experience at the Congress seemed to have the opposite affect.

I will not here comment on Dharmapala's first adventures in America except to say that he regarded it as a great personal success. Of the reception accorded his address to the assembly, he wrote, "some likened me to Christ!!!" (ADC, Sept. 11, 1893) The trip, as well, not only did much to develop Dharmapala's confidence, it also marked the beginning of a certain financial independence for the Mahabodhi Society.

Until this point, the Mahabodhi Society had shared many of its patrons with the larger Theosophical network. Returning to India via the Pacific route, now without the benefit of Mrs. Besant's company, Dharmapala stopped at Honolulu. Here he met for the first time one Mary E. Foster, a wealthy Hawaiian who become his most important benefactress. Mrs.

Foster, of half Hawaiian descent, was born in 1844, and when she first met Dharmapala had been widowed for four years and controlled a considerable estate.

Dharmapala had come to Mary Foster's attention from reports of his speeches at Chicago, and from Theosophical friends with whom she had already been in contact. However, though a sympathizer with Theosophy, she developed a particularly close relationship with Dharmapala, in whose diaries we find the story that she sought out his aid in overcoming her tendency to anger easily. This is somewhat poignant, given that Dharmapala himself was possessed of a considerable temper, and prone, often, to passionate outbursts of anger.

Mary Foster clearly admired Dharmapala, and contributed a great deal of money for his various projects. One of her legacies is the Foster Botanical Garden in Honolulu which contains, among other things, a "Bode tree" via a cutting from Anuradhapura. She died on December 19, 1930, in Honolulu.

Dharmapala's diaries very frequently contain little notes of admiration and gratitude for Mrs. Foster, and, as he continued his return journey from America, stopping en route in Japan and Thailand, propagandizing for the "great cause," he must have felt a great sense of confidence. He arrived in India in the spring of 1894, with something of an international reputation, a new sense of purpose and possibility, and an independent source of financial support for his new society.

Chapter Five

THE GREAT CASE

While in Japan Dharmapala had been given, by Kozen Gunaratna's family, a seven-hundred year old Buddha image that, it was hoped, could be installed in the Mahabodhi Temple. When, however, he attempted to place the image, the Mahant and his supporters objected. Fearing the consequences for the public peace should the Buddhists press their demands, a new District Magistrate, D.J. Macpherson, requested that Dharmapala temporarily abandon his plans to install the image. Macpherson offered the matter up to his Commissioner at Patna, who in turn promptly offered it up to the Bengal Secretariat.

While a suitable response was being formulated, Macpherson took home leave, and was therefore "out of station" when Dharmapala undertook his next move. In Macpherson's absence, Dharmapala received the following assurances from the Government of Bengal.

> There is perfect freedom of worship for all Buddhists at Budh Gaya, and the Hindu Sannyasis who have held the place for over five centuries are ever ready to meet all reasonable requirements of worshippers. Any well-rounded complaint that difficulties were imposed will meet with ready attention at the hands of the Bengal Government. (MBJ, Vol. 3, #3, 1894:22-23)

This is a succinct statement of the confusion that government had achieved with regard to the Bodh Gaya problem. The "requirements of worshippers," subject only to some untested principle of "reasonableness," were removed from the question of proprietorship, which is here implicitly granted to the Mahant as a fait accompli: they have "held the place for over five centuries."

Thereby, the Mahant was granted what had never before been questioned, jurisdiction over the temple. The question remained quite open as to what specific forms of Buddhist worship were guaranteed by the state. After all, "perfect freedom of worship" was formally guaranteed for *Hindus* as well as for Buddhists, and both sets of "purely" religious rights had to be maintained without doing violence to the Mahant's legitimate proprietorship.

In sum, the actual and legitimate exercise of the various rights was subject to validating principles which could only be derived from a great fog of extensive customary practice. As one would expect, then, a number of subsequent actions were grounded in rather different interpretations of what constituted the "reasonable requirements" of worshippers.

An Image Problem at the Temple

In the Theosophical Resthouse at Gaya, sometime after midnight on the morning of February 25, 1895, Dharmapala awoke and "sat in meditation for a little time and then [my] mind suggested [to me] to take the Japanese image to the Maha Bodhi Temple." He roused his companions, two Sinhalese monks, Sumangala and Devananda, and one Sinhalese lay pilgrim, N.S. d'Silva, and "asked them to sit in contemplation for a time."

> Then it was decided that we should take the image early morning. In silence I vowed seven times giving up my life for the Buddha's sake. Before dawn we packed the image and by 7

> we were off to Bud Gaya. (ADC, Feb.25, 1895)

This action, and the Giri resistance to it, led to a series of legal contests which pitted Buddhist rights of worship at the temple against Giri rights of proprietorship. At the conclusion of the legal wrangling, the rights of the Giris were validated, and Dharmapala's reputation was severely damaged. Nevertheless, the terms of the dispute were for the first time clearly set out in a legal arena and, in subsequent negotiations, these terms significantly structured the continuing debate over the proper disposition of the sacred site. Dharmapala came to call this "the Great Case."

The trouble began when, after reaching Bodh Gaya, Dharmapala and his assistants carried the Japanese image up into the second story chamber of the Mahabodhi Temple. As they began to set up the image on the altar, the Special Sub-Registrar and the Deputy Magistrate of Gaya, both Muslims, came into the chamber. They were curious, and wished to observe the proceedings.[1] These two local functionaries were soon joined by Hossain Baksh, the Muslim Mukhtiar,

---

[1] This brief account of the events of the morning of February 25, 1895 has been constructed from Dharmapala's diary account, and from the testimony of principals in the three legal actions that resulted. In the course of this brief account, in the service of clarity, I have not annotated the multiple sources I have used but, throughout the case histories that follow, all of the sources employed have been identified. One of the key sources, Dharmapala's diary entry from February 25, is reproduced below in its entirety.

> At 2 in the morning I woke up and sat in meditation for a little time and then my mind suggested to take the Japanese image to the Mahabodhi Temple. I woke up the priests and asked them to sit in contemplation for a time. Then it was decided that we should take the image early morning. In silence I vowed 7 times giving up my life for the Buddha's sake. Before dawn we packed up the image and by 7 we were off to Bud Gaya. On the way we met two Muhammadan gentlemen driving toward B.G. Soon

or spokesman, of the Mahant, and Jagannath Singh, the Hindu door-keeper of the main shrine. While this little group looked on, Dharmapala's party was arranging flowers, incense and candles in front of the image. Hossain Baksh whispered something to Singh, who promptly left the chamber. Hossain Baksh himself left shortly thereafter. The Sub-registrar and the Deputy Magistrate lingered awhile, then went off to see the Mahant, Krisna Dayal Gir. They later testified that the Mahant had seemed "much enraged and excited," apparently about the installation of the new figure of the Buddha.

Having set up the image, Dharmapala sent one of his companions off to fetch Bepin Behari, the government-appointed custodian of the grounds. When Behari arrived,

---

> after our arrival at B.G. the boxes were carried upstairs and by a strange coincidence these two gentlemen were present and were witnessing the placing of the image.
>
> Bipin Babu was also present and when [we] were going to light the candles the Mahant's Gosains and the Mohammedan Moktiar came up threatening me [and] asked me to remove the image. When I was in silent meditation these men came up and atrociously removed the image. Oh, it was painful! Buddhists not allowed to worship in their own temple. Great excitement.
>
> The Mahant rushes off to Gaya and in the evening the Collector D.J. Macpherson came to investigate the case. When he was leaving he said a great desecration has been committed in the Temple. He ordered the Inspector to take care of our party. We slept in the Burmese resthouse.

It is interesting to note that Macpherson, by Dharmapala's account, was at the outset inclined to side with the Buddhists: in a later passage Dharmapala claims that the Collector took him to the Commissioner of Patna who "asked him to institute a case." If so, and the Collector's, or the Commissioner's, advice was the trigger for bringing criminal charges against the Mahant, the District authorities were responsible for possibly the worst legal counsel ever received by Dharmapala. Throughout the legal action it became increasingly clear that the criminal context was formally inappropriate for a thorough consideration of the issues involved.

Dharmapala asked him to be a witness that the image had been installed, and said that it was a gift from the Japanese. Sumangala Bhikkhu then picked up a candle, and was on the point of lighting it, when perhaps as few as ten and perhaps as many as forty of the Mahant's Sannyasins and retainers, led by Hossain Baksh, burst into the shrineroom. One of them snatched the candle from Sumangala and several jumped up on the altar.

They were shouting in Hindi, which neither Dharmapala nor his fellows understood well, or at all. One witness heard such threats as "Badmash"—rascal—"we will beat you, there are five hundred of us." Hossain Baksh spoke little English, but apparently made his demands clear to the Sinhalese by pointing at the altar. However it was that Dharmapala came to his understanding of the situation, he later complained to the Magistrate that "the Mahomedan Muktiar, Hossain Baksh, told your petitioner to take away the images, and in fact assaulted him by pushing and thrusting him with his hands."

The Sannyasins and Baksh then called for Vijayananda, the Mahant's Hindu Mukhtiar, who apparently had more English.[2] Dharmapala spoke to Vijayananda and protested against the acts of the Mahant's men. Vijayananda coaxed several of the Sannyasins to come down off the altar and then, after some hurried conversation in Hindi with them,

---

[2] It is quite evident that Dharmapala never learned Hindi (ADC, April 6, 1925), although it was part of his hope for a Buddhist mission in India that monks would "learn the Indian vernaculars." As to this last aspiration, in 1927 he wrote "I have not been successful so far." (ADC, Feb. 26, 1927) It is unclear that he ever learned any Bengali, but certainly he never wrote in that language. One entry reads "I will begin to read Bengali with a teacher," but there is no evidence that he ever did so. (ADC, August 25, 1908) All of his Theosophical Bengali friends, and other Indians, spoke English and it seems that Dharmapala was never sufficiently motivated to take up the serious study of any Indian vernacular—linguistically, Dharmapala was a colonial person.

left the chamber, "taking almost all of the assailants with him." Dharmapala then sat down in front of the image, in the lotus-position. He was disturbed, perhaps a quarter of an hour later, when the company of Sannyasins again rushed into the room, took hold of the image, and carried it downstairs into the open courtyard below. They placed it at one end of the line of small shrines that had been dedicated to the Pandavas. "Oh, it was painful! Buddhists not allowed to worship in their own temple. Great excitement." Dharmapala remained seated in front of the empty altar.

The police now arrived, having been summoned by Behari, and the Head Constable sent one of his subordinates up into the chamber to bring Dharmapala down, while he himself took a statement from Hossain Baksh, "praying him to interfere." Dharmapala refused to come down with the subordinate, so the Head Constable finally went up and began to question him in Hindi. Of course, again, Dharmapala did not understand this, or only understood very imperfectly. Eventually, Dharmapala wrote out a summary statement, in English, of the events of the morning. Then the two men came down into the courtyard. There were no arrests.

The Mahant, Krishna Dayal Gir, had not been at the temple during these events, but had been made aware of the disturbance. After the police arrived, he decided to seek an audience with D.J. Macpherson, District Magistrate, who was then off in the larger town of Gaya. The Mahant reached Gaya, shortly after noon, and the Magistrate noted that "I recorded his statement as a basis of the action he wished me to take."

Apparently, the Mahant, and some of those questioned on his behalf by the police in Bodh Gaya, intended at first to deny that the image had been removed at all. Macpherson himself arrived that evening at the temple and, according to Dharmapala, said that "a great desecration has been committed." After Macpherson had reviewed the results of the initial investigation, and had taken some additional statements from witnesses to the events, Dharmapala and his party retired to the Burmese Rest House.

Dharmapala Brings Criminal Charges

Several days later, after the police had finished with their inquiries, Dharmapala filed a petition with the Magistrate, praying that "your Worship will be graciously pleased to issue a warrant against the accused and to decide this case." (MBJ, Vol. III, #2, April 1895:94) Dharmapala was hopeful about his prospects, and wrote, having canceled a date for a Theosophical address that was to have been given in Gaya, "it is not possible to give it on account of the Great Case...we will win. I am only anxious for want of funds." (ADC, March 1, 1895)

Many of his Sinhalese supporters, however, and Colonel Olcott, favored new negotiations and not legal action. "The Ceylon people have telegraphed to the Colonel to go to Gya and reconcile the case. There should be no compromise; and we should press on to the last." (ADC, March 7, 1895) The "High Priest," Sumangala Hekkuduwe, was "against going to the law," and sent a telegraph to Government of India requesting that the Viceroy facilitate negotiations.

Nevertheless, Dharmapala prevailed and, on March 22, he "received letter from Colonel Olcott authorizing me to go on with the case." (ADC, March 22, 1895) All of this activity soon came to the attention of the Viceroy, Lord Elgin—this was, incidentally, the second son of the Elgin who had removed the Parthenon's marble statuary—and, within the week, plans were made for a viceregal tour of the area.

Lord Elgin Pays Respects to his Ancestors

Elgin arrived on March 30, 1895 and, during the course of a reception at the Magistrate's residence, following the standard pattern for the celebration of a Viceroy's country tour, he was presented with an address "on behalf of and as representing the various classes, creeds and communities in the District of Gaya." The scroll was presented in a silver and ebony casket, which bore Elgin's coat of arms and was ornamented with scenes of local temples and landscapes.

The address itself was read aloud by its author, Nanda Kishore Lal, Vice-Chairman of the Gaya municipality. During the course of this oratory, Lal touched on a familiar regional issue, Hindu-Muslim relations. Due to the "uniformly firm and impartial policy," relative to religious difficulties, that had been so expertly carried out "by our sympathetic District Officer, Mr. Macpherson," in dealing with "the unfortunate religious disputes which for a time convulsed the country," Lal was pleased to report that "at the present moment the most cordial relations prevail in this district between Hindu and Mahomedan sections of the community." (MBJ, Vol. IV, #1, May, 1895)

What Lal meant to suggest was that the civil disturbances associated with questions of the cow, the riots that had so vexed officialdom during the period of the last Viceroyalty had at least temporarily abated. The Vice-Chairman might have gone on, had he wished, to bring the Viceroy's attention to a more minor, but uniquely local, example of cordial Hindu-Muslim relations, namely that the Hindu and the Muslim Mukhtiars of the Giri Mahant were about to stand as co-defendants against criminal charges brought on behalf of a foreign Buddhist. However, as the Vice-Chairman of the Gaya Municipality was also the chief legal advisor to the Mahabodhi Society, this example may not have seemed apt to him. In fact, Lal's concluding remarks on freedom of religion might have served as an appropriate opening statement for the plaintiffs in the Mahabodhi case.

> We feel assured that the same feeling of tolerance on the part of the people and the

> same impartial policy on the part of Government will secure to those other creeds which are in a minority amongst us the free exercise of their religion. (MBJ, Vol. IV, #1, May 1895)

To this the Viceroy replied that his visit had no official purpose, that he only wished to see the holy town of Gaya, and the little shrines that dotted the red surrounding hills, in the spirit of a simple pilgrim, "from no other motive except to pay something for his ancestors." Changing roles, Elgin then characterized his visit as one of those "brief holidays" for which he had managed to "snatch a day or two to see for my own gratification the sights of interest which abound here."

Elgin then assumed a genuinely viceregal demeanor, and expressed, in the very general terms most suited to his high position, the spirit of the policy of the Government of India on religious matters.

> Government, as you are aware, must preserve a strict, perhaps even stern impartiality of which you have indicated your appreciation, but it has seemed to me that when we approach spots or deal with institutions which others hold in veneration and affection, our first object should be to do our best to appreciate the feelings inspired by them, and our second to see that we do nothing by word or deed to injure those feelings. (MBJ, Vol. IV, #1, May 1895)

One institution held in veneration and affection, the Mahabodhi Temple, was visited by Elgin that afternoon. It can be assumed from his correspondence that the Viceroy, while circumambulating the shrine, was very much concerned that religious feelings might be injured during the course of the upcoming case: "I managed my trip to Bodh Gaya, though there was very nearly a scene."

Elgin, together with Macpherson, the Mahant, and the Commissioner of Patna, were descending the steps down into the temple courtyard. As the little cluster of Panch Pandava shrines came into view, directly in front of the entrance to the main temple, it was noticed that "lo and behold! the Japanese image had disappeared." Mr Forbes, the Commissioner, quickly took charge of the situation and spoke "very distinctly to the Mohunt."

The Mahant, in turn, spoke very distinctly to one of his retainers and, after the Viceroy's party had taken a turn around the temple, "the image was in the place it has occupied since it was taken from the altar." In the currency of the Viceroy's affections, the Mahant's gamble had failed, and now Elgin, in a letter to Lieutenant-Governor Elliott, seemed to tilt in favor of the Buddhists. "I cannot see how it is possible to ignore the claims of the Buddhists to worship at this Temple, and whatever the rights of possession may be, the rights of the user must not be ignored." (Elgin to Elliott, April 2)

"I am sorry," replied Elliott, "that the Mohunt misbehaved himself." Elliott himself had, on previous occasions, been "much taken with his air of thoughtful sanctity but fear that these contests with the Sinhalese Buddhists have brought him down to a lower level." The preferred outcome would be that the Sinhalese acquire the temple on suitable terms, "but he will never consent and his rights must be protected too." (ECCI, Vol.66, #194)

Aside from any issue of legal rights, both men were concerned with matters of public peace. Nanda Kishore Lal's assurances notwithstanding, the Viceroy had come away from Gaya with the feeling that "on some of the minor points of religious controversy a wrong word might be very unfortunate." (ECCI, Vol. 66 #250) Both the Lieutenant-Governor and the Viceroy, however, had to wait on events that would shortly unfold under the supervision of a District Magistrate, Macpherson, who had his own notion of how to apply the principles of religious tolerance and impartiality. Elliott feared for the Mahant: "I am afraid that Macpherson does not take quite the same view of his rights as I do."

D.J. Macpherson Reviews some Matters of Common History

The case began on April 8, with Macpherson taking evidence and the counsel for the defendants cross-examining the witnesses for the plaintiffs. The defendants declined to be cross-examined and had, on advice of counsel, submitted a written statement to the court. The five co-defendants, three Giri Sannyasins and the two Mukhtiars, had been charged under the Indian Penal Code with damaging religious property, disturbing lawful religious worship, and behaving in a manner likely to "wound" the religious feelings of others. (IPC: 233-236) In addition, all were charged with having formed an unlawful assembly for the purpose of committing the alleged acts.

Also, the Mukhtiar Hossain Baksh was charged with use of criminal force against Dharmapala. The case for the prosecution, as summarized in the court transcript, is as follows:

> The question who is the proprietor of the Temple is, he [the prosecutor] observed, quite irrelevant to this case, but the prosecution must incidentally challenge the assertion of the defense that the Mahanth is sole and absolute proprietor, and looking to all the facts connected with its repair and guardianship by Government, Dharmapala had good reason for considering Government to be the proprietor, and Government, in taking over the Guardianship, undoubtedly continued

> freedom of worship to the Buddhists. Assuming, however, for the sake of argument, that the Mahanth was in some sort of possession, and was allowed to enjoy a certain usufruct in taking offerings, such possession was nevertheless subject to the long-standing right of every Buddhist to worship and perform any ceremony in accordance with the tenets of his religion in the Temple, and neither Government nor the Mahanth is entitled to prevent the full exercise of that right. (MBJ, IV, #6, Oct,1895)

The first point, of course, is that the Government had somehow assumed "guardianship," and that therefore, by definition, Dharmapala's "religious rights" were guaranteed. The fall-back position was that even if the Mahant were in some sense the sole proprietor, this could not alter the "long-standing" rights that had developed there. That is, access to the property, whoever "owned" it, had been subject to easements established by practice.

Furthermore, the prosecution contended, the Mahant could not, to Dharmapala's rights of worship, offer a superior Hindu religious right, it being known "as a matter of common history" that the Mahabodhi Temple was a Buddhist one, and that "no Hindu has ever (unless possibly in the last few months) worshipped or could worship there." There are two points to be made here.

First, the defendants could not in their defense claim that they had intervened with the worship in order to maintain an existing right of possession: this right had been modified either through some partnership with government, which guaranteed the rights claimed by Dharmapala, or had been so modified by customary practice.

The second point is that they could not assert that they intervened in order to maintain an existing right of Hindu worship, as no actual practice could be put forth to substantiate this claim. Therefore, the prosecution argued, the defendants actually had intervened in order to assert an innovative and spurious right against "the actual enjoyment by the complainant of his [actual] right." (MBJ, Vol. IV, #6, Oct,1895)

The argument for the defense, on the other hand, placed proprietorship at the very heart of the case. The accused, acting in the belief that the Mahant's proprietorship was absolute and unmodified by either partnership with government, or by custom, had regarded the plaintiff's behavior as a sham act intended to assert a novel right. Acting consciously as they had, in defense of the Mahant's legitimate property rights, they would not have logically acted to destroy, damage or defile that same property, as had been charged, neither could they, as legitimate agents of the Mahant, have committed any trespass. Finally, what amounted to a novel right asserted by the plaintiff had not, and could not, be established. According to this view, Dharmapala had not been engaged in a lawful act of worship, and no offenses had been committed. After this, the position was summed up by Macpherson:

> The defendants repudiate all guilty knowledge and claim to justify their action on the ground that they had every reason to believe, on grounds stated, that the Mahanth was the sole proprietor of the Temple, and as such, entitled to all offerings made by pilgrims, whether Hindus or Buddhists, whom he permitted to worship according to rules and directions which he alone was competent to frame and give; that the Mahanth had last year forbidden the Buddhists doing anything that might infringe his rights as regards wor-

> ship by pilgrims in any part of the Temple, in consequence of which an attempt by Dharmapala to place this very image in May, 1894, without his consent, had failed, the Magistrate, as they believed, having directed him to desist; and that all they did on the 25th February was done in good faith, under the general order of the Mahanth, to maintain his existing possession and rights and to prevent the enshrining of the image without his consent and without the requisite Hindu ceremony of pranpratista [breathgiving] as they believed that this was merely an attempt on the part of Dharmapala to create evidence of some right adversely to the Mahanth, and that he and his comrades were not *bone fide* engaged in any worship or religious ceremony. (MBJ, Vol. IV, #6, Oct, 1895)

As to the Mahant's proprietorship, the defense put into evidence a number of the documents that had passed between the Government of India and the Burmese during the 1877 negotiations over the temple restoration project. That the Government of India, at that time, had felt it necessary to consult with the Mahant was sufficient proof of legitimate Giri control. In fact, the defense argued, the Mahant's status, as well as the limited claims of the government on the property, was demonstrated in the *Revised list of Ancient Monuments in Bengal,* wherein, under the heading "Custody or Present use," appears "Mahant and a custodian appointed by Government." (Beglar, 1896, 285-87) This seems not too clear an argument, actually, as the precise nature of the "custodian," and the extent of his responsibilities, either to the Mahant or to the government, is not specified.

Perhaps more importantly, the defense placed great emphasis on what they saw as the validation of their proprietary claims by the government during the previous May, when Macpherson had ordered Dharmapala to cease from his first attempt to place the image in the temple. However, Macpherson's recollection of his own order only illustrates that the legal situation at Bodh Gaya had remained largely undefined.

The Giri lawyers held that Macpherson's May 5, 1895 order directed Dharmapala to desist from further attempts to place the statue, "but I may mention," stated Macpherson, that Dharmapala "received no instructions to this effect," though caution had been advised. In the end, Macpherson suggested, Dharmapala "felt that there was nothing for it but to take his stand upon the freedom of worship Government had declared to exist, and which he knew existed." (MBJ, Vol. IV, #7-8, Nov. & Dec. 1895)

It seemed now that Government had committed itself to value the "customary right of worship" over the right of ownership. Defense maintained that the Mahant's proprietorship embraced Dharmapala's "freedom of worship" in the sense that this freedom was a gift of the Mahant. Government of Bengal, however, had declared this freedom to exist, absolutely, while also recognizing that "Hindu Sanyasis" had "held the place for five centuries." By this statement alone Government, in one of its rare comments on the status of the shrine, had separated rights of worship from the question of proprietorship.

Nevertheless, the defense would not relinquish the proprietorship argument, and cross-examined Dharmapala at length to show that he had, in conversations, negotiations and in his journal articles, accepted the Mahant's legitimate control of the place. Why, otherwise, would he have sought to purchase the temple from the Mahant?

In alternative argumentation, the defense attempted to put forward their own purely Hindu religious rights. How they asked, could a Buddhist assert that he had rights of worship in a temple that was demonstrably a Hindu one? "For some time prior to the 25th February Buddha has been regarded as a deity to be worshipped" whether Hindu texts actually justified such worship or not. The defense also denied that they had desecrated the Japanese image in any way, in fact "believing Buddha according to the shastras to be a Hindu Deity, they treated the image with all respect, though it had come from a mleccha [barbarian] country." (MBJ, Vol. IV, #6,Oct. 1895)

In order to underscore a general and legitimate Hinduization of the shrine, the custodian Bepin Behari, a witness for the plaintiffs, was cross-examined with respect to Hindu practices. The defense made much of Behari's testimony that Hindus are seen at, not only a pipal tree near the edge of the courtyard, but also at the Bodhi tree itself. Although Behari saw no actual ancestral ceremony at the Bodhi tree, nevertheless, Hindus did "bow before it."

There had been, within the last several months, a few Hindus inside the temple and they have been seen to "bow before the image." Macpherson was unimpressed. This bowing was "I dare say, of no more significance than my taking off my hat, as I always do, when I enter the sanctum" (MBJ, Vol. IV, #7-8, Nov. & Dec. 1895)

The prosecution retorted that this evidence was only documentation of a recent attempt by the Mahant to Hinduize the shrine in contravention of established custom. There is, in fact, a note to this effect in the *List of Ancient Monuments in Bengal:*

> The collector reports that during 1894-95 certain alterations were made at the instance of the Mahant of Bodh Gaya on the image of Buddha on the ground floor of the temple for the purpose of showing that it is a Hindu and not a Buddhist object of worship. (Beglar, 1896: 285-87)

Not only, claimed the prosecution, was this worship a recent innovation and one designed to wound the religious feelings of the Buddhists, it was also, from the standpoint of Hindu orthodoxy, prohibited. Bepin Behari had, after all, testified that he had heard "brahman priests, accompanying Hindu pilgrims to a pipal tree in the compound, forbid them entering the temple because of its being a 'Jain' one." Also, the Hindu Pandit of the Government Zillah School, although he had been to the place several times, had never entered the shrine itself as it "is a Buddhist Temple and Hindus are forbidden to enter such."

"On the contrary," however, "the fact that Buddhist pilgrims worshipped and made offerings at it [the temple] has been admitted." This point, in combination with the fact that Hindu worship at the site had been recent, and either a sham, a ruse, or disallowed by the shastras—the texts of "orthodox" Hinduism—was claimed by the prosecution to overthrow the notion that the Mahant could regulate and frame rules for worship within the temple. (MBJ, Vol. IV, #7-8, Nov. & Dec. 1895)

Against the notion that Hindu worship at the shrine had been both innovative and a ruse, the defense offered several arguments. To begin with, there was the question of the lingam in the main shrine room. This had certainly been in place in 1872-73 when Beglar visited the site and, possibly, on the authority of the Chinese pilgrim Hiouen Tsang, might have dated from 600 AD. (Cunningham, 1966 [1874]: 67-73) Then too, defense placed into evidence a great number of quotes from Mitra's *Buddha-Gaya* to underscore the general point that the shrine had been Hinduized by a very early date. Thus, considered the Magistrate, defense had put forward a remark, purportedly from Mitra, that "the lingam was worshipped by the Mahanth."

Macpherson was not at all impressed: "a remark of that kind is not regular proof, and it is utterly opposed to all the evidence given in this case"[3] (MBJ, Vol. IV, #9 Jan. 1896)

A second, and rather amusing, line of argument, for the defense, was that Hindu worship of the Buddha *was*, quite clearly, a ruse, but rather than being a recent innovation, it was a ruse of such ancient standing that it had been sanctified as a form of Hindu practice. In fact, in the following argument, it is as though what I called in my introduction the "Hindu mode of encompassment" had been summarized and placed into evidence.

> Though the defendants themselves no doubt would not say so, Counsel pointed out that when the Brahmans were endeavoring to expel Buddhism from India, they found it a matter of policy to convert all images of Buddha into an incarnation of Vishnu, and their worshippers therefore into Hindus; but when they acquired full dominion over the Buddhists, it became unnecessary to continue

[3] The tradition in question, as addressed by Mitra, is that, at the beginning of the seventh century, the great Hindu King Sasanka, had the central image of the Buddha removed from the main shrine room and had an image of Mahadeva (Siva) installed. "How far this story has any substratum of truth it would be hazardous to determine with certainty; but it suggests the idea that some Saivite Hindus wished to appropriate the temple to their use."

> In the eighth or ninth century the last image was evidently lost, and in its place was set up a black stone image, which I believe was removed by one of the Mahants of the math when he again consecrated a lingam in the middle of the sanctuary. The image was not destroyed, but removed to a small temple within the enclosure of the math, where it still exists. The lingam established in the centre of the square area in front of the throne is not an ordinary figure of its kind, but a big votive stupa, which has been made to do duty for it. It is still worshipped by the Mahant of the math. (Mitra, 1878: 84)

> such worship of Buddha, which would account for Hindu worship not having been carried on in the Temple on the same scale as it has been within the last few months. (MBJ, Vol. IV, #6 Oct. 1896)

It seems that Counsel for both plaintiff and defense were happy to accept the point that some Hindus, at some time, in some way, had taken up a deceptive strategy to rout the Buddhists. As a result, both sides placed into evidence a great deal of material from the Puranic texts.

Most of the mythology brought forth emphasized the same point: Buddha had been absorbed into the Hindu pantheon as an avatar of Vishnu. In Bhagavata Purana, for instance, it is said that "after the full advent of the Kali age, he (Vishnu) will be born with Buddha as his name," and that "he will assume the guise of heretics, deluding the mind and attracting the hearts of asuras (demons)". (MBJ, Vol. IV, #10, 1896; BG,1.3.24; 11.7.42) Dharmapala's lawyers felt that this would illustrate Hindu contempt for Buddhism and pose a threat to the defense claim that the Buddha could become an integral part of Hindu worship.

However, most of the material produced by the defense had exactly the same tone. The relevant verse from the Agni Purana illustrates how the Buddh Avatar "deluded the Daityas (demons), and caused them to forsake vedic power," and the demons were thus "rendered impotent." (AP, 14.70-73) In the Mahant's view, the character of the Buddha was ambiguous to be sure, but the Buddh-Avatar had performed a necessary function by undermining the power of the demons, and was therefore to be venerated.

The same set of mythological characterizations was approached by the Buddhists as evidence of an ancient hegemonic plot, conceived in hatred of the Buddha and of Buddhism, and by the Hindus as an integral development of their own religious tradition, through which the Buddha had been legitimately, if cunningly, absorbed into the Hindu fold. Perhaps on the point of remembering that the devil everywhere quotes scripture, the magistrate abruptly ended the debate: "If in any case, it was felt expedient to endeavor to establish Vaisnavite worship of Buddha Bhagavan at Mahabodhi, it was an anomaly for the Mahanth, a Saivaite, to set himself up as its founder." (MBJ, Vol. IV, #11, March, 1896) Actually, there was nothing odd about the Shaivites' appeal to mythological literature as much of it was exclusively neither Shaivite nor Vaishnavite.

In the final analysis, Macpherson wanted what he seemed to have wanted in the first place: he held that "no form of Hindu worship has been carried out inside the Mahabodhi Temple," aside from the current "spurious worship," since 600 AD. The recent worship was intended by the Mahant to provide a "pretext for interfering with the dealings of the Buddhists in the Temple and strengthening whatever prescriptive rights he may possess to the usufruct of the offerings made at the Temple."

Furthermore "this conclusion is not weakened" by evidence put forth about the *avatar* formula. None of the evidence put forth by the defense could, in Macpherson's view, have upset the "essentially Buddhistic character of the Temple." (MBJ, Vol. IV, #10, Feb. 1896) In his judgment, he found that: 1) the defendants did indeed completely believe in the legitimate proprietary rights of the Mahant, "that *the Mahanth did enjoy possessory rights of a certain kind* over the Temple and its precincts," but 2) that they could not have thought these rights "to be of so complete a character as to connote *full proprietorship* or carry with it the right claimed by the Mahanth to do what he liked inside the temple." (My emphasis) (MBJ, Vol. IV, #10, Feb. 1896)

And, on the question of this "full proprietorship," Macpherson denied that the evidence from the Burmese negotiations vindicated this stance: these can "be taken as acknowledging certain undefined rights in the vicinity, which rendered it desirable to consult him." The proprietorship was best characterized as "the dual custodianship," shared between the Mahant and Government, "which has existed ever since its restoration was undertaken." Prosecution had not demonstrated that the defendants had committed either trespass or defilement, but the disruption of a lawfully assembled religious congregation had been amply demonstrated.

The two Mukhtiars were acquitted as they had not been involved in the actual disruption of the ceremony, which was most dramatically marked by the removal of the image during the time that the plaintiff had been in a contemplative posture. The three other defendants, however, all Giri monks, were found guilty of disturbing "an assembly lawfully engaged in the performance of religious worship."

They were sentenced to a month's imprisonment, and fined one hundred rupees. (MBJ, Vol. IV, #10, Feb. 1896) It seems the court had determined that Dharmapala's "posture" of meditation during the ceremony, and not the total ceremony as such, was the privileged "religious" expression. This is one point on which later appeals would dwell at some length.

The First Appeal: "The Limits to which This Criminal Case Must be Confined"

The Giri abbot Krishna Dayal died late in the year of 1895 and his successor, Hem Narayan Gir, made his first order of business the filing of an appeal against Macpherson's decision. This was heard in the Sessions Court of Gaya, in July 1895, by Herbert Holmwood of the Judicial Department of the Government of Bengal.

At this level of the system, justice was no longer administered by a District Collector or Magistrate, in whose office policy, administration and the judiciary were combined, but by a specialized officer who had no local involvement in the affairs he was called upon to judge, and whose time was solely devoted to legal matters. In no time at all Holmwood disposed of Macpherson's amateur status in these matters.

> [the opinion] has fully set out all the facts and circumstances nearly and remotely connected with the case, and his full review of the History of the Temple, and the ancient authorities on Hindu and Buddhistic lore which render his judgment a most valuable state paper and a contribution to the polemic literature on the much vexed question of the respective rights of Buddhists and Hindus will, no doubt, be read with interest long after these questions are settled, either by judicial compromise, or by the only judicial tribunals which can settle them, viz., the civil courts of this country and Her Majesty's Privy Council, has opened the door to considerable discussion in my court as to the limits to which this Criminal case must necessarily be confined, and I think to a good deal of unnecessary animadversion on Mr. Macpherson's assumed unconscious bias in the matter. (TB, Vol. VII, #45,1895)

Holmwood then dealt with the appeal itself. Ghose, for the appellants, argued that a conviction under section 296 should properly depend on: 1) that the offense be voluntary, 2) that the worship involved be a genuine and not a sham act, and 3) that the plaintiff be shown to have been lawfully engaged in worship. The first point was largely unproblematic as the acts, held by the plaintiff to constitute an offense, were fully admitted by the appellants.

> The second point—whether or not the act is a sham—is more interesting. On this, Holmwood felt compelled to note that its consideration would strictly require that "every member of the assembly be perfectly sincere and single-minded in his worship," and this, in turn, was "a matter with which the law can have nothing to do." How are the accused to know what was going on inside Dharmapala's mind and at what particular moment he was in religious contemplation and therefore engaged in worship? Obviously the law can take no cognizance of such distinctions. Either the posture of contemplation is the outward and visible sign of Buddhist worship and the accused knew this, or it is not such a sign or the accused did not know it.
>
> I find, as a fact, that it is the well-known outward and visible sign of Buddhistic worship to sit in contemplation in the attitude in which the sitting Buddha is often depicted and that the accused had the best possible means of knowing this. (TB, Vol. VII, #45, Nov. 19, 1895)

This certainly seems the only pragmatic legal attitude, but it also brings into relief the paradox that faces all governments which profess to protect religious rights: what is protected is only the conventional behavior which is held to mark the presence of religious concern. The third point, then, which involves a demonstration that the worshipper be "lawfully engaged" in worship, has nothing whatsoever to do with religious sincerity. Proprietorship, therefore, which was the most available measure against which "lawfulness" could be judged, would be a crucial issue in Holmwood's court:

> The Mahanth is undoubtedly the "owner" of the place as far as the present knowledge of anybody in the world goes. I use the expression 'owner of the place' advisedly as it is the strongest expression of the Mahanth's proprietary right on the record. It is to be found at page 121 of the Government List of Ancient Monuments in Bengal, 1886.

Although Holmwood admitted that this document might in certain regards be unsatisfactory—it did not really constitute a deed or grant—"this was the authoritative declaration of Government in 1886 and the Mahanth may rely on it as such."

In the original case, and again on appeal, the Mahant's lawyer had attempted to discredit Dharmapala's testimony on the subject of the Mahant's proprietorship. Holmwood, on the contrary, was generally convinced of Dharmapala's truthfulness. Proof of this was evident in Dharmapala's answers to questions put to him about his state of mind while maintaining a posture of contemplation in front of the altar. Dharmapala had testified that, after a certain point, although he remained in the same posture as before, "the outward and visible sign of Buddhistic worship," he was, in fact, no longer in a mental state of "religious contemplation."

Holmwood was also, by the way, inclined to excuse whatever "shuffling" there may have been in Dharmapala's testimony on the grounds that he was "a foreigner and a student singularly ignorant of the world," and also that he had been misled into believing that "it was a matter of supreme importance to deny the Mahant's proprietorship." And, Holmwood concluded, in a culturally relativistic vein, after all, "Oriental standards of truth are not the same as ours." Now, however, the question of proprietorship having been at least arguably settled, it remained for the appellants to demonstrate that Dharmapala's act had been "unlawful." (TB, Vol. VII, #46, Dec. 6, 1895)

In Holmwood's judgment, the appeals argument, that Dharmapala's behavior had exceeded the boundaries of customary usage, ultimately failed. Holmwood found that the Burmese negotiations, although they had not modified the Mahanth's proprietorship in any substantial way, *had* established a right of worship for Buddhists. The Burmese documents:

> Can only bear the interpretation put upon it by the learned Advocate-General, namely the King of Burma has no occasion to look after the preservation of the place, as that is the Mahanth's business, but his priests, Buddhists of course, can remain and do Buddhistic worship there as long as they conform to the "zamindari rules of the zamindar." (TB, Vol. VII, #47, Dec. 13, 1895)

The right that had been extended to the Burmese had to be, and had been in the past, in Holmwood's opinion, extended to Buddhists in general. The case of the plaintiff, that the Mahant had intended to deprive him of "his actually existing right," was born-out by the Mahant's behavior. In particular, Holmwood singled out the Giri offer to enshrine the image on the condition that it undergo the pranpratistha ("breath-giving") ceremony:

> [The Mahant] cannot but know that Buddhism is a religion to which his own predecessors were literally opposed and that all the ceremonies of Buddhism are completely abhorrent to Hindus. Huntley and Palmer's biscuits, candles of lard, and cheap English scent would be profanation to a Hindu deity. When the Mahanth therefore insisted on turning

> this Buddha into a deity, whatever his theories may be as to Buddha being an avatar of Vishnu, he must thereby have intended to prevent Buddhists from ever offering impure articles of food, candles, scent, etc. (TB, Vol. VII, #49, Dec. 27, 1895)

This established for Holmwood the *male fides* of the Mahant and influenced his subsequent ruling. He found, then, that the Mahant's agents, the three Giri appellants, had attempted to deprive Dharmapala of his established right of worship, and upheld the conviction. However, as Dharmapala's behavior constituted an innovation, albeit not an illegitimate one, Holmwood held that the acts of the appellants had been committed within a context that somewhat ameliorated the extent of the offense, and he therefore suspended the jail sentences, while retaining the fines.

Each fine amounted to one hundred rupees, which was then somewhat less than six pounds: by the close of the case, Dharmapala and the Society had spent 22,500 rupees (ADC, July 26, 1895) In fact, the dispute had become something of a windfall for the lawyers of Bengal. Clearly, neither side cared very deeply about the costs and, now, as the Mahant filed a second appeal, to have the conviction overturned in the Calcutta High Court, there was a brief competition for the best talent.

Dharmapala records that when he attempted to hire one of the more celebrated of the Calcutta advocates, Griffith Evans—a well-known Bengal figure and at one time a member of the Viceroy's Legislative Council—he "asked me to go and inquire from his clerk whether he has [already] accepted a retainer from the Mahant." (ADC, August 2, 1895) He had not. Therefore, the Society went into the second appeal armed with Sir Griffith's advice, at a charge of 6000 rupees. The Mahant stuck with Ghose and Cotton, and brought in three others to assist them.

The Calcutta High Court: "No Such Broad Question Arises"

The second appeal was heard before the Calcutta High Court, in August, by Justices William Macpherson, no relation to the Gaya Magistrate, and Guru Das Banerjee (who was a major figure in Bengali letters and politics, and a prominent protestor against the partition of Bengal).

Sir Griffith, for Dharmapala and the Society, took a minimalist line: "Section 296 contemplates that a worship should be disturbed, and when that is done the offense is complete." Possibly, the Mahant, through his agents, had the right to prevent the ceremony of the placing of the image, or, possibly, to have the image removed after the ceremony was completed, "but they were not justified in disturbing the worship during its continuance." (ILR, Calcutta Series, Vol. 23, 1896: 61)

Ghose, for the appellants, put forth the familiar argument that, for an offense to have been committed under the relevant section, the act had to be both lawful and genuine, and that the alleged disturbance had to be voluntary. In fact, Ghose maintained, Dharmapala and his companions "made an attempt to enshrine an image which they had no right to do," and the worship in question was not genuine, as was apparent "from the conduct of the complainant and his men."

The Magistrate of Gaya had characterized the case as being of importance due to the fact that the Mahant, though a Hindu, had claimed the right to regulate worship in a shrine that was "regarded by the Buddhists, that is, by almost one-third of the human race, as the most sacred spot on earth." Justice Macpherson demurred: "No such broad question arises."

> [The Case] has been fought with a persistency and at a cost which would have been more appropriate if it had been brought up in a

> court which could fully determine the rights of the Parties and not in a Criminal Court where the narrow issue is, whether a criminal offense has been committed. (ILR, Calcutta Series, Vol. 23, 1896: 62)

So, once again, the Gaya Magistrate was put in his place by his judicial superiors, who now proceeded to weigh the evidence.

"Each party charges the other with being the aggressor," wrote Justice Macpherson, the one characterizing the worship as "by permission," the other as "of right." The Justice found this to be a question "which it is unnecessary to consider."

> I shall assume for the purpose of this case that the worship which they were in the habit of performing was of right. It will, however, be necessary to consider the nature of that worship, and the nature of the act which gave rise to the disturbance complained of, in order to see whether a criminal offense has been committed. (ILR, Calcutta Series, Vol. 23, 1896: 64-65)

It would also be necessary to take up again the issue of proprietorship.

The complainants had argued that either the Mahant had no legitimate rights of proprietorship, or that, if he had, these rights had been subject to significant modification. Justice Macpherson found two such modifications. The first was that government had been entitled to appoint a custodian "whose principal duty it apparently is to look after the building and relics generally." This, he said, had no impact on the relevant position of the Mahant. The second had to do with rights of worship.

> That position I find to be this, that he held "possession" of the temple and had the control and superintendence over it, subject to the right of Buddhists to worship there in the customary manner, that is to say, in the manner in which they had been in the habit of worshipping. I see nothing in the judgments of the lower courts which goes against this finding. The difficulty is to understand from those judgments where the freedom of worship ends and the right of control begins.

In this regard Justice Macpherson felt it necessary to consider, not only the actual event, but also Dharmapala's intentions. These suggested that Dharmapala was not an "ordinary worshipper," as his counsel claimed, but had shrouded his aim, which was to wrest control of the temple from the Mahant under the guise of exercising a religious right.

There were "good grounds" for questioning Dharmapala's general veracity with respect to his testimony that he did not regard the Mahant as the owner of the temple. Justice Macpherson was of the opinion that it had been amply demonstrated from "his own writings, and from writings published with his knowledge and under his authority" that Dharmapala had always regarded the Mahant as the proprietor. (ILR, Calcutta Series, Vol. 23, 1896: 66-67) Justice Banerjee, in a separate opinion, concurred. As well, Banerjee lectured Appeals Judge Holmwood rather sternly on the subject of cultural constructions of truth:

> The learned sessions Judge, in order to reconcile his view of the general truthfulness of Dharmapala's evidence with the unreliable character of this part of it, has to rely on the erroneous and somewhat mischievous theory of the oriental standard of truth being different from the normal standard, a theory

> the application of which must often lead, as it has in this instance led, to incorrect estimation of evidence. (ILR, Calcutta Series, Vol. 23, 1896: 76)

The correct estimation of this evidence, and here Banerjee was in agreement with Justice Macpherson, was that it revealed a purpose larger than the assertion of an ordinary religious right guaranteed by custom.

Both Justices seemed to argue that the actual act of worship in question could only be understood within this larger context of Dharmapala's objectives. However, at one point Macpherson allowed himself the luxury of indicating that this line of reasoning was superfluous: "I have said that Dharmapala was not in the position of an ordinary devotee, but he is, of course, entitled to have the legality of his act judged as if he were one."

He then turned to the nature of the actual act, which was an "enshrinement" undertaken without permission of the proprietor, and in the knowledge that a previous attempt to place the image in the second story chamber had been forbidden by the Mahant, and that the Mahant's rule on that occasion had been observed.

On these grounds alone, then, the enshrinement party had not constituted a lawfully assembled religious body. (ILR, Calcutta Series, Vol. 23, 1896: 68-72)

Sir Griffith Evans, in the view of Justice Banerjee, "no doubt felt the difficulty of the position." This accounted for the ingenious argument, on behalf of the Buddhists, that the event had to be divided into several constituent sacred and secular moments.

> Even if there were no disturbance of a lawful religious worship or ceremony on the first occasion, when Dharmapala was told to re-

> move the image and was prevented from lighting the candles, there certainly was on the second, when the image was removed, as the Buddhists were then sitting in contemplation before the image and actually and to the knowledge of the disturbers engaged in religious worship. (ILR, Calcutta Series, Vol. 23, 1896: 68-72)

Banerjee and Macpherson both found this to be a choice argument and seemed reluctant to dispose of it too quickly. Banerjee briefly considered the notion "that religious worship, from its sacred character should, while it is going on, be secured against molestation, even though the worshipper be a wrong-doer and a trespasser." But, in fact, "that is not provided for by our criminal law."

Justice Macpherson was prepared to concede that, certainly, had the Mahant's men attempted to effect even a legal object through the disruption of a lawfully assembled body, they could have been found guilty under section 296. And, certainly, it would be no defense to say that the worship was not genuine, as is stipulated it must be under the relevant section.

> It is no excuse for disturbing them to say that I thought they were not worshipping, and that they were thinking of something that they ought not to have been thinking about."

I want to pause here to point out something that may seem obvious to anyone who has thought about the problem of regulating, guaranteeing, or delimiting religious rights as these are enjoyed in formally secular states. British India was, in fact, such a secular state. It had been, in earlier Company times, secular by general practice and inclination, and became more so after Queen Victoria's 1858 proclamation, which announced the transfer of power from Company to

Crown, and which, significantly, contained a strong and explicit promise to refrain from interference in religious matters.

It is not necessary to detail the legal codification of this in British India, only to point out that British India shared, with many modern states, and many contemporary ones, a formal and principled distaste for the regulation of religious matters. This sort of thing is widely celebrated as progress, of course, and rightly so, but it does not on the other hand solve the problem that Macphereson brings up, namely, that in order to protect a religious right, it may sometimes be necessary to determine whether or not a religious phenomenon is actually present, and this involves secular governments in a very uncomfortable bind. Government *should* not, but sometimes *must,* involve itself it judging whether or not something is legitimately religious. In the present case, Macphereson dodged the issue neatly enough:

> Here I think it is quite open to the petitioners to say that there was no real worship, but I do not wish to decide the case on that ground, or to hold that the Buddhists were not really contemplating, and that they merely fell into a posture of worship for appearance's sake. I prefer to hold, as I do, that they were not lawfully engaged in worship, that the disturbances must be regarded as continuous, and that if they were not lawfully engaged at first they were not lawfully engaged afterwards. They went to enshrine an image in place where they had no right to enshrine it. (ILR, Calcutta Series, Vol. 23, 1896: 72)

So ended the third stage of the "Great Case," with the Justices, having ruled that no offense had been committed, setting aside the convictions.

The proprietorship issue had been examined at length throughout all the proceedings and, finally, Macpherson had arrived at the judgment that "if the temple is not vested in the Mahant, it does not appear to be vested in anyone." (ILR, Calcutta Series, Vol. 23, 1896: 65)

Banerjee felt, with his associate, that the question of proprietorship could not be adequately addressed in a criminal action and, further, noted that "the question of what the exact nature and extent of the Mahant's control over the temple is, the evidence adduced in the case does not enable us to determine." (ILR, Calcutta series, Vol.26, 1896: 75-76)

However, Banerjee noted, Dharmapala, through his journal writings and through his attempts to negotiate for the sale of the temple, had certainly acted as if the Mahant were the legitimate and sole proprietor, and that sufficiently established the nature of the property rights for the purposes of the case. In short, Dharmapala had not only lost badly in the criminal proceedings, he had strengthened the general impression that the Mahant was the actual owner of the temple and its grounds.

Chapter Six

LORD CURZON AT BODH GAYA

"When all had deserted me in 1895 I put on the yellow robe and became anagarika [homeless]," wrote Dharmapala (ADC, Feb. 12, 1927). Another of Dharmapala's recollections is that "in May 1895 the Ceylon Buddhists abandoned me because I failed to recover Buddha Gaya." (ADS Vol. 3, 1918) Indeed, Dharmapala had lost considerable prestige as a result of his expensive legal adventure, and he did not fully recover his position as a leader of Buddhist ecumenical interests in India until well after World War I, when he managed to mobilize sufficient funds and support to open Buddhist Viharas in both Sarnath and Calcutta.

In the interim, the Governments of both India and Bengal took up the problem of how best to allocate the sacred resource of Bodh Gaya between Hindus and Buddhists.

Dharmapala out of Favor: "Ah, the Utter Injustice of the British Raj!"

At one level, for Dharmapala, the campaign had been an attempt to achieve, within the context of a community of like-minded believers, perhaps within "a beautiful company of men preaching," a secure and valued position. Just how personal this vision was is apparent in a memory, which dramatically contradicts his earlier diary entry, of the decision to carry the image to the temple.

In his diary, at the time, he had written. "then it was decided that we should take the image early morning," to enshrine it in the Mahabodhi temple. Much later, though, we read that "The Bhikkhus advised me *not* to take the Jap. image of Buddha to B. Gaya." (ADS Dec.19, 1927, my emphasis)

He quickly sought, against the opposition of his erstwhile allies, to recover his influence. His major vehicle for so doing was to propose that the Mahabodhi Society attempt to purchase land in the area at any price. At a Theosophical meeting in Calcutta, Dharmapala urged that thirty thousand rupees be raised, and Olcott had strenuously objected. (ADC, Jan 29, 1896)

The plot in question, again in the Tekari Raj, proved, again, to be unavailable: the Mahant's interests had not altered since the previous offer had been tendered by Dharmapala and Olcott. And, somewhat ironically, in light of later events, Dharmapala held the British responsible for the blocked sale: "Ah, the utter injustice of the British Raj." (ADC, April 7, 1896)

The Mahant, for his part, immediately acted to capitalize on his legal triumph, and requested that the Commissioner of Patna order Dharmapala to turn over the keys of the Burmese resthouse to the Math. (ADC, Dec. 1, 1895) The Commissioner refused to comply, and his decision was upheld by Government of Bengal. In so ruling, the Bengal Judicial Department stated, in May of 1896, that "the Mahanth has no right to close it [the resthouse] against any of the Buddhists wishing to use it." (MBJ, Vol. 18, #6, June 1910)

Through this language Bengal wished to uphold the position that Buddhists had a customary right of worship at the site. In the course of the same order, however, government seemed to commit itself to the proposition that such customary access was limited.

The Magistrate of Gaya was directed to write Dharmapala. (These quotations are from 1896 documents that were reprinted in the Mahabodhi Journal in 1910: these matters were re-fought in that journal for many years.)

> [In order to] instruct him to remove the [Japanese] image from its present place and from the precincts of the Temple within one month, and warn him that if he fails to do so, the Government will take possession of it and deposit it in the Indian Museum in Calcutta, where it will remain until it is reclaimed on such conditions as the Government may think fit to impose. (MBJ, Vol. 18, #6, June 1910)

Buddhists, mainly from Ceylon and Burma, objected and Dharmapala, in his petition to Bengal that the order be reversed, wrote, in language that was obviously in accord with Edwin Arnold's earlier attempts, that "by allowing this great and historic image to remain as it is, you will win the love and esteem of their Majesty's Buddhist subjects and the lasting gratitude of the millions of Buddhists in Asia." (MBJ, Vol. V, #3, July, 1896)

Bengal did reverse the decision, but not, it is likely, only in response to pleas from Dharmapala, who was increasingly regarded as an irritant. Rather, it was pressure from Burma, where some Buddhists were outraged by the decision, that brought about the change.

D.M. Smeaton, the Chief Commissioner, Burma, had sent on to Government of India a number of petitions begging that the image be allowed to stay in the resthouse. Many educated Burmese, it appears, were well aware of the historical links between Burma and Bodh Gaya and felt a national or proto-national pride in the matter. To the Burmese petitions, which were in turn forwarded to Bengal, Smeaton appended an "interesting historical document."

> I may mention that in the "Narrative of a Mission of Mandalay in 1875," which is an enclo-

> sure in Sir Douglas Forsyth's letter to the Foreign Secretary to the Government of India, dated 7th July 1875, there occur the following passages in a conversation between King Mindon and the Envoy Sir D. Forsyth:
>
> King.- "Setting aside all other matters, I am most anxious to repair some pagodas and religious edifices at Gya and I hope to obtain the assistance of the Viceroy.
>
> Envoy.- "I am sure the Viceroy will do all in his power to enable your majesty to carry out your instructions in this respect."
>
> King.- "I attach great importance to this matter, and shall be grateful for assistance."

Smeaton concluded by saying that "King Mindon was a very devout Buddhist and his memory is much revered by the Burmese." (ECCI, Vol. 26, 254a; some of the relevant documents, seen by Smeaton, are available in the *Bulletin of Burma Research*, Vol. 1, No. 2, Autumn 2003, SOAS)

When notice of the reversal arrived from Bengal there was, of course, no reference made to these pressures. Instead, the government attempted to characterize the decision as an expression of "neutrality" in religious affairs.

> The Lieutenant-Governor was under the impression that the image was practically a derelict and in charge of no one, and the object of Government in issuing the orders of the 2nd April 1896 was to prevent any mischief happening to such a beautiful work of art. It now appears that there are in residence at Budh-Gaya Buddhist priests who consider themselves responsible for the image and declare the police guard which is kept over

> it unnecessary. This being so there is no reason why Government should not maintain the only possible attitude which it can properly assume in such a case, that, namely, of absolute neutrality. The guard will accordingly be withdrawn and the image will be left in the Rest House where it is, Government being in no way responsible for its safe custody or preservation. (MBJ, Vol. 18, #6, June 1910)

Predictably, however, the counter-order called forth a new barrage of petitions, from the Mahant, and from his allies, who reacted to the new form of absolute neutrality with some resentment.

Mahant Krishna Dayal Gir, in a letter of November 23, 1896, had put before the Lieutenant-Governor "the grievances of the Hindu community caused by the unjust claims and unlawful attempts of the Buddhists." The proximity of the resthouse and its image, "devoted to the worship of a sect that holds views so diametrically opposed to those of the Hindus must be a perpetual source of dispute, perhaps of breaches of the peace, and should therefore be avoided."

Attached to the Mahant's letter was a Hindu petition stating that the shrines at Bodh Gaya were felt to be so holy that "slight pollution or contamination of them is felt by the memorialists to be a great calamity affecting the salvation of their forefathers and their own well-being in the future world."

Now, of course, the Giris, and as far as is known other Hindus in the area, had never felt that the access for worship granted to Burmese Buddhists had represented any such threats. The real target here was Dharmapala, who was named as the man "wholly responsible for the creation of the recent misunderstanding between the Buddhists and the Hindus." (BIA, 1896: 126)

Amplification of the Conflict: The Mahant's New Allies

At this point it became apparent that the Mahant had tapped into a new source of support; the British Indian Association. This was an organization that represented the interests of large landholders—zamindars—in Bengal and, of course, the Mahant himself was one of these. There is no indication that the Mahant was ever actually a member of the association, but his counsel, Cotton, had a number of clients there and encouraged the Mahant to apprise them of his difficulties.

As well, the Maharajah of Darbhanga, to the north of Gaya District, was a major influence in the association. Darbhanga had a reputation for great Hindu orthodoxy. Having said that, it seems clear that some more complicated combination of wealth and/or orthodoxy brought him, and the British Indian Association, into connection with the Mahant. Certainly, from this point on, and throughout Curzon's Viceroyalty, the British Indian Association were key players in negotiations over the temple.

The association was overwhelmingly Hindu, in its membership, and native Indian, but it also made common cause with landowners throughout India, primarily in Bengal and Bihar. Its members moved comfortably in educated urban circles that included many British, most of whom were not in official government service—though they may have once been, or may have been close to others who were—but in commercial careers.

The first blast from the association appears in a letter to Bengal protesting the reversal order. "Government apparently overlooked the fact that the effect of this order could only be to alter the character of the building and to convert it into a Budhist [sic] Shrine." In response to this, and to other British Indian Association petitions, Bengal refused to again reverse itself, but did note, in replying, that they "denied that the Budh-Gya temple was a Hindu temple in the sense implied by your committee."[1]

The committee, a small group of members chaired by Raja Peary Mohan Mukherjee, an aristocrat and landowner, of considerable wealth with which he became locally quite philanthropic, in his family site at Uttarparah (near Calcutta), recorded that "protest meetings have been held at various centres and there can be little doubt that the decision has been received with disapproval by a large section of the community."(BIA, 1898:15)

Such discontent had been brewing since the first attempt by Dharmapala to set up the Japanese image in the temple. The *Dainik-o-Samachar Chandrika,* a Bengali daily in Calcutta, had editorialized, on May 4, 1894, that "there are a number of Hindu temples which formerly belonged to Buddhists, and none of these can be given back to Buddhists," without it "constituting a grave danger to public peace." (NPRB, 1894, #22:424)

The same paper, after the legal proceedings had run their course, and after Bengal had reversed its decision regarding the image, called on Muslims and Hindus to unite against the order: "if Mr. Dharmapala can today lay his hands on a Hindu temple, he may tomorrow lay his hands on a Musalman mosque." (NPRB, 1896, #11: 278) Another Bengali daily newspaper predicted that the reversal would

---

[1] The British Indian Association on at least one occasion addressed the government to provide for more facilities to Hindu pilgrims at Gaya, the larger Hindu pilgrimage town whose main Hindu priests, the Gayawals, have traditionally regarded Bodh Gaya as an important satellite.

> The committee represented to the Agent, East Indian [railway] Company, that in order to remove grievances of Gya pilgrims, stations should be established at Poonpoon and Palmergunja and that Babu Shewprasad Jhoonjhoonwala had liberally offered to build at his own cost proper rest houses at the places if the Railway would acquire the land required for the purpose. (BIA, 1904: 25)

be a disaster, kindling "the fire of religious animosity in peaceful Budh-Gaya."

Subsequently, the paper *Dainik-o-Samachar Chandrika* weighed in with the theory that since Buddhists and Christians are "natural allies," both being "anti-caste," and since Dharmapala, aided by "powerful patrons such as Sir Edwin Arnold," had been able to threaten the government with "the displeasure of the Buddhist countries," Bengal had been forced to back away from its initial decision, with what could only be the most disastrous consequences. (NPRB, 1896, #25: 616) Finally, the *Bangavasi* of Calcutta claimed that "this cunning priest is trying to revive Buddhism in India and make the Buddhists as a class powerful in this country." (NPRB, 1896, #26: 633)

One paper, the Hindi language weekly *Bharat Mitra* of Calcutta, reported that "the visit of some Japanese gentleman" had prompted official fear that "continuance of Buddha's image in the temple might afford foreigners pretexts for coming to India in large numbers."The paper not only upheld Dharmapala's right to purchase land, but also recommended that the image be allowed to remain. This suggestion was perhaps sarcastic, as the editorial went on to suggest that should foreigners create disturbance government should "keep a Political Officer as well as a military force in Buddha-Gaya." (NPRB, 1896,#18: 428)

Government did, in fact, become concerned about foreign influence, but this was not their primary difficulty. The main task from the point of view of government was to juggle two sets of interests, both of which seemed, at least in part, legitimate. Futhermore, in fashioning a resolution, they had to act in accord with their own legal process.

Government had established, on the one hand, that the Mahant was the de facto proprietor of the temple and its grounds, and, on the other, that Buddhists enjoyed some right of access for worship at the temple. Insofar as government had also, at this time, retreated to a principle of religious neutrality which discouraged formulation of any precise definition of these religious rights, prospects for fruitful intervention became murky indeed. During Curzon's viceregency, however, intervention came to be regarded as both possible and necessary.

Lord Curzon and Things "Intrinsically...of no Value"

In the Winter of 1900, the Lieutenant-Governor of Madras, Sir A.E. Havelock, offered to the King of Siam a relic of the Buddha that had been recently unearthed in Godavari District. The offer came to the attention of George Nathaniel Curzon, then in the second year of his first term as Viceroy, and he had a curious reaction to the news: "I have seen this relic at Madras and, while it is intrinsically, of course, of *no value*, it possesses great *historical and sentimental value.*" (CCIC, Vol. 202, 1900, #163; CCEP, Part IV, 1900:1, my emphasis)

Curzon regarded himself, incidentally, as having rather a knack for symbolic and ritual strategies. He was after all to mount, in 1903, one of the great British "Durbars"—royal assemblages—in Delhi, with the confidence that however much it might cost it would be economical in "binding" the average Indian to Britain. This was because, he thought, the "native mind" was susceptible to the operations of certain "time-honoured" elements of royal ceremony. (Trevithick 1990:567-68) This is symbolic thinking, and imperial symbolic thinking: with regard to the King of Siam, Curzon decided that he had already been well-treated in the way of relics from India, from British India, and should receive no further gifts in this line.

This is the first occasion on record of Lord Curzon's interest in Buddhist affairs, but it illustrates a general principle held by Curzon, and by many in the Government of India, concerning traces of past Indian greatness. As will become clear during the course of this chapter, Curzon held strong views on the recovery and preservation of the artifacts of Indian civilization.

Oftentimes, such recovery and preservation had to be pursued in the face of what the British regarded as Indian ignorance, negligence, and abuse. Shrines, palaces, and relics had to be discovered, classified, recorded, and displayed and, most importantly, held in trust against the neglect and depredation of a heedless population.

This, of course, was precisely the philosophy that facilitated the great heaping up of the world's treasures in British museums, and, to be sure, Indian civilization is not unrepresented in those repositories. Yet, for Curzon, not Britain, but British India, was the supreme field of British greatness, and India's claims on her own past were not to be denied. It was in this frame of mind that Curzon wrote, "in my judgment, these interesting relics should be conserved in the country to which they originally belong."

The relic originally belonged to India, and was thereby immovable. But this little fragment of bone was not merely an Indian relic: it was an Imperial British Indian Buddhist Relic.

> I may add, though this is not for repetition, that my reluctance to let it go to Bangkok is enhanced by the possibility that a day may one day come when whatever treasures there are in the palace at Bangkok are not unlikely to be forcibly removed to the Louvre.

The British resident at Bangkok was instructed to "undo" the offer. (CCIA, Vol. IV, Dec, 21, 1900) The Viceroy's thinking on this minor matter instanciates the process through which an item "intrinsically" of no value can come to be invested with "historical and sentimental"—and political—value.

Let me sum up this strain of British Indian thinking about

"valuable things." Things of no apparent value came to have value through their links with the past. Then too, things properly belonged to the places where they originated. Finally, such things had to be protected by government from those who would wrongly appropriate or abuse them. When Curzon, and the Government of Bengal, turned their minds to the problem at Bodh Gaya, they employed these ideas. Furthermore, their vision of the proper and original nature of *things* was entirely in harmony with their vision of the proper and original nature of *people.*

Curzon first became aware of the situation at Bodh Gaya when, in Mandalay, he received a petition from Buddhists at the Kuthodaw Pagoda, on November 29, 1901. The Burmese expressed some alarm about the fate of presents that had been sent by King Mindon "to the Temple," and which had apparently been seized by the Mahant. In addition, the Buddhists wished Government of India to facilitate the construction of a new Burmese Rest House at the site. Curzon promised to investigate. (CCIA, Part IV, Nov. 21, 1901)

In response to subsequent queries, Curzon received from Bourdillon, the Acting Lieutenant-Governor of Bengal, the response that "the resthouse you speak of at Bodh Gaya is now being built." The gifts that were said to have been appropriated by the Mahant were something of a mystery. "About the gifts in 1875 I have never heard but inquiries will be made."

In fact, the precise nature and final disposition of these gifts were never established. (CCIC, Vol. 205, Feb. 25, 1902) Nevertheless, this communication served as an opening for Bourdillon to discuss with Curzon the nature of the religious situation at Bodh Gaya.

On several occasions during the course of the year, Bourdillon expressed his dissatisfaction with the Mahant's management of the place, and, finally, it was decided that a

Viceregal visit was in order. Just prior to this visit, Bourdillon submitted to Curzon a memorandum on the subject.

> I venture to think that the temple ought to be made over to the Buddhists and the Hindu rites stopped which only disgust and outrage the Buddhist Pilgrims and are revolting even to casual visitors. You will see, I suspect, the colossal form of the Buddha in the basement of the temple, not simple and unadorned, but draped in tawdry tinsel and smeared with caste marks, with Hindu offerings before it, and, at the back of the temple, when I was there with Sir John Woodward, we saw under the sacred Bodhi tree of the Buddhists, where everything should tend to devotion and contemplation, Hindu priests chanting noisy hymns. (CCOC, Vol. 1, 10A, Jan. 9, 1903)

There is not, I would note, in this passage, much in the way of a "legal" attitude towards the problem at Bodh Gaya. Religious rights are not, at this moment, the most salient issue. The problem, from Bourdillon's point of view, was that people were not behaving in an appropriate manner. The defense of the "rights" of the Buddhists to worship, though no doubt a concern of Bourdillon's, was associated, as well, with a bid to defend "casual visitors" from squalid Hindu excess. What happens, in fact, to legal principles, is of great interest.

Hitherto, continued Bourdillon, the government has struck a pose of complete "neutrality," but now the time has arrived for the "righting of a great wrong."

Chapter Seven

THE VICEREGAL COMMISSION

Lord Curzon, prior to his arrival, had satisfied himself that, on legal, historical and religious grounds, the Buddhists' claims were just and he had "resolved...to question the Mahant very closely on these matters," when he visited the shrine. So, the Viceroy, accompanied by the Collector of Gaya and the Commissioner of Patna, descended the steps down into the courtyard of the Mahabodhi Temple and, as the little group paused before the main entrance of the shrine, they were greeted by the Shaivite abbot.

The Viceroy's questioning, and the Mahant's responses, have not been preserved in any extensive form. However, Curzon apparently asked the Mahant how it was that Hindu worship in a Buddhist shrine could be justified, and had received the expected answer that Buddha was a form of Vishnu. Curzon retorted that "if this were so, it was remarkable that for centuries the Vaisnavas had never found it out," by which he meant that, although there might be *Shaivite* Hindu worship going on in the temple, there seemed to be no evidence of Vaishnava worship.

Actually, this is a rather revealing remark, and indicates the extent to which Curzon was capable of hiving off one strain of Hindu tradition from another. His notion was this: the Mahant is a Shaivite, therefore he performs Shaivite worship, but the avatara formula refers to Vishnu, and therefore worship carried out according to this formula by a Shaivite is not legitimate worship. The Mahant responded that he simply followed "ancient custom" at Bodh Gaya.

This is all we have of the actual visit of Curzon to Bodh Gaya, but it is clear that the Viceroy arrived with the conviction that the temple, by right, belonged to the Buddhists, and that he left with this conviction unchanged. Having reviewed the legal history of the place, he saw that the proprietary rights over the place had never been directly addressed in the appropriate arena.

This unsatisfactory outcome he blamed on Dharmapala, who had attempted his enshrinement "without sanction either in precedent or in the consent of the Mahanth." It had been, in fact, "the provocative and irritating attitude of Dharmapala" that had driven the Mahant to his current obstinacy. Now, however, Curzon thought that he had noticed, on the part of the abbot, a certain "hesitancy" in responding to questioning, and this encouraged the Viceroy to think that he might be "malleable." (CCIA, Vol 622, Jan. 16, 1903: 227)

The Lieutenant-Governor was well-pleased with the Viceroy's findings. "I have carefully read the note of His Excellency on Bodh Gaya and I must express my astonishment and gratification at the perfect grasp it shows of the whole question." His Excellency's only significant mistake was to have called the butter offerings being made by Hindus before the main image "grease" and not "ghi," that is, clarified butter. (CCOC, Vol. 1, #19, Jan. 17, 1903) Certainly it would not have been orthodox Hindu practice to offer rendered animal fat before any image.

Either way, however, grease or butter, the attentions of the Hindus to the figure of the Buddha in the Mahabodhi Temple were inappropriate, and the Lieutenant-Governor now had Viceregal sanction to investigate an appropriate adjustment of the situation. The possibility that a special commission of inquiry should be formed had been discussed, and also the possibility of "legislation," that is to say an executive order. But, this sort of problem at Bodh Gaya, being a local matter, was best managed at the local level and, so, some days after the Viceroy had returned to Calcutta, the Collector of Gaya sent the Mukhtiar Vijayananda off to fetch the Mahant.

Worship "According to Custom"

Bourdillon had, prior to the Viceroy's trip, praised the talents of the new Collector of Gaya, Charles Evelyn Arbuthnot Oldham, a valued correspondent of the archaeologist Sir Aurel Stein and the Sanskritist Sir Ralph Turner, among others.

"You will find him full of information," wrote Bourdillon, but he is a "particularly sensitive and diffident man, and may require a bit of drawing out." (CCOC, Vol. 1, 10A, Jan. 9, 1903) He may well have been diffident when in the company of the Viceroy, but with the Mahant he seemed, at least at first, though cautious, quite confident and forceful. Oldham had seen the Viceroy's note, and now wished to follow up on Curzon's line of questioning. The following is from the Collector's summary of his audience with the Mahant.

> Had it occurred to [the Mahant] that the Viceroy seemed much astonished to see the image of the Buddha decorated and besmeared? That from his tone he seemed amazed? The Mahanth would not admit this altogether, but evidently had noticed HE's manner.

Surely the Mahant had noted His Excellency's grasp of the situation, and surely he knew of the Viceroy's opinion that the temple "was a really a Buddhistic shrine." Of course, the Viceroy respected the feelings of the Hindus, and earnestly desired to work in cooperation with the Mahant on this matter, but, after all, in the course of several legal cases, "the question of proprietary right had really not been decided at all." Furthermore, the High Court, even while overturning the criminal convictions, had expressed strong disapproval of the "spurious worship" of Hindus at the shrine.[1]

Oldham then brought up the "temporal aspect" of the case. Had it occurred to the Mahant that, these days, many more Buddhist pilgrims were visiting the temple than in previous years?

It had, replied the Mahant, and Dharmapala himself was to blame for it. But here Oldham took up a more social and a more global perspective. On the contrary, claimed Oldham, "Dharmapala's advent was really but a result of the same causes that tended to bring a much larger influx of pilgrims in the future."

These causes were manifold: various religious revivals in Ceylon, Japan and Siam, western style education with the consequent creation of a larger reading public that could read about sacred destinations in books that were increasingly available through improved printing and distribution methods, and the establishment of reliable rail and steamship services. So, in effect, here was Oldham practically endorsing, or at least supporting by reference to general historical processes, the sorts of international efforts that

[1] This is a reference to evidence first brought out in the case heard by the District Magistrate. In the Calcutta High Court Appeal case brought by the Mahant, Justice William Macpherson wrote:

> The evidence shows, and the Magistrate finds, that since July 1894, the Mahant and his disciples have been carrying on a sort of spurious Hindu worship of the great image of Buddha on the altar of the ground floor, and that the image has been dressed in a way which renders it repugnant to Buddhist worshippers. The Magistrate regards this a stratagem on the Mahant's part to strengthen his position against, I suppose, some threatened danger. This was extremely wrong, but it does not, I think, affect the present case. (ILR, Vol. XXIII, 1896: 71)

Dharmapala—and, it is true, the Theosophists—had been working at.

Well, in matters such as this, Oldham, who was a very intelligent and well-informed man, was absolutely correct. In truth, his prediction is fully borne out by contemporary experience: more Buddhists than ever had been imagined in the Mahant's time now visit and spend money in Bodh Gaya. This was what Oldham was getting at: considerable monetary benefit might accrue to the Mahant from these developments should he soften his line somewhat to provide for the sensitivities of Buddhist pilgrims, who now were outraged by the Hindu treatment of the shrine and its main image.

On the other hand, continued Oldham, were the Government forced to the remedy of "special legislation," who knows what might happen? The Mahant promised to give it some thought. Oldham then proposed the following terms: 1) that the temple be regarded as "a purely Buddhistic shrine," 2) that it be handed over to government "in trust," 3) that the "Western Bo-tree be reserved exclusively for Buddhist worship, 4) that the Northern Pipal tree be reserved for Hindu worship, and 5) that the Mahant, as "ground landlord," continue to receive "customary fees and gifts of visitors." (CCOC, Vol. 1, #45, Jan. 2, 1903)

Mr. Oldham pointed out that Babu Hariharnath, the government pleader, was in the next room and that it would be quite convenient for him to prepare a draft agreement. The Mahant thought it would be best if he consulted his own legal advisor, Mr. Cotton of Calcutta—the man with the long connection with the British Indian Association. At the close of this interview, Oldham tossed in a suggestion that, were the Mahant to cooperate he might be granted an esteemed mark of prestige, exemption from personal attendance in the civil courts. In a letter to the Viceroy's private secretary, Oldham was optimistic. "In the end [the Mahant] appeared to agree, and even went so far as to promise he would do what I might suggest."

At their next meeting, Oldham presented the Mahant with a draft for his signature. The Mahant, however, protested that the terms had to be drafted "ke hamko koi ninda la kare," so that "no blame will attach to me." On being asked the meaning of this, the Mahant said that, were Hindus to be actually barred from the temple, "all Hindus in India" would blame him. This triggered an inconclusive debate. Hindu worship in a Buddhist temple is not orthodox, claimed Oldham. You should, retorted the Mahant, ask Mr. Beglar of the archeological survey, about what is and what is not orthodox. Mr. Beglar has testified that Hindu worship in the temple is of long standing. Furthermore, The Maharajah of Darbhanga, a pillar of orthodoxy according to the Mahant, came into the temple "with his Gayawal" (his priest, in this case one of the Vaishnava priests associated with the Vishnupad Temple in the larger town of Gaya).

Not happy about the proposal in general, the Mahant was quite irritated with certain of the details. Why should the Hindus only be allowed to worship at the so-called Northern tree? The Northern one is younger, this in itself was sufficient to injure Hindu feeling. No, it was *not* younger, claimed Oldham, the Western tree was younger, having in fact been planted by Sir Alexander Cunningham not thirty years prior. "He then hinted that we were all biased in favour of the Buddhists, that the English read only the Buddhist scriptures and not the Hindu scriptures." Oldham claimed neutrality.

Buddha Dev was a Hindu deity according to the Mahant, and was worshipped by Hindus according to the shastric authorities. Perhaps, said Oldham, Buddha is in some sense a form of Vishnu, but surely, at a temple as clearly Buddhistic as the Mahabodhi, the Buddha in question was Gautama Buddha, and thus an improper object of Hindu worship. We worship according to "custom," said the Mahant and, after all, had the Maharajah of Jammu not been recently told by his pandit that it was proper for a Hindu to worship in the shrine? Oldham was unconvinced: we cannot establish what is properly "custom" by reference to "the mere fancy of an individual."

No agreement was signed. Certainly, said Oldham, he would be happy to see a draft proposed by the Mahant, but the Mahant should realize that the next officer might not be so accommodating. The Mahant said he would have a draft prepared in such a way that no blame would attach to him. Oldham's communication with Calcutta after this was that "the Mahant is a hopeless person to negotiate with verbally." The Collector now favored the formation of a commission, with the proviso that it "be able to elicit sufficient Hindu opinion in the course of its proceedings." (CCOC, Vol. 1, #45, Jan. 2, 1903)

The "Right Hindus" Produce the Wrong Report

No sign of the Mahant's agreement was forthcoming for the next month, and Bourdillon began to think about the possibility of an executive order. This was dangerous as there might well arise, "in certain quarters," the perception that "the Hindu religion is being damaged and so forth." In this regard the Lieutenant-Governor was keen that the British Indian Association "be kept out of the dispute."

This group, as well as the Bankipore Hindu Sabha, had "interfered" during the controversy over the disposition of the Japanese image in 1897. Now, both these organizations were represented by the Mahant's legal advisor, Mr. Cotton, and it was Bourdillon's own opinion that Cotton was the motive force behind their expressions of solidarity with the Bodh Gaya Giris, which took the form of telegrams and newspaper editorials. How it was, in the absence of draconian press legislation, that Bourdillo thought they might then be "kept out of the dispute" is not quite clear.

In any event, government had the reasonable expectation that an executive order might promote some negative Hindu reaction, and Bourdillon had formulated a tentative response.

> Government will answer that the worship is spurious and impure in itself, that it is revolting to the Buddhists who are the undoubted authors, and should be the owners, of the shrine, and that in order to prevent this offense being perpetuated, the Government merely intends to supervise the proceedings in a building which they themselves rescued from ruin, and in which they have ever since maintained an interest. I believe that the agitation will be short-lived and unimportant. (CCOC, Vol. 1, #76, March 9, 1903)

In the meantime, it was important to get on with the formation of the commission, which would be able to provide suitable grounds for an order. Bourdillon thought that it would be best to have two Hindu commissioners. "The difficulty is to get the right Hindus." S.C. Mitra, from Calcutta, was such a candidate, respected, knowledgeable, and a lawyer who had been designated for the High Court. As well, "we should endeavor to strengthen our position by obtaining the opinions of learned Pandits whose view will carry weight, to the effect that Hindu worship in the Buddhist Temple is spurious and impure." (CCOC, Vol. 1, #76, March 9, 1903)

There was a point at which this strategizing became highly manipulative, and exemplary of the worst sort of imperial smugness, in the sense that it was assumed that government could always come up with a good compromise, given the right selection of antagonists. One advisor to Government of Bengal, for instance, J. Munro, suggested that the Commission, in taking opinions, set in motion some agitation "amongst the [Hindu] parties themselves."

"Make the parties get their vyavasthas [opinions] and then let Govt. come in as the peace loving Buddha!" (CCOC, #76, March 4, 1903) On the other hand, government did in fact realize that only responsible and knowledgeable people could get the job done. It would be ideal, they thought, if someone from Benares could act as one of the commissioners, someone "who would take a broad and sensible view."

Unfortunately, wrote Bourdillon, "I know no one who answers that description." Having failed to locate the correct Benares candidate, Bourdillon settled for Hari Prasad Shastri, a highly respected Sanskrit scholar, and the principal of the Sanskrit College at Calcutta. Shastri had demonstrated his suitability by claiming that "the transfer of the temple to the Buddhists is a very important work in which the whole of Asia is interested." (CCOC, Vol. 1, #76, March 9, 1903)

On March 15, 1903, Bourdillon informed Curzon that the Commission was prepared to begin. The Lieutenant- Governor promised to limit the circulation of certain memoranda to an inner circle of advisors as, otherwise, "I shall find it difficult to keep Your Excellency's name in the background as much as you should suggest." (CCOC, Vol. 1, #85, March 15, 1903) The concern was, that if there were to develop a perception that the Hindu religion was being "injured," that blame at least be confined to Bengal and not seen to involve Government of India.

Several days later, Bourdillon wrote Curzon to indicate that the composition of the commission seemed most favorable to the desired outcome: "The opinions of the Pandit [Shastri] we already know, and I was glad to find that S.C. Mitra was equally favourable." Both felt that the terms offered by Oldham to the Mahant were "eminently reasonable." On the other hand, the lawyer for the commission thought that "the Buddhists would not likely gain much out of a civil suit." (CCOC, Vol. 1, #87, March 17, 1903)

The commission's findings confirmed this impression that the Buddhists had no actionable rights that would gain them significant concessions in the civil courts. The first finding, not surprisingly, was that since 1875, that is to say, since the Burmese negotiations, the Mahant had been "explicitly" recognized as the owner of the place. The temple, "no doubt originated in the piety of the Buddhists," but it had been, as had similar temples and grounds throughout India, "practically abandoned" by the twelfth century. "We do not see how the Buddhists can legally put forward any claim to what they abandoned or were compelled to abandon centuries ago."

In the fullness of time, the distinction between theft and other forms of acquisition can become rather foggy, but whether they "abandoned" it or were "compelled to abandon" it, the Buddhists had not "held" the temple for many centuries.

The issue now was that rights of "ownership and possession," had been pitted against "rights of access and worship." (CCBG: 4) Having failed to locate even the slightest grounds on which to devalue the Mahant's claims of ownership, the Commission then took up the issue of religious legitimacy. It was true that the Northern Pipal tree, the so-called Mahabodhidruma, had always "attracted a large number of Hindu pilgrims," and that Shastric authority for the practice was readily available in the Vayu and Agni Puranas. On the other hand, the temple itself had never been "particularly attractive" to Hindus.

As well, "the majority of the witnesses examined by us declare that the sight of Buddha's image is sinful to a Hindu." (CCBG: 4-12)

The commissioners gave out only the sketchiest of details on the selection and questioning of their informants, but it seems that not more than two dozen Hindus, in Gaya and

ceive offerings be affirmed. This was in line with Oldham's first proposal. However, contra Oldham, he stipulated that 1) he be declared "manager," 2) that both Hindus and Buddhists be allowed to worship inside the temple, and 3) that Hindus be allowed access to both the Northern and Western pipal trees. (CCOC, Vol. 1, #98A, April 5, 1903)

The Lieutenant-Governor took the Mahant's proposal to be a negotiating instrument and, in a turn-about from his previous position, now attempted to recruit the British Indian Association. Raja Peary Mohan Mukherjee, the "moving spirit" behind that society, now expressed a desire to see that an amicable outcome be arranged. The Bengal government hoped that by winning over the association they could put some pressure on the Mahant to yield on several points. What Bourdillon wanted was for Mukherjee to ask the Mahant to amend his agreement to 1) assure that the "Buddha in the Temple is not to be painted or clothed" and 2) to declare himself agreeable "to be bound by decisions of the board." (CCOC, Vol. 1, #98A, April 5, 1903)

With Mukherjee dispatched on his mission, Bourdillon apprised Curzon of the latest developments, and found the Viceroy dissatisfied. "I regret," wrote Bourdillon, "that your excellency thinks the agreement suggested in my previous letter so little advantageous." It was not everything that might have been hoped but, for instance, the right of Hindus to worship under both trees *had* been found by the commissioners to be legitimized in sacred texts. There were simply no grounds for excluding them from worshipping at the Bodhi-tree. As for the revised proposal itself, there were, in truth, certain gaps.

> I would have added that offerings of ghi shall not be made, but I am informed by the Commissioners and by Mr. Oldham that some sects of Buddhists do make offerings of that material nature.

Indeed, it is difficult to imagine a Tibetan Buddhist ceremony *without* the use of butter. Oldham was therefore quite correct in addressing the anti-butter bias of Bourdillon who, in any case, came to see that there were things to said in favor of the current proposal.

"First of all, we gain the benefit that the Buddha image be neither clothed nor daubed." This was a step towards the restoration of decent British Buddhism. The real sticking point would be the tilak problem. The commissioners had told Bourdillon that the tilak on Gautama's forehead *"is utterly abhorrent to all Buddhists"* (my emphasis) and that "this appears to be the crux of the whole controversy."

True, the Mahant stubbornly insisted that "that placing the Tilaka mark on the forehead of the image is an essential part of the Hindu Worship." (CCOC, Vol. 1, #113A, April 14, 1903) It was devoutly to be hoped that this marking came under the general category of "painting" or "daubing," and that the proposed agreement might put an end to this objectionable practice.

Sadly, however, a week later, the Bengal government received a short and rather somber memorandum, taken by Mukherjee at the Mahant's dictation, and Bourdillon felt obliged to pass it along to the Viceroy. Unfortunately, Curzon's reaction is not available to what are a sort of alternative commission's findings. Many Tibetan and Nepali Buddhists, according to the Mahant, "anoint the forehead of the image with sandlewood paste," and Ceylonese people routinely sprinkle eau-de-cologne on that same part of Gautama's head. The Burmese and the Siamese clothe the image.

One Siamese priest was said to have clothed the image at a cost of 2500 rupees. The tilak marking was, indeed, an essential component of the Hindu form of worship, and could not be dispensed with, but, "*a number of Buddhists do the same thing.*" (CCOC, Vol. 1, #113A, April 14, 1903, my emphasis)

Bourdillon was disheartened by the Mahant's obstinacy. Barring an agreement, "we have only the alternatives of legislation, or of abstention from action." He was further disheartened by a new communication from the Mahant, again through Mukherjee, which now expressed complete opposition to the formation of a board of any kind. "Dharmapala," claimed the Mahant, will assume that the board has been created for his benefit," and the Giris, and their legal advisor, were against the establishment of any board that would allow this.

Bourdillon took courage from the surprising offer, from the Mahant, that a tilak no longer be placed on the image. Also, the Mahant offered an arrangement whereby, from time to time, if "a large body of Buddhists so require it," the image might be disrobed. "It should be mentioned," however, that certain Buddhist princes "have clothed the image in the Mohunt's presence, and have asked him on such occasions not to remove the clothing."

Bourdillon immediately responded that he was well satisfied with the resolution of the tilak problem, but that it was essential to form some sort of advisory board and, finally, that it would be best that the image never be clothed as this "offends a large part of the community." (CCOC, Vol. 1, #119A, April 24, 1903)

Government of India having been duly informed, Denzil Ibbetson, Minister, Home Department, was "decidedly of the opinion that we should accept the agreement," still, however, with the proviso that the ban on the tilak be made "complete," and that it be designated what exact number of Buddhists be required to demand that the image be disrobed. "Large body" was both unreasonable and imprecise. Some small, specific number should be designated. The number five was suggested, but Curzon himself seems to have wished to leave the language less precise, directing that "large body" or "considerable number," be changed to "reasonable number." (CCOC, Vol. 1, #126, May 4, 1903)

The Patience and Powers of Government Exhausted

Bourdillon was seeking yet further concessions from the Mahant, when, on June 17, 1903, a letter was received from Cotton. "The Mahanth and I have been friends ever since I appeared on behalf of his men in the criminal proceedings at Gaya in which Dharmapala cut so dubious a figure." As his friend, and as his legal advisor, Cotton had recommended that the Mahant not accept a board of whatever composition.

Furthermore, although the Mahant himself had been willing to cease the practice of placing the tilak on the image, "the Mahanth's brother [sic] Sannasis have raised the strongest objections and they have certainly satisfied me from texts that the placing of the tilak mark is an essential part of the worship."

Were the Mahant to accept Bengal's suggestion, he would "render himself liable to dismissal from his office." The Lieutenant-Governor passed this on to Curzon with the note that "Your Excellency will notice that the Dharmapala Bogey again appears in Mr. Cotton's letter and I will take care to see that he is finally laid." (CCOC, Vol. 1, #157, June 17, 1903)[3]

However, Dharmapala was not to be "laid" as a source of concern to the Mahant and his men. The government had, after all, practically turned over the Burmese resthouse to the Mahabodhi Society. At the present time, there were two

[3] Dharmapala had become decidedly a problem in the eyes of Government. From the last letter on the subject to Curzon that I have been able to locate, from A.H.L. Frazer, Lieutenant Governor of Bengal: "we have been greatly troubled by that intolerable person, the Dharmapala. He has done all he can do to cause friction and ill-feeling; and the Mahant's obstinacy has been mainly, I believe, due to this cause." (CCIC, Vol. 211, #29, August 2, 1905)

of the Society's representatives occupying the rest house, and they were now collecting pilgrimage fees, pronami, that rightfully belonged to the Mahant. Buddhist pilgrims had been "a source of handsome income to the Mohunt, but for the last two years [he] received nothing from them."

Now, furthermore, the District Board had agreed to accept 15000 rupees from Dharmapala for the construction of a new resthouse, and this certainly indicated that government was willing to help Dharmapala in his quest to deprive the Mahant of even more income. The Mahant would only consider an agreement if this plan were halted, the money returned to Dharmapala, and the construction of a new resthouse entrusted to the Mahant. Also, the Japanese image had to be removed from Bodh Gaya. (CCIC, Vol. 194, #36, Aug. 11, 1903)

A month later, having heard again from Cotton and Mukherjee, Bourdillon telegraphed Curzon to say that "Mahant of Bodh Gaya declines all terms." (CCIC, Vol. 194, #84, Sept. 13, 1903) This triggered talk of executive action. Ibbetson, the Home Department Minister, wrote Curzon to say that, while any resolution "had better issue from the Bengal Government, we should certainly see the draft." There was, of course, some case to be made for a resolution, issuing from either government, as the Mahant had "at one time or another promised everything that we ask." At the same time it had to be admitted that there was very little compelling reason for government to interfere.

In spite of the commission's best efforts to show otherwise, in fact, "the public peace is in no way threatened, and we have had no complaints on the part of the Buddhist worshippers." This is most interesting—*no* complaints on the part of Buddhist worshippers—and it underlines the extent to which British colonial officials were capable of complaining about what they thought that Buddhist worshippers *ought* to complain about. At any rate, Ibbetson was beginning to have serious doubts:

> It may be said that our proposal will arouse little or no opposition. But it may, on the other hand, be made the pretext for an agitation which may become serious...we are already at variance with the European community about the Bain case. [This involved the murder of an Indian servant by his British master.] We shall have to fight the educated natives over the Universities Bill, and if an agitation amongst the bigoted Hindus arise from this Bodh Gaya case, we shall be at variance with every section of the Bengal community.

There was possibly one benefit, thought Ibbetson, in formulating an executive resolution in the cloistered safety of the Governor-General's council: the proposal might, properly managed, never see the light of day. "As you yourself suggested," he wrote Curzon, "it would be easy to let the Secretary of State know privately that we wished him to disallow our proposals."

This gambit might go some way toward soothing the ruffled feathers of the Lieutenant-Governor, for whom the project of "restoring the shrine to the Buddhists" had become something of a personal obsession.

A month later, Ibbetson had not altered his opinion that some terrible reaction might greet any interference at Bodh Gaya. The native press had been fairly silent, but this was "no index whatever to the way in which the great mass of Hindus would regard it." (CCIC, Vol. 193, #88e, Sept. 16, 1903) Bourdillon pressed on with his looping, pointless negotiations, even at one point telegraphing Curzon that "Mohunt is disposed to sign agreement, and is about to submit it with letter." (CCIC, Vol. 193, #97, Sept. 25, 1903) But no agreement was forthcoming.

There was no cause for the Mahant to yield on rights that had been established to be legitimate, and the government had exhausted its powers of leverage. When, therefore, Bourdillon agreed to prepare a resolution, "stating the facts and laying the matter before the Government of India," it was clear that another stage of developments at Bodh Gaya was coming to a close.

In the Bengal resolution, still in the process of being formally promulgated, Bourdillon promised "to place on record distinctly my views on the whole matter." These were, largely, those views with which the Mahant, during the previous months of fruitless negotiation, had become familiar. Furthermore, Bourdillon could not accept Ibbetson's apprehensions about Hindu agitation.

Finally, the Lieutenant-Governor attempted an appeal to Curzon's imperial sense. "Your excellency has no doubt considered the effect which a spontaneous concession to the Buddhists would have at a time when our relations with China and Tibet are so strained." (CCIC, Vol. 193, #120, Oct. 9, 1903)

All negotiations for an agreement with the Mahant came to a complete halt a fortnight later, after Bourdillon received from Cotton what appeared to be a convincing review of how a future civil action might be organized. The crux of Cotton's argument, as it reflected on the government's claims, was that, whatever assistance had been rendered during the Burmese project, no part of the Mahant's proprietorship had been in any way ceded.

> The proposition is quite untenable from a legal point of view that a man by coming forward to repair, and even to rebuild, the property of another, acquires any right of any kind over the same. There are many temples in India, where worship is carried on by men of

> different sects and religious faiths, but nowhere have the Government ever desired to exercise any control or superintendence, either direct, or through any Board or Committee appointed by them.

Cotton's last point might have been argued: nevertheless it reflected well a policy that many administrators, Ibbetson, for instance, felt to be quite sound. But Cotton was not satisfied merely to outline his defense of the Mahant's rights. Now, he asked Bengal to *enforce* those rights: the Mahant's income had been reduced by the "interference of the Sinhalese agent [Sumangala]." Sumangala, wrote Cotton, must be evicted from the Burmese resthouse he had illegally occupied. (CCIC, Vol. 193, #156, Oct. 24, 1903)

It had become plain to Bourdillon that "a very strong argument would be required to deprive the Mahant of his proprietary rights by legislation." It had proved impossible to develop such an argument and negotiations had therefore been entered into. "It is manifest that the negotiations for an amicable agreement for the future control of the worship at Bodh Gaya in accordance with the views of the Lieutenant Governor have completely failed."

The patience and powers of the Government of Bengal had thus been "alike, exhausted." Mr. Bourdillon "has no further remarks to offer on the matter," and the case had now to be "laid before the Government of India for their consideration and orders." (PHDI, Vol. 6805, #15, Jan. 15. 1903) Of course, the matter had lain before the Government of India for months, and before Lord Curzon as well. The Mahant, it seemed, could not, and would not, be budged.

Chapter Eight

A JAPANESE VISITOR

"I ought never to have abandoned my original position that the only safe course is to abstain absolutely from all interference in matters of religion." (CCIC, Vol. 194, #88c, Sept 15, 1903) This was Ibbetson's comment on the failure of the temple negotiations that had been initiated by Curzon. Indeed, bureaucratic pride had been wounded and, now, the matter was allowed to drop back to the level of local administration, which had been, by default, judged competent to deal with it.

Meanwhile, Mr. Cotton, for the victorious Mahant, began to prepare a case against the Mahabodhi Society for illegally occupying the Burmese Resthouse.

Before, however, the Mahant's new case came to trial, a Japanese pilgrim arrived in Bodh Gaya, and he had a new formula for Hindu-Buddhist cooperation. At the core of this chapter, then, will be the visit of Kakuzo Okakura, his friendship with the Hindu reformer Vivekananda, and an approach to the Buddhist-Hindu relationship that contrasted dramatically with Dharmapala's politics of confrontation.

A Japanese Pilgrim on the Mahant's Veranda

The following entry from Dharmapala's diary will serve as a convenient introduction to the "Japanese pilgrim":

> A Japanese by the name of Okakura visited India in 1903 and associated with a number

> of Bengalees to establish a center of Japanese Buddhism at Buddha Gaya. He with the help of the Bengalees belonging to a neo-Hindu school opened negotiations with the Saivite Mahant stating that Japanese Buddhism is similar to Hinduism, and that they have no relationship with the Buddhists of Ceylon, and urged the Mahant to grant the Japanese a plot of land at Buddha Gaya to build a Japanese Temple." (Dharmapala, 1918: 205)

This was Kakuzo Okakura, an art historian and philosopher, and popularizer of Asian ideas. His work *The Book of Tea* (1906)—composed in Boston when he was Curator of Chinese and Japanese Art at the Boston Museum of Fine Art—is selling well even today.

Okakura had, prior to his India trip, "declared sententiously and quite inaccurately," as Reischauer puts it, that "Asia is one." (Reischauer, 1980: 415) This certainly, by the way, is a Japanese variant of the Orientalist project. However, sententious and inaccurate though it might have been, it also facilitated Okakura's way into friendly relationships with Hindus. He was a friend and correspondent of many Indians, including the Tagores, but the most significant of these relationships was with the "neo-Hindu" Vivekananda, the Vedantic activist who had been Dharmapala's more famous rival at the World Parliament of Religions in Chicago in 1893. (Horioka,1963:49) According to Vivekananda:

> Japanese Buddhism is entirely different from what you see in Ceylon. It is the same as Vedanta. It is positive and theistic Buddhism, not the negative atheistic Buddhism of Ceylon. (Vivekananda, 1926: 139)

This idea of Vivekananda's, of a "theistic Buddhism," is very likely an outgrowth of his conversations with Okakura. For the Japanese aesthete, "the great Vedantic revival of Sankaracharya is the assimilation of Buddhism, and its emergence in a new dynamic form." (Okakura, 1903:80) Vivekananda expressed this notion of the kinship of Buddhism and Hinduism more robustly: the two great faiths were from the same tree but the branch of Buddhism "degenerated and Sankara lopped it off!" (Vivekananda, 1926, Vol. 6: 86)

Nevertheless, the umbrella of a common origin was broad enough for both Vivekananda and Okakura to sit comfortably beneath its shade. Some such language of commonality was necessary in order to facilitate a renewed Buddhist presence at Bodh Gaya, and, it will become clear, such a language did in time develop.

Vivekananda's approach, however, served only to enrage Dharmapala. In a letter from William James, who corresponded with both men, Vivekananda was told that Dharmapala was "very wroth" about the remarks on "degenerate Buddhism." Vivekananda responded that "Mr. D- is a very good man and I love him, but it would be entirely wrong for him to go into fits about things Indian." Buddhism in Ceylon was moribund—"the only living people there are the Hindus."

According to Vivekananda, Sinhalese Buddhists, even within their own degenerate tradition, were enfeebled: "The Buddhists there are all much Europeanized—even Mr. D. and his father had European names, which they have since changed." Finally, in a splendid but unintentional pun on the Buddhist doctrine of *anatman* —"no soul"—Vivekananda claimed that the Buddhists in India were "non-entities." (Vivekananda, 1926, Vol. 7: 434-35)

Okakura was free to choose between Dharmapala and

Vivekananda, and he chose the latter. This makes sense from his perspective. Okakura was, while nominally a Buddhist, primarily an aesthete with pretensions to having developed a pan-Asian philosophy. He had, for instance, broken away from the Imperial Art School, which he himself had founded, when he came to the conclusion that it was "too western." (Okakura, 1904: ix)

Actually, Okakura's outlook is very similar to Dharmapala's early Theosophical "pan-Aryan" philosophy, a philosophy that had, for a time, facilitated association with a wide variety of allies, that had emphasized, at least at the "esoteric" level, commonalties rather than conflicts.

Now, however, Okakura's approach could not have been more different than Dharmapala's public Buddhist militancy.[1] (Okakura, 1903, 80) Okakura did not, as Dharmapala did now, regard Hinduism to be a hegemonic plot. Rather, he thought of the two great religious traditions as entirely complementary. In Okakura's language, Buddhism was related to Hinduism in an almost genetic manner, but he avoided the implication that one or the other tradition represented either immaturity or decay:

> The great Vedantic revival of Sankaracharyya is the assimilation of Buddhism, and its emer-

---

[1] It should not be thought that Dharmapala was anti-Japanese, except with regard to his occasional diary outbursts of anger against a number of named ethnic and/or religious populations. Really, the Japanese, though, were seldom featured even in these entries. He visited Japan several times—as had many South Asian "colonial" intellectuals and activists—and, after all, he had begun his Bodh Gaya campaign in the company of the Japanese Shingon Buddhist, Kozen Gunaratna. He wrote several articles, of an anti-imperialist nature, for Japanese publications, and this no doubt brought British official interest. One such article, in 1913, was entitled 'A desperate warning for the Japanese People." (Barnett 2004: 6) Having said this, he never made common cause with Okakura at Bodh Gaya, and found Okakura's overtures to the Giri Mahant unsavory.

> gence in a new dynamic form. And now, in spite of the separation of ages, Japan is drawn closer than ever to the motherland of thought. (Okakura, 1903, 81)

This sort of language is clearly capable of promoting dialogue in a way that confrontational tactics, such as those used hitherto by Dharmapala, cannot. So, in late summer of 1903, Okakura found himself "seated on a spacious veranda of the Mohant's guest house at Bodh Gaya."

> It was 108 degrees and the conversation between the Mahant and Okakura was occasionally interrupted by the latter's moans of "too hot, too hot!" He was discussing with the Mahant the possibility of a grant of land for a resthouse and the proposal that an old Japanese priest be stationed there—"until the first batch of pilgrims could be sent along."
>
> The Mahant professed his delight at being able to "welcome a distinguished representative of Japan," and readily expressed his willingness to cooperate with the scheme. On the other hand, the Mahant was concerned that the District Officer might not approve a proposal for the transfer of land to "an Asiatic alien." (Tagore, 1984: 236)

Government could not legally prevent the transfer of land, and, as I have indicated, there is no evidence that they had attempted to do so in the past. Now, however, in the wake of acrimonious legal proceedings, and in reaction to the commission's report, Bengal began to focus on two concerns: 1) that foreign influence in the area might exacerbate existing tensions and 2) that within the "Buddhist Community" itself, dangerous rivalries obtained.

In line with this, Bengal had recourse to the one legal instrument available: denial of a building permit for the resthouse. When, therefore, the Commissioner of Patna approached Bengal about the wisdom of building such a structure, the response was that "Government is not satisfied that there is any necessity for another resthouse at [Bodh] Gaya, and moreover is of the opinion that the multiplication of interest there is undesirable." (PRO. of the JD, Bengal IOL Vol. 6569, B, Dec. 1903)

"Things had much better be left as they are at Bodh Gaya"

Returning now to the unsettled question of the Burmese resthouse, the Mahant, in 1906, petitioned, in the Court of the Subordinate Judge of Gaya, Saroda Prasad Basu, that Sumangala and the other Sinhalese monks be ejected therefrom, that the Japanese image be removed, and that the Mahant be declared "sole owner" of the structure. (MBJ, Vol. 14, #9, Sept. 1906)

The case was not acted upon until 1909, but, when it did come up, the Subordinate Judge made very short work of it indeed. There was, he found, "no evidence that the house had been used by Buddhist monks and laymen before 1890." This is unsurprising: as I have shown, the Burmese for whom the structure was originally intended apparently had preferred to take advantage of the hospitality offered by the Mahant, and had lodged at the Math.

No law of limitation therefore applied, as the Mahant "had been in possession down to 1896." There was no evidence, either, that the resthouse had been built directly with Burmese funds; rather, it had been built, by the Mahant, in consideration of gifts received from King Mindon, but with the understanding that the transaction did not entail either a sale or permanent lease of property. Judgment was given, on January 19, 1909, "for the plaintiff with costs on all issues." (MBJ, Vol. 17, #1, Jan. 1909.)

A month prior to the close of hearings, the Lieutenant-Governor, as was by now customary, made a tour of the troubled area. At that time, the Mahabodhi Society wished, again in line with custom, to present Sir Edward Baker a petition. Bengal declined to receive it, on the very technical and convenient grounds that such petitions had to be submitted, in writing, fifteen days prior to being presented.

Dharmapala, planning to approach the Lieutenant-Governor personally, was checked in his intentions by an order from the Collector, who wrote him to say that "whereas it has been made to appear to me that if you approach or enter the Temple at Bodh Gaya there is likely to be a breach of the peace, you are hereby required to abstain from entering the temple up to the hour ten (10) a.m. today," (MBJ, Vol. 18, # 1, Jan. 1910)

These actions marked Bengal's firm resolve not to become again entangled in the matter at any but the most local level. At that level, the decision of the Subordinate Judge of Gaya prevailed and, when Dharmapala attempted an appeal in the Calcutta High Court, it was dismissed without discussion. (MBJ, Vol. 18, #4, April 1910)

Over the course of the next several years, Government took a number of steps to disengage itself from even a potential involvement in adjudicating or administering temple affairs. One such step was to define with some precision the status of the temple as an archaeological monument.

On September 11, 1914, J.F. Blakiston, an Archeological officer, sent to the provincial government a list of properties considered by the Archeological Survey of India to be protected under the Ancient Monuments Act of 1904. Included was "Bodh Gaya and everything within the compound, Gaya." Bodh Gaya was now, after the second partition of Bengal in 1911, under the newly created Government of Bihar and Orissa, and the Lieutenant-Governor of that province, H.G. Hallett, forwarded the Archaeological list to his Commissioner at Patna. (EDBO, Vol. 9792, A, Sept. 1915)

In the context of the previous forty years' experience at the site, the inclusion of Bodh Gaya in Mr. Blakiston's list made little sense. Since the Burmese restoration project, three Governor-Generals of India, and three Lieutenant- Governors of Bengal had considered proposed changes in the management of the Mahabodhi Temple. In each case, it had been determined that Government had no grounds to take executive action, and in each case the wisdom of this determination had been enhanced by the fear of negative Hindu reaction. At both provincial and central levels, and in spite of occasionally very strong sentiments for change, government had demonstrated an inability to establish a new configuration of rights.

Naturally, then, Bihar and Orissa had to respond to the aspirations of the Archaeological Survey. Oldham, now Commissioner of Patna, accepted all of the buildings as falling under the act "except the Mahabodhi Temple at Bodh Gaya and the images, sculptures, carvings, inscriptions, etc., within the compound of that temple."

This was the final and definitive disavowal, by a British Indian executive, of any power to affect a new arrangement at Bodh Gaya, and it was briefly elaborated in terms by now familiar:

> The District Magistrate of Gaya very properly points out that to declare the Mahabodhi Temple and its surroundings to be a protected monument under the act might give rise to serious complications. Things had much better be left as they are at Bodh Gaya at present. (EDBO, Vol. 9729, A. Sept 1915)

And so, government did indeed leave things as they were,

content to take on only the responsibility for ensuring that local peace was not disturbed. The larger questions of management and proprietorship were no longer asked by government but, over the next thirty became subjects of discussion within emerging Indian legislative bodies and political organizations.

Government having finally achieved, after much fruitless experimentation, its preferred posture of religious neutrality, Dharmapala and his supporters were called upon to work within a new arena, that of negotiations with Indian politicians, and to develop a new language, not confrontational, but ameliorative.

Chapter Nine

OUR HINDU BROTHERS

Gandhi, wrote Dharmapala, "has no knowledge of Buddhism and the only book he had read on the subject was *Light of Asia.* (ADC, May 7, 1925) This comment is a telling measure of the distance Dharmapala had traveled since, as a young man, he had read Sir Edwin Arnold's *Light of Asia* and felt it to be a "light from heaven." So, Gandhi's grasp of Buddhism was less than satisfactory—Dharmapala elsewhere dismissed Gandhi as "a God-believer," and added that "God is a nightmare" (ADC, June 11, 1924; May 7, 1925). However, this judgment could not obscure the necessity that Dharmapala and his successors would have to work closely, now that Government had withdrawn, with Indian politicians.

From the year 1911 until after independence, the claims of foreign and Indian Buddhists for control of the Mahabodhi Temple were taken up, often sympathetically, by the Indian National Congress, the All-India Hindu Mahasabha, and in legislative assemblies. However, the discussion was usually embedded in a larger context of Indian nationalism, and this required that any proposed resolution satisfy a variety of overlapping interests.

A review of the Indian legislative debates and maneuvers, as well as an examination of certain informal processes that guided the public discussion, will help to illuminate the Indian cultural climate that has, at various times either facilitated or frustrated Buddhist goals.

The Bodh Gaya question had first come before an Indian nationalist representative body at a Gaya session of the Bihar Provincial Conference of the Indian National Congress. The chairman at that conference was none other than Nanda Kishore Lal, the Mahabodhi Society's chief legal advisor. Lal, as chairman of the reception committee for the conference, had this to say about the Gaya and its environs. The tone of his remarks is in marked contrast to the legal language of opposition that had been employed during the temple case.

> Gaya...has been one of the principal centres of the Hindu Religion from time before the Royal Recluse Prince Sakya Sinha...became Buddha and to this day, to the followers of that Lord of Compassion who number not less than one third of the human race, Gaya and its neighborhood are as sacred as Mecca is to the Mussalman and Jerusalem to the Christian. Nor does the Hindu of the day look upon it with any less reverence than the Buddhists. (MBJ, Vol.19, #12, 1911)

This invocation of the Hindu-Buddhist veneration of a common sacred ground, while it produced no specific proposals for joint administration of the temple, nevertheless exemplifies a discourse of mutuality that became a staple in debates on the issue.

The Congress, The Mahasabha, Gandhi, and The Question of the Cow

While the Mahabodhi Society, and Dharmapala, continued to editorialize for complete Buddhist control, the language of mutual interest and cooperation began to shape Buddhist strategy for proposed legislative solutions. Dharmapala himself began to see the wisdom of seeking out support from

Hindus and nationalists, and even invited Gandhi to attend the opening of a new Buddhist Vihara in Calcutta. When this proved impossible, Dharmapala lamented that "I have not entered into his heart." (ADC, Oct. 18, Nov. 12, 1920) In fact, despite Dharmapala's often vitriolic treatment of the Hindu tradition, Gandhi's personal magnetism could not always be resisted: "Wonderful is the spiritual power of Mahatma Gandhi." (ADC, Dec. 28 1920)

Gandhi did finally respond to repeated requests by the Mahabodhi Society to take up its cause, but he seemed content to register sympathy and to blame the impasse on the iniquities of British India. "Much as I should like to help you, it is not possible for me to do anything directly at the present moment. The question you raise can be solved in a moment when India comes into her own." (MBJ, Vol.30, #7, July 1922) In truth, Gandhi was prescient about the solution, although it came, not quite a moment after, but only two years after India "came into her own." The eventual legislation, however, was shaped by a long process of public discussion and negotiation.

At the Cocanda Conference of the Indian National Congress, Burmese delegates proposed that a committee be formed to investigate the situation at Bodh Gaya. The resolution was carried and the committee assigned to Rajendra Prasad, a Bihari lawyer and academic from Saran District, abutting Gaya District. Prasad was one of Gandhi's favored lieutenants, and the future first President of India. However, the Mahabodhi Temple issue being of very marginal concern to the Congress in the context of the total nationalist struggle, it was not given great priority, and the committee had not met once before the opening of the following year's joint session of the All-India Congress and the All-India Hindu Mahasabha.

Dharmapala was convinced that the key to success lay in winning the sympathy of Gandhi. Gandhi at this point had been in prison since March of 1922 and, just prior to his release, and prior to the conference at Belgaum, Dharmapala had written that "when Mahatma is released the Bud [sic] Gaya Temple will be given over to the Buddhists." (ADC, Jan.14,1924) With this hope in mind, a special Buddhist delegation, largely underwritten by the Mahabodhi Society, was dispatched to the conference. The delegation consisted of four members, two from Ceylon, and one each from Burma and Nepal.

The Ceylon delegates urged the Congress to directly support the Buddhist claims, but the Indians were concerned, as had been the Viceroy and Lieutenant-Governor in previous years, that vesting control of the temple in the hands of foreign Buddhists might give rise to certain "international complications." Like the Government of Bengal in 1905, Lajpat Rai was concerned about the "multiplication of interests"—" foreign" interests—at Bodh Gaya.

Having for all practical purposes abandoned the demand for exclusive control of the temple, the Buddhist delegation at Belgaum managed to garner much conservative Hindu support by skillfully manipulating negotiations on two emotional issues: cow-killing and beef-eating. Both things, of course, are generally anathema to Hindus. Swami Vishwananda, president of the Mahavir Dal, one of the many constituent groups of the very loosely constituted Hindu Mahasabha, had spoken to the Buddhist delegates of his concern that Buddhists were not sufficiently committed to the veneration of the cow.

Now, of the twin evils of boviphagy and bovicide, only the latter, as a variety of the taking of life, would be formally anathema to most Buddhists. I use the term "formally" as it is manifest that most Buddhist traditions have come to terms with the eating of flesh and, either reluctantly and by their own hand kill beasts for their meat, or entrust this task to others, who may be Muslims, Christians or other "defiled" categories of people. The point being that, for Buddhists, the killing and eating of cattle is neither more nor less problematic than the killing and eating of any other class of animal.

Dharmapala, on this issue, was somewhat idiosyncratic. At several points in his life he took up the anti-kine killing standard. In his diary, for instance, is a note, from January 5, 1897, recording that he had sent a letter to Queen Victoria to ask that, "on account of her affection for her Indian subjects, she will abstain henceforth from taking the flesh of cattle, etc." (ADC, Jan. 5, 1897)[1] The "etc" is interesting here, and it recalls his feeling, developed during a period of experimentation in the United States, that "beef and pork" were injurious. In both statements there is no clear status assigned to the cow.

Was Dharmapala toying with the idea of vegetarianism? It has often been a Buddhist method of resolving what may appear to be a moral dilemma: if the taking of life is forbidden, should not the enjoyment of the products of death likewise be forbidden? At any rate, for Buddhists, the flesh of beasts is in some way all of a kind, and they had no special category for the cow.

How, then, could the Buddhists make bovicide an issue of joint concern with the Hindus whose support they required? The two Sinhalese delegates, and one Burmese, argued quite implausibly, but with great effect, that beef- eating had been introduced into their countries only in recent times, and by imperialist Europeans. D.A. Dharmacharyya,

[1] Dharmapala could not, himself, reach a final resolution for the problem of meat-eating, but on a number of occasions was disgusted by the behavior of others. "The Burmese priests are fond of meat-eating; they find it difficult to stay here hearing that they would not get meat!! Priests of Buddha, the embodiments of gentleness, have become carnivorous!!! Shame on them." (ADC, Feb. 13, 1896) Nevertheless, Dharmapala himself ate meat, and fish, and, particularly when ill, felt that meat was therapeutic.

the Nepali Buddhist delegate, had assured Vishwananda that meat-eating was "strictly prohibited to the Buddhists of the pure Mahayana Buddhism."

This prohibition, actually a feature of very few Buddhist sects, including the Nepali's own heavily Brahminized Newari Group, was backed up, in Nepal, by legal force. In fact, said Dharmacharyya, any one guilty of either cow-killing or beef-eating in Nepal could be put to death. The truth, of course, is that the force of these prohibitions and laws issued from Nepal's *Hindu* monarchs, and had nothing whatsoever to do with Mahayana Buddhism. Nevertheless, Dharmacharyya's grim assurances, coupled incongruously with an evocation of Gautama Buddha as a gentle crusader against blood-sacrifice of all varieties, gained the Buddhists a new measure of respect from the Sanatan, "orthodox," Hindu "community."

Having agreed to celebrate the notion that the murder of a cow properly requires the sacrifice of a human being, the Buddhist delegates and Viswananda drew up a joint memorandum for distribution at the conference. This appeal, distributed widely at Belgaum and to groups associated with the Hindu Mahasabha, urged the abolition of kine-abuse, not only in India, but in all Buddhist countries as well. Beef-eating was characterized as a practice "introduced by the people of the west," and due only to "Christian influences on our people." The reaction of Muslim congressmen to this news has not been preserved.

In crafting their appeal, the Buddhists relied on rhetoric that encompassed the widest possible mutual interests, even, as I have suggested, inventing a few ornaments for the Buddhist faith. The Vaishnava and the Indian character of the Buddha was now emphasized: "Our Hindu brothers worship the lord Buddha as the 9th avatar, and historically Gautama Buddha is the Greatest Figure in the Motherland." They asked, "will not our Hindu Brothers join hands with us and give us our shrine, at which all are free to worship. the one condition being that Ahimsa shall rule at the Holy site of Him who was the Lord of Compassion?"

This invocation of Vaishnava tradition and of a joint Hindu-Buddhist ethic of ahimsa, or "non-harming," was designed by the Buddhists to ease the way for their strongest claim in the document:

> We agree that a controlling board of equal numbers of Hindus and Buddhists be appointed, provided that the shrine itself be presided over by Buddhist Bhikkus alone." (MBJ, Vol.33, #3, Feb. 1925)

In fact, the consensus reached at the conference was in support of guaranteed access for the Buddhists under a system of joint control, and not in favor of exclusive Buddhist control of the shrine. The sole outcome of the Buddhists' lobbying efforts was that Dr. Prasad's not-yet-convened committee, mandated at Concanda, was now expanded to become a joint committee of the Indian National Congress and the Hindu Mahasabha.

Dharmapala Disengages: "There is Hope" for Bodh Gaya

In the following year, the Mahasabha held several public meetings on the issue in Calcutta and other cities. Dharmapala, newly alarmed by the possibility that Hindus would consolidate their hold on the temple, editorialized vigorously against the rhetoric that he saw as most damaging to the Buddhist cause.

> The attempt is made foolishly by interested people to show that Buddha is the ninth avatar of Vishnu. But they do not care to analyze whether the Buddha of Vishnu avatar is the Buddha Gautama of the Buddhists. The

> Buddha as depicted in the Vishnu Purana has no characteristic feature to show that he is the Buddha Gautama. (MBJ, Vol.33, #4, April,1925)

Even so, in the face of Hindu sensitivities, Dharmapala felt increasingly obliged to ameliorate his criticism of the Hindus, and to emphasize certain links between the two faiths.

> To the Buddhists the Lord Buddha is the Supreme One. The Hindus have many devatas to receive their worship. The Buddhists do not worship Vishnu; neither do they worship Siva. But Ceylon Buddhists hold Vishnu as the patron God of Ceylon. (MBJ, Vol.33, #4, April,1925)

Notice, by the way, that here Dharmapala was perfectly happy to admit that Sinhalese Buddhists, in spite of formally recognizing no supreme divine entity or pantheon, were indeed able to find some use for the gods. It is just another irony that Dharmapala, who in so many ways was not at an "orthodox" Theravadin, had for so many years, in public, made "god' and "soul" and so-forth such crucial points of disagreement. However that may be, his bid for Buddhist-Hindu solidarity was designed to appeal to the Hindus who would attend, that month, a Mahasabha Conference in Calcutta, over which Lala Lajpat Rai was to preside.

Lajpat Rai was characterized in the Mahabodhi Journal as "a man of truth and Courage and we trust that he would act heroically in doing that which was right and just." (MBJ, Vol.33, #4, April, 1925) Actually, at the meeting, Dharmapala could not be quite sure just how the President of the Mahasabha was coming across: "Lala Lajpat Rai spoke in Hindi. Didn't understand anything. A man moved for a committee to manage temple with 6 Hindus and myself." (ADC, April 6, 1925)

This of course meant that an overpowering Hindu majority would control the board but, given the fierce opposition that the Giris at Bodh Gaya had developed to the notion of having Dharmapala involved in any management structure, it is not surprising to read that "the Mahant's men protest."

In spite of the opposition, a version of the resolution was passed. Dharmapala felt that it represented something of a victory. "There is hope." Nevertheless, Dharmapala was unhappy with the support for such an overwhelming Hindu representation on the board.

At the close of the Mahasabha conference, Dharmapala feared that the Mahant and his supporters might yet manage to scuttle any settlement at all. Against this eventuality, Dharmapala summoned divine aid: "I asked Vajrapani [a Bodhisattva] to use his vajra [lightening bolt] to frighten the Mahant's people." (ADC, April 5, 6, 1925)

Prasad presented substantially the same proposal at the next INC Conference, but, in the less than urgent tone that characterized most of his committee's directives, recommended that any action be postponed "until a more opportune time." (Prasad, 1957:233) The substance of the proposal was that the temple be entrusted to a "Joint Committee" of Buddhists and Hindus, two members of which should be the Mahant and a Hindu Minister. "The idea was that we should not have Buddhists from outside the British Empire, e.g. from Japan or China or Tibet." (MSBG)

Dharmapala, that May, achieved something of a public relations victory when Gandhi accepted, finally, an invitation to visit the Mahabodhi Society Vihara in Calcutta.[2] However,

---

[2] This temple had been opened in 1921, and at its opening, Dharmapala made the following comments, in thanks to the Government of India for a gift of relics that had been unearthed by the Archaeological Survey. Notice that here he is in a Bud

Gandhi's attitude was, again, non-committal and, furthermore, as I noted earlier, his grasp of Buddhism was unsatisfactory to Dharmapala. In one construction of his life's work, of course, Dharmapala had arrived at Bodh Gaya precisely in response to Edwin Arnold's Buddhistic best-seller but now, however, a familiarity with *The Light of Asia* seemed rather a thin foundation for an understanding of Buddhism.

Fundamentally, Gandhi's problem was that he was a theist: "He is a God-believer," wrote Dharmapala, lapsing away from the brief relaxation on such issues he had shown just a little prior—his remark about the Sinhalese esteem for Vishnu as a "patron god." (ADC: May 7, 1925)

Dharmapala, at this point quite ill with heart disease—the result of rheumatism —sciatica, and a host of other lesser ailments, left India for Europe. At the expense of one of his American patrons he was, for a time, treated at a Swiss sanatorium, after which, until early in 1928, he devoted his energies to the affairs of the London Mahabodhi Society.

Shortly after his return to India, he was ordained a Bhikkhu, at Sarnath, and took the name Devamitta Dhammapala. He worked with great dedication, until his death, primarily on improving the society's properties in Sarnath, and was largely uninvolved in the final phases of the actual negotiations over the temple. I have provided more detail about Dharmapala's

---

dhist *and* an imperial mood:

> Even the most sacred places connected with His life and teachings had been forgotten, and the significance of the ruined sites was not realized until the researches of that great band of Oriental Scholars headed by Prinsep had shown the universal prevalence of the religion of Compassion throughout the length and breadth of this great empire. (AD 1921: 24)

In the same address, Edwin Arnold was also credited with having done much to foster understanding of Buddhism, as was Sir John Marshall (by then director of the Archaeological Survey). Also thanked was the Bengali artist Manmohan Ganguly, author of "Orissa and Her Remains" and designer of the Calcutta temple, which was meant to be in the "style of Ajantan architecture." (BAC 1921:23-36) This latter is in, shall we say, the Pan-Indian and Historico-cultural Buddhist mode.

life, and some analysis of his career, in the last chapter of this work.

"Hindus and Buddhists are Culturally One"

Returning to the subject of the temple itself, the Congress as a whole did not again address the issue until 1939. This, however, was simply a proposal to reconsider the question and even this was not taken up, as, after 1939, the Congress was completely involved with non-cooperation tactics that precluded any legislative action. On the other hand, Burmese members of the Legislative Assembly, acting on their own initiative, were able to lobby for control of the temple by presenting their own schemes for a cooperative management board.

In 1928, MLA U. Tok Kyi moved, unsuccessfully, for the introduction of a bill that would provide for a board "to be elected by Buddhists of India, Burma and Ceylon," with the Mahant as an ex-officio member. The bill stipulated that the rights of Hindus to worship at the shrine, except by blood-sacrifice, would be protected. The Burmese initiative was, in some ways, an extension of the tactics used at the Belgaum initiative. There was an attempt made to woo Hindu opinion through the advocacy of ahimsa[3] and through a guarantee of Hindu rights of worship at the temple.

However, there was continued opposition from some seg-

---

[3] I have no evidence that blood sacrifice was ever performed by anyone at the Mahabodhi temple. On the other hand, of course, blood sacrifice is an integral part of innumerable folk Hindu traditions in India, and this raises a conflict with regard to the appeal to ahimsa. The Mahabodhi Society at one point attempted to "solve" the problem by drawing a sharp distinction between Shaivite and Vaisnavite religions. "The God Siva is a tamoguna deity. The Vaisnavas abstain from blood sacrifices. Siva as Rudra is the god of destruction and darkness, as Vishnu is the God of light. There is sympathy between Vaisnavas and Buddhists." (MBJ, Vol. 30, #1, Jan., 1922) This sort of language was a minor theme in the Mahabodhi society campaign of emphasizing commonalities between Buddhists and Hindus, no doubt because many Hindus would not have made such sharp distinctions.

ments of the Mahasabha. Just prior to the Cawnpore Hindu Mahasabha Conference of 1935, for instance, there was a gathering, at the Trikeneshwar Temple, of Bengalis associated with the local Hindu Sabhas of Calcutta and environs. At this meeting a resolution was passed urging the Mahasabha to reject any change in the proprietary or religious status of the Mahabodhi Temple.

The temple was characterized as one "with which the religious faith and practices of the whole Hindu world have been bound up for ages." Buddha, "from time immemorial," had been worshipped as the ninth avatar, and Buddhism regarded "as a branch of the *Aryan Religion of India.*" (my emphasis) Hindus, they claimed, offered oblations at the Mahabodhi Temple in the same spirit as they did at the Vishnupada Temple at Gaya. "The exclusive claim of the Buddhists is untenable." (HMBG)

In spite of this attitude on the part of many Hindus, Buddhists succeeded to a very high degree in cultivating Hindu sensibilities and, remarkably, two weeks after the Trikeneshwar meeting, a Burmese Theravadin Bhikku, U Ottama, was elected Chairman of the Hindu Mahasabha at Cawnpore. The Cawnpore conference also featured a large Buddhist delegation, composed of Burmese, Japanese and Indian MBS members. In the introduction to the report on the Cawnpore session, the Buddhist presence was noted.

> The sixteenth annual session of the All-India Hindu Mahasabha was held at Cawnpore on the 20th April 1935 under the presidency of Rev. Ottama Bhikku. Welcome song by women volunteers from Baroda in picturesque uniforms and the chanting of Buddhist prayers formed the preliminary ceremony. The presence of a fairly large number of

> Burmese and Japanese Monks, in yellow robes, added a distinct oriental touch to the meeting. (HSIAR, Vol. I, 1935: 42)

I must conclude, by the way, that the Hindu member who was so struck by the "oriental" flavor of the proceedings—added by the Burmese and Japanese—was clearly using an orientalism that was neither Okakura's nor Edward Said's. At any rate, on the third day, a resolution on the temple question (not recorded) was moved, with regard to a bill that had been proposed, again by Burmese members, in the Indian Legislative Assembly. This gave offense to Sanatan Hindus who made angry demonstrations and rushed to the dais in order to prevent the passage of the resolution.

> Great confusion reigned for nearly a quarter of an hour. The President then left the meeting but was brought back in order to adjourn the session. The session was adjourned til afternoon.
>
> The Bodh-Gaya temple question which caused so much confusion in the morning session was settled at last and the following resolution agreed by the Subjects Committee and the opposition was put from the chair in evening session and passed.
>
> "The Hindu Mahasabha is of opinion that efforts should be made to arrive at an amicable settlement of the question which was arisen (sic) the management of the Bodh-Gaya temple between Sanatanists and Buddhist Hindus and is therefore of opinion that the proposed bill for the management of the

> above temple be not proceeded with by its authors in the Assembly."

A second committee was formed, comprised of five members, three from the Hindu Sabha and two Buddhists, the Indian Buddhist Ananda Kaushalyana, and the new General Secretary of the Mahabodhi Society Devapriya Valinsinha, Dharmapala's ne-phew. (HSIAR, Vol. I, 1935: 335) The members were directed to work in cooperation with Prasad's long-standing Indian National Congress committee.

The Mahabodhi Society, under Valinsinha's leadership, now heavily relied on the language of compromise and brotherhood, and attempted to put as favorable a face as possible on the negotiations.

> The tolerant and friendly manner in which a Buddhist was allowed to occupy the chair of the most influential, and, at the same time, somewhat orthodox organization of the Hindus, marks a further stage in the liberalization of Hindu ideas. The session also demonstrated that *Buddhists and Hindus are culturally one* and that there should be complete harmony between them, if the true spirit of Arya Dharma is understood. (MBJ,Vol.43, #5, May, 1935) (my emphasis)

In the same spirit, in June, Valinsinha asked MLA U Thein Maung to not move the bill in the Assembly. (HMBG)

The Mahasabha committee quickly began to receive complaints from both Buddhists and Hindus. A Hindu newspaper in Delhi, the Swarajiya Naiwara, editorialized "we should not give any rights to the Buddhists in the Gaya temple so long as the Buddhists did not concede the rights of Hindus to the Kataragama temple." (Prasad, 1957:234) (Kataragama is a pilgrimage center in Ceylon, important to Buddhist and Hindus, and even to some Muslims, that has been the subject of jurisdictional disputes.)

For their part, the Burmese Buddhist delegates, who had promoted the temple management bill in the Assembly, felt left out of the proceedings. On July 3, 1935, two Burmese Barristers, U Thein Maung and U Ba Thoung, wrote to ask that they be allowed to give evidence before the committee. "As it is, the Burmese Buddhists are quite in the dark as to the intentions of your Committee and the procedures they propose to follow" (HMBG)

The joint committee was charged with traveling to Bodh Gaya in order to negotiate with the Mahant. It was specified before hand that they should not concern themselves "with the existing legal rights of the Mahant over the temple," but should attempt only to arrange "an amicable agreement." It was further stipulated that the findings of the committee should be subject only to the approval of, for the "sanatanists," the Sankaracharyya (sic) of Govardhan Math, and for "the Bodhists, the Sangraj of Bikshu Sangh." Notice here the assumption, shared by British colonial officials, that "orthodox" Hindus and Buddhists were subject to a unitary and unbroken authority represented by clearly defined ecclesiastical leaders.

There is no adequate record of the Mahant's response to the proposal, which was substantially the same as the recommendation produced by Prasad, in consultation with the Sabha, in 1925.[4] The new proposal called for a manage-

[4] In a letter dated July 31, 1937, from Prasad to Roy and deSilva, Prasad claims to have approached the Mahant with an offer to "buy him out." On what authority the offer was made, and from what source the transaction was to be financed, is not specified. Prasad, at any rate, reported that the Mahant was holding the temple "for the honor it brought him" and not for the money it provided. (HMBG)

ment board to include four Buddhist and four Hindu members, including the Mahant of Bodh Gaya, and an additional Hindu member, a provincial minister, to be appointed by the "sanatan members." (HMBG)

However, the recommendation was not given the form of a specific legislative proposal. The Mahabodhi Society regarded this as a delaying tactic, and responded by urging the Burmese MLA, Thein Maung, to carry forward with his own bill in the Assembly. This was, in fact, the same bill that had been introduced by the Burmese in 1928, and it called for a much more expanded Buddhist presence on the management board than anything that had been entertained by the INC-Hindu Sabha committee.

Thein Maung had his own reason for wishing to move quickly on the bill: the Union of Burma was to be split off from the Indian Dominion by the terms of the Government of India Bill of 1935, and the influence of the Burmese members of the Assembly was therefore about to become a non- phenomenon. In the event, the bill was accepted for consideration but never debated. Then too, several requests by MLAs to Government of India met with the assurance that government had no precise information, had no interest in the matter, and considered it to be a provincial issue. This marks the last occasion on which the Mahabodhi Temple situation was considered in an all-India legislative body.

After this time Buddhists were unable to have any significant formal impact on the debate from within an Indian Legislative body, but were forced to rely on informal discussions, negotiations, and petitions. Once again, all-India legislative and administrative institutions, in this case, the Indian Legislative Assembly and the Government of India, were happy to let the matter drop to a provincial level. This being the case, whatever Indian Buddhist representation as might eventually been heard in assembly, from, say, Chittagong, was disallowed. Nevertheless, very shortly, a new sort of Indian Buddhist voice *was* heard, and it often seemed more "Indian" than "Buddhist."

"Buddha Gaya Belongs to India"

By late June of 1927, however, it was not yet apparent that the issue had run its course at the all-India institutional level, and Rajendra Prasad continued, sporadically, to collect testimony. Much of the opinion gathered by Prasad's committee indicates that, not only were there continuing Hindu objections to any plan that would cede control of the temple to Buddhists, but that, amongst Buddhists themselves, there were serious divisions. In this latter regard, the most intriguing documents are several letters, received by Prasad in the period from June to December, 1937, from two Buddhists. These were Anagarika Suhrit Ranjan Roy, a Bengali, and Vincent deSilva, a Sinhalese, joint secretaries of an ad-hoc organization, "The Buddha Gaya Defense League."

Roy and deSilva quoted, at length, the writings of Edwin Arnold, in order to show that the dispute was not of recent origin. They claimed to have set in train a movement "to mount a Satyagraha" for Buddhist control of the temple. The satyagraha was, of course, one of Gandhi's trademarks, the "weapon of truth," a mass display of peaceful civil disobedience. It was necessary to resort to these measures, according to the League, because no help had been forthcoming from either Government of India, the Indian National Congress, or the Hindu Mahasabha. Buddhists from Burma and Chittagong had expressed a strong interest in the proposed demonstration, which was to take the form of a long march, from Calcutta to the Mahabodhi Temple. "Many Indians" as well had offered their support. The issue was of all-India importance as Bodh Gaya was "the emblem of the greatest civilization in India, nay, of the whole East."

Prasad responded to these claims by apologizing for the inaction of the Congress, which were, he claimed, a result of the realization that "it was necessary to carry the Hindu Mahasabha." Prasad had placed his report before the All-India Congress at Delhi, on March 6, 1937, and he intended to see that the committee recommendations were taken up in the appropriate manner. "I cannot approve the programme of satyagraha which you are contemplating," concluded Prasad, but, as the Congress had decided to take office under "the new constitution," he would see that it was referred to the appropriate ministers. (HMBG)

Months later, from Colombo, Prasad received another letter signed *only* by the Bengali Roy, who, while still championing the cause of a *Buddhist* Mahabodhi Temple, now made it plain that he very much resented the attitudes of the Sinhalese: "The Indian Buddhists who come here on pilgrimage are not given even as much attention what common courtesy demands (sic)." Moreover, "you will be astonished to hear that caste system is practiced even among the Bhikshus, what we are trying to eliminate from India (sic.)" Other foreign Buddhists were no better: "the tendency of Burma is still worse."

> Buddha Gaya belongs to India though it is a Buddhist temple. It is now in the hands of a Saivite Mahant. We the Indian Buddhists want some concessions to do our "pujas" in our own way. But will it be discreet to pass the temple to the foreigners - Ceylonese, Burmese, Chinese or Japanese - cleanly (sic) forgetting the Indians? Buddhya Gaya affair is between Indian and Indian. [sic]

Roy styled himself a "Theravadi" but claimed that the Sinhalese "are fanatic Theravadis [sic]." The temple, he wrote, should be made over to India "Mahayani and Theravadi

Buddhists," and he maintained that he had accepted the secretaryship of the Buddha Gaya Defense League only on the basis that the organization would agree that the temple "remain in the hands of Indians."

Roy also abandoned the proposed satyagraha, and was of the opinion that such a course would only become necessary if the temple were made over to foreigners, in which case "a grave injustice will be done to the Indian Buddhists." A future satyagraha, he claimed, might be led by Buddhists from Chittagong, Nepal, Sikkim, Bhutan and Kashmir.[5]

Let me pause here to point out that none of these Buddhists, save the Chittagonians, would have been in any very accurate sense "Indians." They would have been, variously, Buddhist citizens of either a Hindu or a Buddhist Kingdom, or of a Hindu Princely state. In short, they stood outside the political arena of British India and were not entitled to membership in any of the nascent Indian representative bodies.

This in itself goes a long way towards explaining why the Indian Buddhist community was unable to mount a vigorous campaign for temple control from a position within the legislative context. As small and ill-defined a population as it was, however, it *was* able to affect the thinking of others. For instance, notwithstanding the dearth of information on Roy, his shadowy organization, and his Sinhalese ally, deSilva, consider Prasad's response on the "Indian" question.

It had been expected since 1925, wrote Prasad, that any future settlement, while excluding "foreigners," would include all Buddhist from within the British empire, that is to say from India, Burma and Ceylon.

---

[5] Also, most, who would be Newaris or Tibetans, would not be, as Roy styled himself, "Theravadi," but Mahayana Buddhists. This attests to Roy's own Chittagonian Buddhist history; while that area had been, since the early 19th century "purified" by Burmese Theravada reformers, it is clear that most of the affected groups retained significant Mahayana elements. (Chaudhuri, 1982, 24-45 & passim)

> It appears from your letter that you would like the Committee to have only Indian Buddhists. Personally, I do not mind, but I fear we may not get a committee which would be acceptable to the community as a whole unless we included Buddhists from Ceylon and Burma.

Prasad was here confronting, as had Curzon's commissioners before him, the problem of the "community as a whole," and he was, as a result, perplexed. "I am aware that there are different schools among Buddhists, but I did not know that there was such racial cleavage."

Prasad ended with an expression of regret that the problem had not been settled by Dharmapala at the turn of the century. It might have been resolved, he wrote, "if the situation had not become complicated by international considerations on account of the arrival of the Japanese priest. I hope no such complication will arise this time." But my point right now is this: for an Indian politician, at the time, to have only Indian Buddhists? "I don't mind." Why would he?

Reactions of "the Buddhist Public"

The Mahabodhi Society, of course, had always regarded itself as the prime mover in the campaign to recover the temple, and the society's representatives were keen to maintain this status. In response to the pressure being placed on Prasad for an "Indian" solution, then, a representative of the Colombo branch of the Society wrote him to say that they were satisfied that the claims of the Buddhists had been "fairly dealt with by both the Congress and the Mahasabha.

"I have come," wrote Laksman Seneviratne, "as the advance guard of a delegation with a mandate from the Ceylon Buddhists to see you." The rest of the delegation, which was scheduled to arrive shortly, would be joined in Calcutta by

Kalidas Nag (historian and Bengali politician and intellectual), who would present a letter of support from Rabindranath Tagore.

Anagarika Roy was outraged by the Mahabodhi Society delegation, and wrote Prasad immediately on reading the news of their arrival. "I have a got a letter from the Mahasthavira of Calcutta." This latter figure would have been the chief monk for the community of Chittagong Buddhists resident in Calcutta; unfortunately, Roy never sent along a copy of the letter. "Who will like our Dear Leader to give away one's own property to the outsiders? (sic)" (HMBG)

To complicate matters, deSilva, Roy's compatriot in the Buddha Gaya Defense League, now wrote to say that there was "great dissatisfaction in the country as to the method that the Mahabodhi Society is adopting in this matter." Rival groups, such as the All-Ceylon Congress of Buddhist Associations and All-Ceylon Women's Buddhist Association, had not been consulted, and the "so-called Buddhist deputation" represented only the Mahabodhi Society and not "the Buddhist public." (HMBG) This is interesting, by the way, in light of Dharmapala's reputation in some circles as a predominantly *Sinhalese-Buddhist* figure: no doubt he was in some sense at some times exactly this, but Sinhalese objections to the Mahabodhi Society's role points out that the unity of religious nationalism was subverted by intra-religious-national disputes: also, of all the groups mentioned above, the Mahabodhi Society, Dharmapala's highly ecumenical and internationalist project, was the *least* nationalist in character.

Finally, among the materials that were assembled by the Congress and Mahasabha committees, was a newspaper article from the Ceylon Daily News, which bore further testimony to the fissionable quality of the Buddhist community "as a whole." This is a letter from a Burmese resident in Colombo who had attended a meeting held at the Maligakanda headquarters of the Mahabodhi Society: Maung Maung Khin complained bitterly that the delegation being sent to Calcutta included no Burmese members, and represented only Sinhalese Buddhists. Furthermore, the Maligakanda proceedings were conducted entirely in Sinhalese, "and I could not follow a word of it." (HMBG)

Prasad nevertheless met with the delegation, on Dec. 18, 1937, and explained to them that the 1924 committee recommendations should be implemented and that they would be pursued, if necessary, either in the Indian Legislative Assembly, or, perhaps more appropriately, in the Bihar Assembly. As the possibility of legislation became more real, elements within the All-India Mahasabha hardened their stance.[6] In the end, although the bill was mooted, under Prasad's sponsorship, in the Bihar assembly, because the Congress ministries, en bloc, resigned in protest in 1939, the bill never came to be debated seriously in any assembly prior to Independence.

"Inheritors of One Great Aryan Culture"

In 1946, the Mahabodhi Society again tried to garner Hindu support by sponsoring a joint conference at Patna, in the Birla Temple, under the chairmanship of Prasad, then President of the Constituent Assembly. Jagatnarayan Lal, President of the Bihar Provincial Hindu Mahasabha, expressed his conviction that Buddhists should be given some measure of control over the temple. At the same time, Prasad publicly urged the Mahant to accept the principle of joint control. (MBJ, Vol. 54, #3-4, 1946 40-41)

---

[6] At the 1938 All-India Hindu Mahasabha Conference, a resolution was passed that repudiated completely the prior prevailing spirit of compromise. "Hindu Temples and places of worship that have been converted into mosques or converted to other uses should be restored to the Hindus, and calls upon the Provincial Hindu Sabhas to prepare an exhaustive list of such temples in their respective provinces and to press this demand before their respective Provincial Governments." (AIHMS, 1938:3)

Although the ultimate legislative solution of the problem was decided at the provincial level, the debate remained alive in a variety of forms. Internationalist Buddhist interest in India and its Buddhist geography was approaching a high degree of intensity in a movement that was to peak during the 1956 celebration of Buddha Jayanti, the 2500th anniversary of the Buddha's nirvana. Also, in her new role as a leader of the post-colonial non-aligned movement, India became a favored location for the staging of various pan-Asian conferences.

At the Inter-Asian Conference, held in Delhi in March of 1947, Buddhist delegates formed an All-Asia Buddhist convention. Delegates, from China, Burma, Thailand, Nepal, Bhutan, Tibet, Ceylon, and India, appealed to Prime Minister Nehru to "hand over Buddhagaya Temple to the Buddhists of Asia." While Nehru had no more power than had Curzon to do any such thing, he promised "all support for the restoration of Buddhagaya to the Buddhists." (MBJ, Vol. 55, #5-6, 1947)

The Prime Minister of Bihar, S.K. Sinha, was certainly aware of this international interest in Bodh Gaya when he introduced a bill in the Bihar Assembly for a joint management scheme. Sinha even used Dharmapala's, and Arnold's, favorite language for characterizing the site: the temple was sacred to Buddhists as Jerusalem to the Christians, as Ayodhya to Hindus, as Mecca to Muslims.

This bill, in line with most previous proposals, provided for joint administration, and not for Buddhist control, and Sinha's rhetoric revived the Vaishnava linkage between the two religions: "Hinduism took itself into Buddhism and accepted Lord Buddha as one of the ten avatars. To Hindu it was his right to worship one of the ten avatars equally with Buddhists.[sic]" (MBJ, Vol. 56, #10, 1948)

An amendment was passed, moved by C.P.N. Singh, to circulate the bill for public comment. Singh, in spite of a provision in the bill that assured a Hindu majority on the board of management, was anxious that the bill not be viewed as a repudiation of Hindu interests in the temple. "After all - what were Hindus - they were neither Shaivas, Jains, Buddhists or other branches of religion but *were inheritors of one great Aryan culture.*" (my emphasis)

The initial reaction of the Mahabodhi Society, in a final show of the sort of pugnacity that Dharmapala had habitually employed, was hostile. The bill was styled "an example of the most one-sided legislation it has ever been our misfortune to see." (MBJ, Vol. 56, #10, 1948) Resolutions were passed, at a public meeting in the Mahabodhi Hall at Calcutta, calling for a number of amendments to the bill, including provisions for a board with a Buddhist majority. The Assembly Select Committee that was charged with hearing public opinion heard testimony from the District Collector that the bill's provisions for a permanent Hindu majority would prove "an unnecessary irritant" to Buddhists.

Sinha did act to partially satisfy Buddhist claims for a larger role by moving an amendment for the establishment of a separate "advisory board" to be appointed by state government but, importantly, to be comprised of a majority of Buddhists "who may not all be Indians. The bill was passed in this form on June 19, 1949, and the Mahabodhi Society put the best face on things by describing the victory as one of the society's "proud achievements." (MBJ, Vol. 58, #4-5, 1950; BLA, 1950, Vol. I: 215-20)

A Ceremony of Transfer at Bodh Gaya

I will close this chapter with a simple description of the ceremony which transferred jurisdiction of the temple, in 1953, from the Giri Mahant to the new temple management board. The ritual can serve as a sort of mnemonic though which many of the themes of the dispute may be easily retrieved.

On May 28, 1953, a procession of Buddhists moved from the Mahabodhi Resthouse to a dais in front of the main temple. At its head was a contingent of trumpet-playing Tibetan monks. These were followed by monks and laypeople from Ceylon, Burma, Cambodia, and India.

In all, perhaps somewhat more than 5000 people attended the event, although the Mahabodhi Journal account claimed attendance of as high as 100,000. (TOI, May 29, 1953: 7)

The actual ceremony commenced with the intoning of Sanskrit hymns by an assistant of the Mahant. He was followed by a Mahabodhi Society official, who recited Buddhist sutras in Pali. Then, very appropriately, given the role of the Vaishnava rhetoric which so routinely marked the debate over the temple, a Hindi recording star, Shrimati Malati Sarve, sang Vaishnava Bhavans—hymns to Vishnu, usually in the form of, not Buddha of course, but Krishna.

Messages of congratulations were read out, from foreign and Indian notables; the Prime Ministers of India, Thailand and Sri Lanka, India's Foreign Minister, The Maharajah of Sikkim, Japan's ambassador to India, and others. S.K. Sinha, Chief Minister of Bihar, in his address before the crowd, expressed his hope that Buddhists would attend in great numbers during the 2500th Buddha Jayanti Celebrations that were being planned for 1956.

The Mahant then presented a declaration to the Chairman of the Temple Management Committee, which promised full cooperation with the new arrangement, and expressed the hope that the committee "would look after the various traditions of this temple." Following the Mahant's acceptance message, a Mahabodhi Society monk again read out short excerpts from the Pali Suttas. This, had it marked the close of the ritual, would perhaps have marked a very clear transfer from Hindu to Buddhist jurisdiction.

The final bit of ceremony, however, was more suited to both

the diverse nature of the assembly, to the history of the temple campaign, and to the flavor of the resolution: a Hindu employee of the Bihar Education Department brought the celebration to an end with readings from Edwin Arnold's *Light of Asia.*

Chapter Ten

CONCLUSION : CIRCLES AROUND THE TEMPLE

Circumambulation of temples—walking around them in circles—is a common Hindu and Buddhist practice, and the term is evocative, to me, of certain strategies 1) that can be used to pull people into a common orbit, and 2) that can continue to be used for an indefinite period of time. In my introduction, I explored a "Hindu mode of encompassment" which took form centuries ago and which seemed to be at work throughout the modern events I have described.

In fact, the Bodh Gaya case is rich in illustrating the ways that an encompassing strategy can be deployed. Everyone, Hindus, Buddhist, Theosophists, British colonialists, and Indian politicians used some such device, and I therefore wish now to summarize a few main instances of such behavior.

Hindu Encompassment Language

It seems that this language, and particularly the doctrine that Buddha is the 9th avatar of Vishnu, was the most important element in the negotiations and final settlement at the temple. Having said that, it can no doubt still be mildly irritating to some Buddhists to read, for instance, on an Indian travel website, that "Buddha, the 9th incarnation of Vishnu, was born at Lumbini in Nepal." As well, one reads occasionally about minor disturbances at the temple site, such as "Buddhists protest projection of Buddha as Hindu god's incarnation." (Imran Khan, Indo Asian News Service, Patna, May 27, 2002). Below is an excerpt from this news story which reveals some interesting things.

> Minor skirmishes broke out Sunday over the issue between Buddhists and Hindus gathered in Bodh Gaya, the pilgrim town 110 km south of this capital city, where Buddha is said to have attained enlightenment.
>
> This month the All India Monks' Association asked Shankaracharya Jayendra Saraswati of Kancheepuram in Tamil Nadu to intervene in the tussle between Hindus and Buddhists over the control of the temple.
>
> As per the 1949 Temple Management Act, a Buddhist cannot become committee chairman as the post is reserved for a Hindu. If the district magistrate happens to be a non-Hindu, the state government has to nominate a Hindu.
>
> . . . Bodh Gaya remains the most important Buddhist pilgrimage centre, attracting a large number of pilgrims and tourists from across the world.

Notice, first of all, the phrase "minor skirmishes." This has, thankfully, remained the same throughout Bodh Gaya's modern history. Indeed there have been tensions, but in comparative terms these have never been, and we should expect that they will never become, in the wider context of such things, more than minor.

Also, notice the phrase "most important Buddhist pilgrimage center." That, really, is simply a fact of the modern world, and minor squabbling has not affected it at all. The "recovery" of Bodh Gaya, the thing that Dharmapala hoped for since 1891, has been facilitated, I think, as much by the 9th avatar doctrine—it provokes the occasional minor skirmish, but encourages the longer term sense of common value—as much as by any other device.

Encompassing and Ecumenical Buddhist Language

Dharmapala, just a year prior to his death, had written in his diary that, at Bodh Gaya, "Burmese, Japanese, Chinese, Siamese [and] Tibetans should have cottages built for each country." (ADC, Dec. 20, 1932) This is precisely what has happened within the last fifty years. In fact, all the Buddhist traditions mentioned by Dharmapaḷa, and others, are well represented at Bodh Gaya. Tibetan Buddhists have built three temples, Japanese Buddhists, two, and Vietnamese, Thais and Koreans one each. Indian neo-Buddhists have also built at the site.

The temples have been built, then, in various "national" traditions, and also in specific denominational traditions, Gelugpa, Kargyupa, Karmapa, Zen, Soka Gakkai, and so-forth. This fits well with what Dharmapala had once proposed: the establishment of *discrete* and *separate* "cottages" for different traditions, even though the Mahabodhi Society had been established as a Buddhist *ecumenical* organization, chartered to represent "Buddhism in general, and not any single aspect of it." (MBS1:1-2)

I suppose this is ecumenicalism as we generally employ the term, rather blandly "religious," dialogic, reasonable, non-hierarchical, and generally non-threatening to any specific tradition. There were, as well, other ecumenical processes working at Bodh Gaya.

The Theosophical Circle

The Theosophists, during the period I have documented, were most interesting in respect of their operations as a young and expanding cult in the service of which Colonel Olcott and Madame Blavatsky cast their ecumenical net very wide indeed. The raison d'etre of the group was, we know, the discovery of those "natural laws" which were known to "priests of ancient Persian, Indian, Egyptian, Hebrew, Chaldean, Grecian, Roman, Keltic, Scandinavian, Peruvian, Mexican, and other religions," and which were used by said priests to produce "weird and occult phenomena." (Olcott, 1880: 26)

For all practical purposes, then, every nation and culture of the world was said by the Theosophists to be worthy because every nation and culture had produced individuals who were capable of producing the valorized occult phenomena.

One must say, on the other hand, that sub-Saharan Africans, Chinese, and Jews seem to be missing from the list: I do not believe that the early Theosophists were particularly racist in the European context of their times, but surely something must be said about a movement that made so much of so-called "Root Races" and "Aryans." That, however, is a topic I will leave to others. For now, I wish to note that there is a point of reference in the Theosophical formula, the "ancient world," from which distance is measured, and the ecumenical force of the Theosophy is based on the assumption of an underlying unanimity which extends from this point, and transcends, or should, cultural and religious distinctions.

Yet there was also a clear anxiety on the part of Olcott and the European Theosophists that the original identity of specific religious traditions be preserved. An example: In 1898 Dharmapala and Olcott were approached for help by representatives of a so-called "fifth varna" community in Madras, an "untouchable" group which was seeking to upgrade its status through the assertion of a Buddhist identity. Olcott characterized this bid in the following terms:

> The movement inaugurated among the

> Pariahs....for the *return* of their great community to Buddhism, the alleged religion of their Dravidian ancestors, proceeds slowly but surely. (TT, Vol. XIX, No. 12, Sept 1898: 766, my emphasis.)

What is intriguing is that the Colonel expressed, in the next issue of the *Theosophist*, his concern that Buddhist "conversion" of the panchamas be legitimized by a demonstration that the group had suffered an actual "loss of religion." So, in truth, he wished to support a "re-conversion." This demonstration was not forthcoming because, although the panchamas had based their claim on "an ancient [Buddhist] work," the palm leaf manuscript in question had disappeared. (TT, Vol. XX, No. 6, March 1899: 384)

So, in Olcott's mind, an authentic "return" was preferred to simple conversion. By contrast, when an "original" Buddhism could be demonstrated to Olcott's satisfaction aid from the Theosophists aimed at "recovering" the *primal* religion was immediately forthcoming. "The Arakan people," wrote Olcott to Max Muller, "have urgently called me to Akyub to explain Buddhism to them, and I sail this week." (MC, Oct. 6, 1892) Arakan (part of modern day Burma) was for Olcott an appropriate and natural setting for Buddhism.

By the way, why did Olcott never express a desire to see any particular community simply convert to some form of unmarked, unhyphenated Theosophy? That seems to have been an option for individuals, but not for communities. I have characterized the Theosophical Society as a "franchise operation." The organization of branch societies was structured by geography and by "original" religion. The "ancient wisdom-religion," a unified esoteric philosophy, could have multiple concrete expressions which mirrored mundane "exoteric" diversity. Elite Theosophical ideology had no interest in dissolving *actual* distinctions. Indeed, they may have wished to strengthen them, not least of all so they—the small mostly European (or, some, Europeanized) core of early Theosophists, those who formed "councils" to confer honors, for interest, and those who wrote nooks—could continue to control the prestige esoteric philosophy.

Theosophical and British Imperial Encompassment of Distinctions

Naming different communities, or freezing different communities into rigid categories while at the same time positing integrative or unifying principles, is a behavior often associated with governments, and particularly imperial governments, if only because these are generally faced with problems stemming from a great multiplicity of social and cultural differences. Compare, then the Theosophical strategy I have presented with some actions of British imperialists in India.

During the period of Curzon's intrigues in pursuit of the correct resolution of the temple problem, his advisor Ibbetson had expressed fear that government action would bring them into "variance with *every section* of the Bengal community and, particularly, with the "bigoted Hindus." (CCIC, Vol. 194, #88c, Sept. 15, 1903, my emphasis) As well, Curzon's government, at both Viceregal and provincial levels, was routinely required to intervene in disputes such as those which divided Hindus and Muslims on the "question of the cow."

Furthermore, there was much confusion and anxiety about whether or not there was such a thing as a unitary Buddhist community, within or outside of India, and whether or not any person or group could adequately represent such a community. I am not now interested in establishing the true answers to any such questions, only that British officialdom was convinced that India (and South Asia generally) was marked by a rich and potentially fractious diversity.

At the same time, however, this same government had prepared a gaudy state ceremony, one in a long series of such rites, the great 1903 "Coronation Durbar" at Delhi, predicated on the notion that all Indians (and "Orientals' in general) were susceptible to rituals built up around the insignia of royal power. In short, there was an "exoteric" outward diversity—and nothing could or should be done to homogenize this, as its existence was a powerful grounds in itself for foreign imperialism: they are too complicated to govern themselves—but this diversity could be domesticated through a ritual form which would promote, in Curzon's words, "a sense of common participation in a great political system in and of fellow citizenship in the British Empire." (Trevithick, 1990: 567)

Every section, that is to say, of British India, could be seduced into a celebration of Empire, through the appropriate ritual incorporative means. But this integrative rhetoric did not mark in Curzon's thinking a desire that the "exoteric" distinctions could themselves be dissolved. Quite to the contrary, for instance, he rejected entirely an earlier Viceroy's proposal for an Indian "Herald's College" of native aristocracy precisely because he felt that regional and linguistic variations would foredoom any such new integrative all-India institution to "impotence." (CC, FD, Secret 1, Sept. 1902, Nos. 2-3: 15-16) That this native variation and its associated "impotence" were to a great extent legitimating inventions of an Imperial government, is obvious.

India, then, had been, and should remain, divided up into various communities only unified ideologically by an imperial apparatus which was uniquely capable of defining, celebrating, and administering them. This in itself is the strategy, now well known through the works of various scholars of colonialism (see for instance Hobsbawn and Ranger, 1983; Cohn, 1985), of classify, invent, and conquer.

To our main subject now, these communities, although only

"apparently" or "exoterically" distinct, were nonetheless best confined to those categories. Neither the Theosophists nor the British much cared for the idea of innovation. Here, for instance, is Olcott's account of Catholic perfidy: "With a flippant unconcern for detection by posterity," medieval priests had converted Gautama Buddha himself and, "at this very day, there stands in Palermo a church dedicated to Buddha under the name of Divo Josaphat." (Olcott, 1880: 37) The form of this last complaint is replicated in a comment from Macpherson, the Collector who presided over the first temple case. Macpherson characterized the Hindu Mythology of Buddha a "politic device" and, referring to an ancient identification of the Madonna with the Goddess Diana, the sort of thing "not unknown in uneducated Christendom." Innovation, in general, is either manipulative or foolish.

Theosophy, read in this context, emerges as an occult satire on British Imperial statecraft, in that Theosophical and British Imperial thought shared a pronounced disinclination to dissolve *actual* distinctions between "included" groups.

The "Homo Hierarchical" Encompassment of Distinctions

Similar styles of thought allowed both the British Government and the Theosophists, both "non-Buddhist" groups, to take up without irony the recovery of the Mahabodhi Temple for the "Buddhists." Their efforts may have been in part, as Curzon's advisor had put it, based on a desire to right "a great wrong," but even to the extent that this is so, most of their efforts seem derived from the conviction that people ought to behave in accordance with the names they have been, by various means, provided. When faced with unsettling discrepancies between their categories and practice, Theosophists and officials alike tended to defend the categories, because, in discrepant cases, people were stepping outside of the categories that had been designed to mark their distinct "inclusion" within the larger configuration.

Recall Dumont's insight that "in the hierarchical scheme a group's acknowledged differentness whereby it is contrasted with other groups becomes the very principle whereby it is integrated into society." (Dumont, 1966:191) There are many things that may be associated with this formula, but a fundamental requirement of it is that "differentness" must be maintained. When this "differentness" is lost or obscured, the very system is threatened. It appears to me that Theosophical and British anxiety about "differentness" is very like the "homo hierarchical" philosophy. This is so whether or not one is swayed by the argument that Dumont's scheme is an "orientalist" formulation.

APPENDEX

THE LIFE HISTORY OF ANAGARIKA DHARMAPALA

What follows is an essay[1] on the life and significance of Anagarika Dharmapala, the figure who was so active in the chain of events that led eventually to the regularization and popularization of modern Buddhist pilgrimage to Bodh Gaya. Readers who have stayed with me thus far will, I think, also be interested in this essay, but I should warn them that it is written, more so than the rest of the text, with considerable attention paid to special issues in sociocultural anthropology, the discipline in which I was trained. That is, it may seem both technical (unnecessarily) and tedious (as an unhappy consequence) to non-specialists: to social and cultural anthropologists, particularly, I make no apologies and believe that my argument is timely and important.

I also believe that even readers who will not be interested in the more technical issues—in the main these have to do with how remarkable individuals and their biographies should be handled in the context of a discipline that focuses on the collective and the social—will be willing to skim over these

[1] A shorter and more specialized version of this essay was originally published as "Anthropological 'Life History' and the 'Life Histories' of Anagarika Dharmapala" in *Journal of Anthropology*, (1992) Northern Illinois University, Vol. 7, Nos. 1 & 2:91-111.

to glean a better picture of the life of Dharmapala who was, it must be said, a remarkable and important figure.

Life Story as Charter

I begin with a traditional anthropological notion, that specific narratives in specific cultures operate as charters for the guidance and evaluation of appropriate or moral behavior. Thus, one strategy for the representation of some "other culture" is to translate, or interpret, for that culture, some highly salient narrative and then to characterize those normative attitudes with which the story seems to be associated.

My double intentions, now, are to explore the use of narratives by a single individual, as he recalled, constructed, and maintained a series of responses to the conditions of his life, and to complicate this exploration through an analysis of the traditional anthropological attitude towards life-history narratives as they may or may not be used to comprehend and present the experience of others. In effect, this is an experiment during the course of which I contrast problems associated with the interpretation of one class of narratives—the diary and the autobiography—with those of another class—the anthropological life history.

What is of prime interest to me here is that Dharmapala's construction of his life-history, in the service of his own moral and "identity-constituative" purposes, might exemplify precisely that form of the biography that has been most appealing to anthropologists for analytical purposes, primarily the validation of culture and personality models. I shall, however, before proceeding with these considerations, provide a skeletal biography of Dharmapala.

Don David Hewavitarne, Anagarika Dharmapala

Dharmapala is well known, in Sri Lanka and throughout the Buddhist world, and in India, as the man who inaugurated a campaign, in 1891, to reclaim for Buddhists the Mahabodhi

Temple at Bodh Gaya and who, in the course of that campaign, founded the first international and ecumenical Buddhist organization, the Mahabodhi Society.

He was born Dom David Hewavitarne in 1864: this name provides a partial index of Ceylon's colonial history, and his life is replete with the sorts of difficulties, opportunities, paradoxes, rebellions and multiple perspectives that mark the biographies of thoughtful and talented "colonials" everywhere. Born into a Buddhist family, he attended English-medium Christian schools and, as a boy, participated in both Catholic and Buddhist rituals.

As he grew older, he came to question the proselytizing of his Christian teachers, and yet, did not embrace an orthodox Buddhist perspective. Instead, at the age of sixteen, he was "adopted" by a very unlikely set of surrogate parents, Madame H.P. Blavatsky and Colonel H.S. Olcott, founders of an occult organization, the Theosophical Society. Had he not met these figures, Dom David might never have left Ceylon.

He learned from Madame Blavatsky, an obese, chain-smoking Ukrainian mystic, with no real knowledge of Buddhism,[2] of the existence of "The Masters," ethereal adepts normally resident in the deep Himalayas who made their desires known through raps on window panes or through "precipitated" letters. Don David, from about the age of twenty years, began to augment his education with readings in a rapidly

[2] Max Muller wrote of Madame Blavatsky that "to quote her blunders would be endless."(Muller, 1901: 104) I concur, and shall content myself with just the following example, from Blavatsky's *Isis Unveiled:*

> [Nirvana, in Esoteric Buddhism] means the certitude of personal immortality in spirit not in soul. When we use the word Buddhist we do not mean to imply by it either the exoteric Buddhism of Gautama Buddha, or the modern Buddhistic religion, but the secret philosophy of Sakyamuni, which in its essence, is certainly identical with the ancient wisdom-religion of the sanctuary, the pre-vedic Brahamanism. (in Sinnett, 1969 [1880]: 143)

growing Theosophical literature.

The Theosophists transported Dharmapala across many national, religious and cultural boundaries and, with Colonel Olcott, who had left his law practice in New York City to become a sort of impresario for the Theosophical movement generally and for Blavatsky in particular, the young man traveled extensively throughout India and the Far East. From the Colonel he learned such things as the principles of "mesmerism" and "animal magnetism," and was, as well, introduced to a global network of mystical confederates. When Dharmapala first arrived in Bodh Gaya, he considered himself a "Chela"—a student—of the "Master Koot Hoomi," about whom, more anon.

Shortly after his pilgrimage to Bodh Gaya he took on a new title, "Anagarika Dharmapala"—the homeless protector of the Dharma. He thus moved closer to a "recovered" Buddhist identity. The title, in fact, is not validated as an actual ecclesiastical designation by any Theravadin canonical source. That is, it is not an *institutional* title or role.

At Bodh Gaya, Dharmapala felt that he had re-entered a sacred space the recovery of which was congruent with his search for an authentic identity. This last phrase is no doubt too programmatic: I do not read in any of Dharmapala's writing the words *I am seeking a new identity*, but I do know, on the other hand, that his life story reads as though this were the case.

By stages, Dharmapala disowned many elements of his Theo-

Blavatsky's attempt to rescue "personal immortality" from the orthodox Buddhist teachings on the concept of an-atman (Pali: anatta), or "no soul" is weak in its attempt to juxtapose to "soul" the term "spirit." This is an old crypto-Vedantic "solution" of the problem, and it has been energetically battled by Buddhist thinkers since at least the time of Asoka, when Pudgalavadins attempted to introduce into Buddhism a soul-like and perduring structure, the "pudgala," which adheres eternally to unique individuals. The notion of "pre-vedic Brahmanism" is, of course, an oxymoron.

sophical past and, finally, he broke off formal relations with the organization, having established, on the Theosophical model, his own Mahabodhi Society, which was formally constituted to promote Buddhist ideas and practices. However, and very importantly, he retained until death his faith in the Theosophical "Master K.H."

For forty years, through fund raising and propaganda in a dozen countries, through legal and legislative work, and through endless rounds of negotiation with British Indian authorities and Hindu religious leaders, he worked for the recovery of Bodh Gaya. Dharmapala became, at an advanced age, a Theravadin Buddhist monk and took the unequivocally Pali ordination name "Devamitta Dhammapala," clearly a major step in his "recovery," or construction, of a Buddhistic identity. In one sense, his is the story of a private impulse that was transformed by him into a mission that carried and created meaning for others. Yet he never, even after ordination, neglected to open a diary entry without invoking the name of the Theosophical "Koot Hoomi," and this is well worth examining.

The "Master's" name, as glossed by the English Theosophist A.O. Sinnett, from whom Dharmapala most likely first heard it, yields a neat portrait of the Theosophical eclecticism which was so important a component of the Sinhalese activist's life: the Master was "a native of Punjab who was attracted to occult studies from his earliest childhood," and was generally known by his "Tibetan Mystic Name"— Koot Hoomi Lal Sing. (Sinnett, 1969[1880]: 84, my emphasis)

I have, frankly, devoted very little time to the establishment of a lineage for the "Master," but, while "Koot Hoomi" might, I suppose, be found to preserve some "Sanskritish" and mantraic quality of the sort not unknown in Tibet, "Lal Sing," I am bold enough to say, has not the slightest mandate to form part of a "Tibetan Mystic name."

I want to be on record as being of the following opinion: when in doubt, the Theosophists, for the most part, simply made up whatever it was they needed. I do not believe that this necessarily means that their ideas or intentions were always fraudulent, but, on the other hand, my basic approach preserves some considerable space for these possibilities.

That the Sinhalese Dharmapala, even after his Theravadin ordination, retained his allegiance to an unseen hybrid adept, whose qualities were most comprehensively described by Sinnett, an English newspaper editor from Allahabad, says much about the heterogeneity of Dharmapala's spiritual progress.

That, in a nutshell, was Dharmapala's life, and, while this life has been presented by others, and most notably by Obeyesekere, who for the most part was concerned to demonstrate that Dharmapala's identity crises were exemplary symptoms of the Sinhalese colonial experience, I shall approach the subject from a different perspective. First, however, as a way into a brief review of anthropological life history methods, let me characterize Obeyesekere's findings.

In his several articles on Dharmapala, Obeyesekere emphasizes the degree to which the activist's life was exemplary of the social history of a group, in this case the emergent Sinhalese or bi-lingual Buddhist intelligentsia of colonial Ceylon. Expressed in terms of the search for an authentic identity, "Dharmapala's own problems of identity represented in exaggerated form the identity problems of a larger society." (1976: 250)

However, this approach, which makes Dharmapala's life central to the creation of "a new and unified Sinhala Buddhist identity," (Obeyesekere1976: 225) has more to do with the appropriation, by a group, of his identity than with Dharmapala's actual lived experience of colonial times.

Indeed, I think there is on this specific issue no very substantial quarrel here with Obeyesekere, who in one article notes that Dharmapala "is more a symbol than a person for contemporary Buddhists [in Sri Lanka]" (1972: 70) I do however, wish to critique some of what Obeyesekere has written about Dharmapala and I follow, in significant part, a prior critique by Michael Roberts, whose article "For Humanity, For the Sinhalese—Dharmapala as Bosat" recognizes as significant, more than Obeyesekere, such non-Sinhalese things as Dharmapala's *English* language diary-keeping, and his long career outside of Ceylon. (Roberts, 1997:1007)

One of Robert's main points, and it is well made, is that it is "too facile" to speak about "a Sinhala Buddhist revival headed by Anagarika Dharmapala," while ignoring the degree to which Dharmapala was not at all motivated purely by Sinhalese nationalism. (Roberts 1997:1010) However, another subject—Dharmapala's name change—which is misapprehended by Obeyesekere and not, I think, thought very important by Roberts, requires extensive comment.

When and Why did Dharmapala become "Homeless"?

In 1927, Dharmapala wrote the following in his diary: "When all had deserted me in 1895 I put on the yellow robe and became anagarika [homeless]," (ADC, Feb. 12, 1927) Roberts, on the other hand, believes that 1891 is the more proper date, though he takes authority for this from the same diaries I have used, and writes as follows: "In my incomplete reading of this data it appears that he pledged to himself (and his father?) that he would follow the anagarika (i.e., brahmacharya) path in 1891."

I did not find "anagarika" that early, and do not, by the way think that "anagarika" is simply equivalent to "brahmacharya."[3] I must say I also quite agree with Roberts

[3] It is also interesting to read Amunugama on this, incidentally, given that he largely defends the thesis that Dharmapala was throughout his life an exemplary Buddhist figure: "In fact, the Brahmacari role is specifically a *Hindu*,

that Dharmapala's "periodic autobiographical reviews"—he did this very often in his diaries—do not always agree one with another (Roberts 1997:1016) Importantly, both Roberts and I date the name change much later than does Obeyesekere, who writes that Dharmapala adopted his new name in 1881:

> In 1881, coming under the influence of the theosophists, Col. Olcott and Madame Blavatsky and prominent Buddhist monks who were engaged in a famous religious debate with Christians, he adopted the role of Anagarika. (Obeyesekere, 1972: 68; also see Obeyesekere, 1976: 236)

Perhaps Obeyesekere means only that the "role" and not the name was adopted but I think not, and also think, again, that "anagarika" is not simply a different name for a conventional role. However that may be, it is certainly the case that in 1895, and even into the next year, he continued to sign his correspondence "H.D.," or Hewavitarne Dharmapala. (MBJ, Vol V, # 3, July, 1896)

Before I investigate the name itself more extensively, it is important to squarely address Dharmapala's continuing and apparently life-long devotion to some aspects of Theosophy. Malalgoda, in harmony with the general trend of Obeyesekere's ideas and, indeed, in line with what seems to have been conventional wisdom onthe subject, has written that the Buddhist Theosophical movement in Ceylon "had very little Theosophy in it; what it did have was a good deal of Buddhism." Malalgoda goes on to agree with Obeyesekere that this Buddhism was "not of the traditional type, it was

---

not a Buddhist one, being a stage in the progress of a man from childhood celibate to householder." (Amunugama 1985: 725, my emphasis) Quite so, and, in fact, therefore, the traditional Brahmacari role, leading as it does to legitimate settled household life, is thoroughly *opposed* to the "homeless" role that Dharmapala actually adopted.

rather of the type that has recently been called Protestant Buddhism." (Malalgoda, 1976: 246, and see Obeyesekere, 1972 and 1976).

This seem not quite accurate: Dharmapala clearly adhered, for a long period, to Theosophical notions, and never, as far as I know, relinquished his belief in the "Masters." While Malalgoda observes that, "by Olcott's own admission, only one monk in the whole of Ceylon believed in the existence of the "Mahatmas" (Malalgoda, 1976:252), Dharmapala, not a monk of course, seems never to have *disbelieved* in "Master Koot Hoomi," to whom his allegiance remained strong until his death—this loyalty may even have strengthened after his internment in Calcutta during W.W.I.

It is fair to say, though, that he thought of "K.H." as an ethereal Buddhist of some sort. "Reading the Mahatma Letters," he wrote in 1924. "They criticize Christianity and Hinduism." (June 11, 1924) And, from another entry, from 1927, we read that "K.H. is the humble follower of the former Gautama Buddha" (ADS June 4. 1927)

Certainly, during this same period, there were many criticisms of Theosophy and of Theosophists. For example, "The Bhagavad Gita, Bible and the Koran satisfy the religious instincts of the people. The last hope has been destroyed by the charlatanism of the Theosophical imposters." (ADS August 25, 1924) However, more frequently one reads such things as "The only refuge for him who aspires to true perfection is Buddha alone. K.H."

Buddha alone? Bu the authority for this statement is Koot Hoomi. "The writer of the 'Mahatma' letters clearly indicates that he is a Buddhist. His status cannot be discovered. Is he a Bhikkhu or a Bodhisattva? Where does he reside?" (May 7, 1931) This is a subject, about the reality and nature of the "masters" that came to Dharmapala, not from Sinhalese Buddhism at all, but from his late-nineteenth century contact with the western Theosophists. All of this serves well to illustrate the extent to which Dharmapala was not firmly rooted in whatever might be presented as "Sinhalese Buddhism." "I shall listen to the voice that speaks to me in silence," he wrote in 1891 (ADC, March 4, March 9, 1891), and referred in his diaries to Koot Hoomi ever after.

Now, however, to return to the *anagarika* problem: what's in a title? The theoretical significance of this documentary matter, for Obeyesekere's argument about "this-worldly asceticism" and its association with the anagarika role, is that Hewavitarne Dharmapala had *already* been involved with political, social and legal matters prior to his adoption of the new title. But this seems problematic.

He had been *deserted* in 1895 and then became homeless. Elsewhere he writes "in May 1895 the Ceylon Buddhists abandoned me because I failed to recover Buddha Gaya." (ADS3, 1918) So it seems as though, at the time, the decision to take on the new title of homeless one came as a reaction to the *failure* of this-worldly activity and not as a warrant for further such activity. Perhaps Obeyesekere credits the anagarika concept with a content with which it was not invested by Dharmapala himself until years later.

For instance, in 1925, Dharmapala called, in a journal article, for the establishment of "an Anagarika order of Brothers." In his characterization of the role at that time, Dharmapala does indeed seem to make a commitment to "this-worldly asceticism." Members of the new order would be trained in three languages, Pali (the Theravada canonical language), an Indian vernacular, and English. Significantly, Sanskrit, the language of the Indian Mahayana texts, would be optional. The new mendicants would "live with the poor," an impossibility for traditional Bhikkhus, and "teach their children morality, to be loving and kind to all living things, and also arts and crafts."

This plan was formulated by Dharmapala after much thought, and after considering many models for social aid organizations—including the Red Cross, the Salvation Army and, interestingly, the work of the African-American social activist Booker T. Washington, whose Tuskegee Institute in Alabama he visited in 1904. In one fascinating letter (December 1903) to Washington, Dharmapala wrote:

> Dear Mr Washington, I invite you in the name of 50 millions of neglected children of illiterate, destitute and starving parents to visit India, if possible next year and bring to them the joyful message that there is hope through a life of education and training in the arts and crafts. I have gained from my visit to Tuskegee an experience that I shall never forget and when I saw the Tuskegee Institute with its manifold branches under enlightened teachers I rejoiced that you have made all this glorious work a consummation within a generation; and thought of the Viceroy in India who with the millions of children starving for education and bread that he should waste in sky rockets and tomfoolery and vain show to please a few loafing lords who came from England last January six million dollars in thirteen days! He is not worth to loose the latchet of your shoe. Yours Sincerely The Anagarika Dharmapala. (ALS Con. 255 BI-W Papers DLC. (BTW)[4]

Certainly, with Obeyesekere, I would accept that the kind of practical social work admired by Dharmapala harmonizes well with "this-worldly" asceticism. I am also comfortable with

---

[4] Washington replied that "such a visit as you mention is quite out of the question for anything like early consideration . . . could not spare the time from my exacting duties here." (December 31, 1903, BTW)

the idea that "anagarika" is a way of introducing a third term between the traditional Theravada categories of "upasaka," or pious layman, and "bhikkhu," fully ordained monk. However, there are several further issues.

First, in reference to the proposed Anagarika Order, notice that there is a requirement that the new aspirants learn English and an Indian vernacular. The fact is underlined that, in his own construction of his life's work, and in his late construction of the anagarika role, India and the British imperial world generally played a greater role than did Ceylon. The second point is that it was *specifically under Indian conditions* that the anagarika role was considered to be important.

> The Vinaya rules appointed for Indian Bhikkhus of old are not possible to be observed by non-Indian Bhikkhus living in India today. There are no Buddhist kings in India, and the only Buddhist King lives in Siam, and it is not possible to get help to establish the Sasana in India from the Buddhist world today. The establishment of a Bhikkhu order in India is therefore at the present time an impossibility. (MBJ, Vol. 33, #4, 1925)

The implication can only be that, aside from any new content of "this worldly asceticism" that may appear in the anagarika role, the prime reason that Dharmapala championed it at this time was to fit Indian conditions. He was not introducing "this-worldly" elements because he thought them an improvement on tradition, but because he thought he had no other good choice.

This well matches what I have heard from Sinhalese monks of the Mahabodhi Society in India. One told me that he abandons his robe upon reaching India because he wishes not to be confused with various orders of Hindu ascetics.

Another stated that, while the anagarika role was a useful wedge into Indian society, now that Sinhalese centers have been established at the more important Buddhist shrines, and now that Indian neo-Buddhists have set up proper ordination regulations for new monks, there is no longer a necessity to have recourse to the intervening term.

Very significantly for this theoretical point, and also as a measure of Dharmapala's integrity, he refused to become a fully ordained Bhikkhu until very shortly before his death. Monks in India have told me of their conflicts in juggling Vinaya regulations with their roles as managers, fee-takers, and landlords. "We shouldn't do it," said one monk, "but we do because we must." That is to say, what contemporary Sinhalese monks in India regard as an unfortunate necessity, Dharmapala had attempted to routinize and validate with the innovated status of anagarika.

Turning now to another matter, what is of interest to me is that Obeyesekere's approach to the artifacts of Dharmapala's life employs a certain kind of narrative, the life history, in much the same manner as life histories were employed, early on, in American anthropology: this involves, 1) the presentation of a specific individual as the exemplification of his culture and, 2) the minimization of the particularities of that same individual. There is, in fact, an anthropological anxiety, of long standing, about the status of individuals, and this is often "managed" in a manner that can misrepresent the nature of specific individuals.

The "Figure" of the Individual and the "Ground" of Culture

The particular individual, and his "life-history," have been almost continuously suspect to those who maintain anthropology's traditional generalizing aspirations—either with comparative intent or with the intent to offer portraits of "whole" cultures—since Radin, in his collection of material for *The Autobiography of A Winnabago Indian*, claimed, in what seems to have actually been a *defense* of some sort, that the object of the study was "*not* to obtain autobiographical details about *some definite personage*, but to have some representative middle-aged individual of moderate ability describe his life in relation to the social group in which he had grown up." (Radin, 1920:384, my emphasis) Thus, the well-chosen individual was to serve as an exemplification of his culture.

Yet, certain aspects of even the "representative" life were seen to pose a threat to the *prior* conception that individuals should exemplify their cultures, and the proper method of handling this was to depress the particularities of an individual consciousness. This explains Sapir's peculiar praise of Walter Dyk's *Son of Old Man Hat*: "It is a sequence of memories that need an extraordinarily well-defined personality to hold it together, *yet nowhere is this unique consciousness obtruded upon us.*" (Sapir, in Dyk 1938:viii, my emphasis) I am not sure how that is possible, but my point is to underscore the anxiety that has often attended the use of the life history.

Boas, in fact, in a posthumously published review article of 1943, seemed genuinely distressed about the great numbers of life histories, overwhelmingly of Native Americans, that had appeared since Radin's pioneering effort. He felt that their main excuse had to be that they might shed light on those ways of Native American life that had disappeared from the continent, but that, in the service of this admirable goal, treacherous memory would play too great a part. This represents a significant shift in the distrust of the individual life history: the problem is no longer merely the matter of exemplification, the choice of the "representative" subject, but one of *reliability*.

In short, wrote Boas, life histories were "valuable primarily rather as useful material for a study of the perversion of truth brought about by the play of memory with the past" (Boas, 1943:334). Actually, at one level I quite approve of this insofar as it indicates a faith in the notion that some things really *do* happen and some things really *don't*. That sort of thinking has not been popular in the better universities in recent decades, Nevertheless, Boas also seems to be saying that the major problem is that people really *were* one particular way at one time, but that we cannot on the other hand trust one of the main sources of primary data available to us—their own memories—as we set about the important business of determining what that one particular way was. This is difficult.

These brief remarks on the life history should be understood within the context of Boas' more general attitude toward the role of the individual actor which, again, feature the exemplification urge. This emerges, in the same posthumous review, in a curious fashion.

Boas begins with a discussion of findings in *physical* anthropology concerning race, to make the splendid and well-known Boasian point that racial "type" is "a construct that has no reality," and that "to identify the construct type and the individual, to ascribe all the characteristics of the type to the individual," is a "fundamental logical error." (Boas:1943: 312-313) The unique biological individual was the fundamental biological fact within the virtually useless context of biologistic racial categorization. However, from the *cultural* point of view, the individual tended to disappear:

> The impressionistically derived concept of typical cultural behavior has a much higher degree of reality than that of a physical type. The pattern of culture has greater reality than the biological types because *the cultural pattern exerts its influence equally upon every individual,* while biological descent produces individuals of different qualities.(Boas, 1943: 313, my emphasis)

In sum then, his specific criticism of the life history, that it tends to be unreliable, does no theoretical damage to the standard defense of the form: that, properly handled, it might provide an *individual* exemplification of a *general* cultural pattern.

However, Boas was not, to his credit, satisfied to leave aside completely the problem of unique individuals, whose lives might be poorly contexualized through the use of bounded cultural models: "Nevertheless, we must recognize that individual variations in behavior exist, dependent on personality and individual experience," and that the investigation of such variation is vital to an understanding of "the dynamics of culture change." (Boas, 1943:314)

Culture change, then, is the domain within which the really different individual might be recognized. Now, this might have signaled a genuine shift in how the life history was to be viewed, not exclusively as an individual exemplification of a general cultural scenario, but possibly, with regard to appropriate individuals, as illustrative of more dynamic processes. After all, it is just such figures as Dharmapala—and Nehru, Gandhi, Jinnah, Nkrumah, Kenyatta, etc—who are, precisely because of inter-cultural clashes and confrontations, and the crises and innovations these routinely inspire, so often initiators of significant change in societies which anthropologists were largely content to describe in atemporal and "cultural" terms. Well, the initiators or perhaps just the most visible carriers of such change, but in either case we need to take their lives seriously.

By rejecting, as a simple "perversion of truth," the "play of memory with the past," Boas rejected a potent tool for the analysis of such individuals. As it happened, anthropologists only later began to direct their attention to the on-going construction and invention of national, or ethnic, or religious histories, mythologies and identities. Had they been less wary about the use of life-historical material, anthropologists might have sooner come to confront the fact that their "cultures" and "configurations" and so-forth were very approximate models abstracted from messy and dynamic social fields.

Now, Kroeber, in considering Boas' approach to the life history, nuanced the problem of "reliability" in a somewhat different vein. The autobiography—and many life histories of Native Americans, however collected, had been presented as such—was not only "subjective," and therefore problematic, it was also, as a form, rather new in human history and generally, as well, a western phenomenon. The suggestion, of course, was that such narratives were less than appropriately employed as vehicles for understanding traditional anthropological communities. (Kroeber, 1945:321)

> Perhaps we shall have an answer to the problem of the question raised by Boas [the "reliability question"] when someone—if there ever is such —who has done a first-class, full-length portrait of a culture, and who has also *edited* a full- length autobiography from that culture, will pronounce an inside verdict on the relation of the two endeavors. (Kroeber, 1945:321)

I have, so far, characterized the reaction to the individual, as marked in the debate about the use of life histories, as one of anxiety, but perhaps now it becomes obvious that this anxiety was sometimes expressed in a most presumptuous tone. In general, there seems to have been the casual expectation that individual lives and narratives were to be "verified" by the cultural model, and that if they could not be so verified, it could be safely concluded that the subject had been acculturated to a state not of interest to serious anthropologists. This is implicit, I think, in the following excerpt from Kluckhohn, who was writing in the same year as Kroeber, on "The Personal Document in Anthropological Science."

> At the end of the introduction the reader should be shown that the individual's life will gain its full meaning only if seen against the background of his own culture. In the second chapter *the anthropologist will therefore construct the ground (culture) upon which the figure (personality) will emerge.* (Kluckhohn, 1945:152, my emphasis.)

If the figure does *not* emerge from the constructed ground, I assume, the fault is likely in the choice of figures. What happens to anthropology—and in the social sciences generally—then, when certain individuals, qua individuals, are simply too important to ignore, is the subject of my next section.

Remarkable Individuals

When we turn explicitly to this problem, the problem of "remarkable," or "distinctive" individuals, certain difficulties are multiplied dramatically. In one account of a remarkable individual, for instance, David Mandlebaum's "The study of Life History: Gandhi," here is how the problem of dealing anthropologically with a renowned figure is approached:

> The more serious research question for our present purposes is whether the life of so singular a man can be a useful source for general concepts about method, culture, society, personality. No person can be labeled "typical" in all respects, and students of life history must always grapple with the question of the typicality of their subjects. As a renowned leader, Gandhi is by definition atypical. (Mandlebaum, 1973:183)

This apology, it seems to historians, psychologists, and political scientists, is designed to acknowledge, for anthropologists, that M.K. Gandhi was not Radin's "representative middle-aged individual of moderate ability," and that Gandhi therefore had to be reformatted as a proper object for anthropological research. What was the warrant for the investigation? It was that Gandhi "evoked ideas and emotions so deeply characteristic of his countrymen that millions of them recognized in him their own deeply rooted feelings."

Finally, then, Mandlebaum arrives at the statement, which ropes together several truisms into a paradox, that while Gandhi was one among millions, "like all other men, he was both typical and atypical, though each in an uncommon degree." (Mandlebaum, 1973:183) This statement is, 1) an attempt to reduce Gandhi's singularity, with the observation that all folk are to some extent atypical, and 2) a bid to magnify the representative quality of his life, by presenting an individual in whose life is encoded, in a condensed and potent fashion, some general cultural logic.

At the conclusion of his article, Mandelbaum notes that Gandhi's "cultural life plan" is a thing sometimes easily traced out, with "cultural expectations" being "sharply drawn," while at other times this "plan" is only "dimly indicated." (1973: 193) So, at any rate, the plan is *there*, somewhere, and that's what matters.

I would not have undertaken this brief review, which must appear to some readers to be somewhat antiquarian, had I not thought that significant and vexatious anthropological continuities could be thereby addressed. So let me take up the subject of how the role and value of the life history has been more recently conceived, in this case by Marcus and Fischer in their *Anthropology as Cultural Critique.* In praise of several life-historical works, the authors mark certain promising tendencies:

> Life histories become the means to explore the discourses of a particular strata of a soci-

> ety and arenas of political competition between strata, and to ask questions about the processes of cultural hegemony, as well as about the didactic norms of character, maturation, and morality which become mass cultural models. Life history here is no longer simply a narrative frame for stringing together life-cycle rituals, socialization patterns, and a generational history as experienced by one individual; nor is it left to unique individuals. Indeed, life history deconstructs in the fullest sense: not making the subject disappear, but rather illuminating the social and constructive elements of an individual that make him or her potent in social context. Insofar as a life is the locus of experience, it is important to specify the cultural meanings that figure and compose it.[5]

I must say that I think that a life is the locus of experience whether or not cultural meanings figure and compose it, but still, much here is laudable, particularly the implicit recognition, now of course conventional in anthropology dis-

---

[5] Elsewhere, Marcus and Fischer recommend that the life-history not be "forced into inappropriate, Western-biased molds," but that they should instead "*emphasize the native conventions, idioms, or myths* that compose the ideas of life histories or similar meaningful narratives about individual experience, growth, the self, and emotions, as they are formed in the conversations and interviews of fieldwork." (Marcus and Fischer, 1986:58, my emphasis) Of course, I am not presenting fieldwork data here, and the comments on "native conventions" etc. are directed to Shostak's *Nisa,* the life history of a Kung woman, arguably, that is, a subject belonging to one of the traditionally bounded "anthropological communities." Nevertheless, this sort of either-or language —the history is either "western-biased" or it is built up from "native conventions"—hints at what is, at best, a rather romantic presupposition about the ongoing strangeness of "primitive" life. Perhaps more seriously, to be directed at the outset to *emphasize any particular aspect of the life history* smacks of precisely the sort of selective, exemplifying and "representative" approach that so characterized earlier American anthropology.

course, that the field within which an individual operates is vastly more complex, heterogeneous and open-ended—and, by the way, includes evolutionary as well as cultural influences, natural as well as social history—than could have been comprehended through the use of older cultural models to which I have alluded: a life history cannot be simply "read off" as the enactment of a cultural script.

Nevertheless, are we still being warned that "our individuals," to the extent that their lives turn out *not* to be useful for an analysis of norms, cultural hegemony, mass models and so-forth, are *not* legitimate objects of anthropological research? In what sense, as well, is the "life history" not to be "left to unique individuals?" Is it that there are no such beings, or is the force of the statement to indicate that, if there are, they had best be left alone by anthropologists? One aspect of this that concerns me is the implication that we ought to be concerned with unique individuals *only* to the extent that they become "potent in social context."

This is not deconstructive in *my* fullest sense. I think we should all be allowed to demonstrate, as seems in fact quite natural to our own social position, a fascination with that which renders an actor, or some part of an actor's life, impotent, or irrelevant, or marginal. In short, I fear that there may yet survive features of the old exemplification pressures, which often predetermined that a distinctive individual should be domesticated for use as "a sort of 'typical personality' writ large" (Angrosino, 1976:134)[6]

The life history should be taken up in a manner that is at least not hostile to the task for which it is arguably best-fitted,

---

[6] Angrosino writes of his life-history method, which involves analysis of a politician from Trinadad, that it has "the disadvantage, of course, of leading one to deal with a figure who is, by definition, distinctive." The way out of the problem then, is to note that perhaps "because the remarkable life is a fulfillment of a culture's highest, it can be seen as a sort of "typical personality" writ large." (1976: 133-35)

which is to provide an account of the lived experience of a particular human being. If we find that "culture," say, or "society," are constructs in a way that an individual is not, we have in no fundamental way brought into question the legitimacy of designating certain representations as collective, but we have begun to explore the limits of such representations and, in doing so we have preserved, perhaps more accurately than in the past, an image of a single experiencing mind.

My feeling is that any life-history approach which demands, at the outset, that an individual exhibit type-typical behaviors, denies, in an unearned and premature fashion, the very possibility of the individual. I recognize, of course, that this denial is a classical stance within the social sciences and that, within anthropology, it has become conventional to characterize "the individual" as a "Western" concept. Indeed, very often the "problem," the individual, can be quite neatly suspended in the solution of some more or less well-described collectivity, but for social scientists to demand across the board for all others what they would by reflex and reflection, I think, resist for themselves, is bad business.

Furthermore, I do not want to grant, as Geertz has, that the "natives" should be free "to call their souls their own," and that we should be content to catalogue not *what* they perceive, but what they perceive "by means of," "with," "through," and so forth. (Geertz, 1974: 125) I really want to know *what* the natives perceive, and I am sure they feel the same way about me.

Now, we may, I admit, have to be content with the "symbolic form" approach when faced with the traditional ethnographic task of constructing aggregate portraits of societies from limited field observations, but that is simply because we will not be able to find out and analyze what each and every individual is perceiving.

However, now that, at least in some quarters, history has been made safe for anthropologists—and in any case the natives themselves produce more and more of their own documents, the lack of which was, in the past, displayed as almost the constitutional *warrant* for social anthropology—we find that for Dharmapala, say, and for other "distinctive" individuals," very rich biographical and autobiographical documents are available, and it is possible, at least, to approach rather closely their "souls," as well as to challenge the sorts of culture and personality models that seem never to lose their anthropological appeal. Let me try to demonstrate this. What follows are treatments of several narrative, from Dharmapala's diaries of 1909 and 1920, and from a largely autobiographical article published in 1927.

"Queen Mab"

"I read many English poets, but I would always go back to Shelley," wrote Dharmapala, and of Shelley's works, "Queen Mab" was his favorite. (Dharmapala,1927: 723) "Read Queen Mab," wrote Dharmapala, and "it should be placed in the hands of young men. (ADS, Oct. 9, 1909) What to make of this affection for Shelley, a seer from the Mystic West? Or, more precisely, what to make of this affection for "Queen Mab?"

To begin with, the tone and structure of the narrative are in harmony, in many respects, with the astral fantasies of the western Theosophists with whom Dharmapala was associated. At the commencement of the story, Queen Mab, an ethereal personage capable of acting as an intermediary between this and the world beyond, awakens the slumbering *spirit* of a young girl, Ianthe. Ianthe has been "judged alone worthy of the envied boon," to be transported beyond the boundaries of the mundane world. This, in order that the spirit, clothed only in its "changeless purity, may know how soonest to accomplish the great goal for which it has its being."

(Shelley, 1972 [1812-13], I:123,180-184) At a remove of several heavenly levels, then, Queen Mab reviews for Ianthe the past, present and future shape of human history.

Mab's history of the world does not flatter humankind. It has been the unwavering instinct, of kings, courts and kingdoms, to achieve, through cruelty, greed and ignorance, a richly deserved oblivion. The present is no improvement, being marked chiefly by war, tyranny and drunkenness. The world is the plaything of dictatorial leaders who rely on a wretched citizenry which has, "in soft childhood's unsuspecting hour," learned the "forms of fawning loyalty." (IV:113)

Selfishness, "the cause and effect of tyranny, unblushing, hardened, sensual and vile," has, at the present time, appeared in a new form. This is commerce, a "venal interchange" of that which "natural kindness should hasten to supply." Commerce, actually, is precisely the career that, following in his father's footsteps, Don David might have been expected to take up. He would have received little encouragement, in this regard, from the fairy Mab, for whom it was a dread prospect that the "corrupted impulses of youth" might "prepare a life of horror from the blighting bane of commerce.". (V:38-40,190-93)

In fact, there is good evidence that Don David did not, in his youth, regard commerce as a blight to virtue and self-fulfillment, and that his failure to take up a career in his father's furniture business is best referred, not to *his*, but to his father's, decision.

> He did not care to have me following to learn his business and he had a clerk to do all the correspondence. Of course in those days the furniture business was not what it was ten years later. (Dharmapala, 1919, ADSU)

So, he was not at all horrified at the thought of a business career, but was prevented by his father from involvement with the management of the family firm. Here, for instance, from an unmarked notebook at the Sarnath Mahabodhi Society Library, is Dharmapala trying his hand at commercial sloganeering:

> We have been foremost for 59 years in the furniture trade. Our house has been an unrivalled reputation for the excellence of the work done. By supporting our firm you will help home industries and charitable institutions founded by us. (ADSU, unmarked notebook, probably from the 1920's)

Instead, his father had Don David placed, first, in a job in a notorial office and, later, in a clerkship at the Department of Public Instruction. The picture of Don David that emerges is of a rather passive young man, and one who, in spite of his spiritual aspirations, had retained career expectations conventional to his class.

His passivity was, I think, validated by such writings as "Queen Mab." Ironically, however, in his most expanded statement on the poem, he celebrates a theme of self-help that I could not locate in the poem.

> I have never ceased to love its lyric indignation against the tyrannies that man heaps on himself, and its passion for individual freedom. With its theory that man by his own efforts can lift himself to higher planes of spiritual happiness, Queen Mab was particularly appealing to a thoughtful Buddhist boy. (Dharmapala, 1927: 723)

Ianthe, of course, does *not* by her own efforts lift herself, but is conducted to those higher planes by an altruistic figure who arrives serendipitously at her side, rather, indeed, in the same way that the Theosophists arrived at Dharmapala's side. I think it is clear that, in his recollections of the impact and attraction of the poem, the man is attempting to recover, as decisive and self-motivated, a boyhood and youth that was contingent, dependent, and uncertain.

History, Culture and Religion: "Life Histories" of Dharmapala *by* Dharmapala

Perhaps there is something left over from Queen Mab in the following selection, written by Dharmapala in Calcutta during a period when he was under political internment at the request of the Ceylon Government, which had accused him of having supported anti-Muslim riots in Colombo in 1915. His brother, Edmund Hewavitartne, was one of many Sinhalese arrested in the wake of these riots, and he died in prison, which no doubt exacerbated Dharmapala's reactions. In the section that follows, written four years after the riots, Dharmapala placed events in a colonial and precolonial context:

> Why should the Ceylon Government continue to persecute me? I have done an act which they think I should have refrained from doing. The great crime of which I am guilty is that I wrote a few lines in the Sinhalese newspaper advising the Sinhalese people to train their children to be brave, and to retaliate if they are given a blow, and that they should train their children to show no fear to the white alien, and to give exercise to their arms by giving daily blows to a dummy figure of straw dressed in coat and trousers. Why did I write in this strain? In 1911 a letter appeared in the Times of Ceylon signed by an Englishman wherein the writer advised his compatriots to kick the Sinhalese and break their teeth if ever any one dares to approach an Englishman. When I read this letter my in-

dignation rose to a high pitch. And to take the brutal attack lying down I thought meant cowardice. In reply to the villain's letter I wrote in the Sinhala Bauddhalaya the few lines of exhortation. This was several years before the war.

Pale faced aliens did not like this and they wrote against me in their newspapers that Mr. Dharmapala by his preaching to the villagers that they are equal to the European [?] where formerly the villager salaamed him, now they do not. The European, when he lands in Ceylon, forgets his home surroundings and adopts an arrogant attitude towards the sons of the soil. This is quite unnecessary, for it eventually brings pain. The Sinhalese have been a democratically independent race for 2258 [?] years. In their history there is no mention made of caste differentiation. No-where do you find that there had been any kind of mutual animosity as you find in India, or in Ireland, or in the United States.

The King [of Kandy] was one of the people. He did not live a barbaric life of splendour. What he loved best he presented to the Sangha [the monastic community], or to the tooth-relic of the Buddha. He wore the simple garb that every well [to-do person?] wears. He visited the temple and was one of the crowd. Only on state occasions he would assume the crown and the royal robes.

As a boy, the crown prince even had to attend the Vihara to study under the Mahatheras [elder monks]. Everyone had to go through in the same manner in the

> Vihara. The psychology of the Vihara discipline must be investigated. Regularity, cleanliness, strict obedience, humility, were the ethics enforced by the Vihara. This early discipline had a remarkable effect in molding the habits of the tender body and mind. (Dharmapala Sarnath Diary, unmarked, 1919, see also Roberts' interesting comments on the events treated here by Dharmapala, Roberts 1997:1026)

"It is strange," wrote Shelley, that people are so often ruled by some tyrannical king and that "on this earth, not one wretch...rears an arm to dash him from his throne!" And so, apparently, thought Dharmapala. Yet is also clear that Dharmapala yearned for a king, the proper king, and it is interesting to see that the values he attributes to some unspecified Sinhalese monarch are those that he imagines would arise from a course of training, "in soft childhood's unsuspecting hour," that is quite unlike the regimen he proposed, in a preceding paragraph, and in rage, for children in colonial Ceylon. The problem, of course, is that he imagines a world of "us," where the king is "one of the people," but lives in a colonial world, the sort of world that Fanon claimed could only become a "Manichaean world," of "us" and "them." (Fanon, 1968:41-42)

He did not know, though, what world he was living in all the time. For instance, he was estranged from the remembered world extensively enough—traditional Buddhists had never before, as Dharmapala had, visited William James' psychology classes at Harvard—to import into his "memory" of the golden past a hint that "tradition" ought to be verified by western science: "the *psychology* of the vinaya discipline must be investigated." *Why* must it be *investigated*—which here appears to mean verified—if it is unproblematically the case that the traditional methods had a "remarkable" and wholly salutary effect on the young mind?

At the core of the conflict, I think, is that the "history" of the preceding passage is insufficiently distinct from Dharmapala's own *developmental history*. *This* is well illustrated in a third narrative segment:

> My family, which is Sinhalese, has been Buddhist without a break for twenty-two hundred years. I was born in Colombo, the capital of Ceylon, in the ancestral home, where my old mother still lives. My earliest memories are of cool coconut groves, fanned by breezes from the Indian Ocean, and of broad verandas overlooking gardens luxuriant with cinnamon and orange trees, Vermillion and purple rhododendron, and the blazing scarlet of the coral plant. The Garden was a paradise for a child. Humming birds hovered over giant blossoms, land-turtles basked in the sun and even snakes glided gracefully through the tangled underbrush; for, they knew they were making their home with Buddhists, who would not disturb them. (Dharmapala, 1927: 721)

Sinhalese and Buddhist without a break—this is truly the Dharmapala of Sinhalese nationalism, and he certainly did on occasion regard himself as a Buddhist figure in the style of an ancient Buddhist saint:

> May I pass away at the holy spot [Sarnath]. May my body be burnt there. May the ashes be distributed to be buried at Calcutta, Gaya, Bud Gaya, Colombo, and Kandy. (March 8, 1929)

This is also Dharmapala at his most grandiose, imagining himself as a modern day Sinhalese Buddhist saint, having brought the Dharma back from the place where it had been best protected and practiced: "The Sinhalese are the oldest historic Buddhist Aryan race, their history is the most authentic of Aryan history."

This went along with a great deal of ethnic and religious prejudice. Of course the British, for obvious reasons, "pale faced aliens," came in for abuse. as did other religions. "Don't trust the Brahmans, don't trust the Moslems, don't trust the British (ADSU: Oct 23, 1931) "How can the British fight or win a war, he asks, "when their leaders are all sexual perverts?" (ADSU: no date, Vol. 3) "My prayer is never to be born in a place where a Christian or a Mohammadon is born." (ADSU: mid-1920's?)

On occasion, though, *all* religions seemed to him to be false, as in the following list:

> Heathen religions: Christian, Mohammudan, Jews, Taoist, Confucians, Jains, polytheist, Scientific religions, Buddhists, Jains and Parsees (AD, August 27 1917)

But also consider the non-Sinhalese Buddhists. "The Tibetans were "dabbling with tantra," "the ancient Mahayanist forgot their Mahayana and went after tantra and mantra. They forgot our lord." (ADSU: April 8, 1933). "Went with Chinese monk to the Chinese restaurant. The Chinese are devils." (May 21 1918) The Burmese are "morons," with disgusting meat-eating habits. (June 12, 1918)

On the other hand, the same peoples were sometimes admired and respected in Dharmapala's diaries. And the Sinhalese, "his own" people, themselves came in for considerable abuse:

> Our Bhikkus are a set of indolent hounds, utterly indifferent to the people. They only know how to fill their stomachs and to repeat Pali gathas in a gramaphone fashion. Their

brains are atrophied." Jan 24 1916

Elsewhere, we read that the "Bhikkhus are drones. They are violating the vinaya." (Sept 25, 1930, Oct 3, 1930).

Returning to his father's garden, there are interesting things to be considered. For instance, he reports that he carried flowers to *both* Christian church and Buddhist temple. On Buddhist holidays, he carried flowers to the temple and laid them beneath an image of the Buddha," where the lotus and the white flowers of the iron tree were already piled high." and for his Catholic tutors, Joshua, Cassion and David, "I brought flowers from my father's garden to decorate their altars on feast days," (Dharmapala, 1927: 721)

There is, for 1925, a poignant diary entry written in Switzerland, where Dharmapala spent six months, at the expense of one of his American supporters, recovering from what seems to be—it is difficult to get a diagnosis from this distance—a nervous and physical collapse. The crisis began in Switzerland, where Dharmapala was meeting with a wealthy American patron and friend, Charles T. Strauss, who had first met Dharmapala after the World Parliament of Religions in 1893. In a Lucerne Hospital, and complaining of a variety of ailments, "palpitations, inflamed testes. piles, swelling feet, anemia and sciatica." (July 16, 1925) He reports taking sleeping medications—not specified—but that he still is "waking at 3 am often." (July 23, 1925).

He was the beneficiary of various of the treatments of the day, "carbonic acid baths," for instance, and "electrical treatment, wrapped in four blankets, etc." (ADSU: July 14, 1925), He had an operation for the hydrocele, but it continued to bother him until the end of his life: In 1929, for instance, he was hospitalized (in Calcutta), and given morphine for pain. "I feel disgustingly loathsome that I shall have to die with a swollen scrotum. The people would blame me that I had not died a pure brahmachari." And, in general after his collapse in Switzerland, he continued to suffer painfully from a range of chronic problems.

Here is one list, from among many that he entered into his diaries: 1. swelling of feet, 2. shortness of breath, 3. distension of stomach, 4. decrease of urine." He recognizes these latter as symptoms of serious heart disease. (ADSU: various entries, July-September 1929). Throughout, he is thinking about the "Mahatma Letters" and invoking Koot Hoomi. Returning now to Lucerne, a month prior to his leaving the hospital, he reports attending a church service:

> Father Kugler spent much time at the altar in worshipping the relic. I told Jehovah to practice Loving Kindness, and wished St. Anna should see the coming Budhha Mettyyo [Maitreya]. How carefully the R.C. priests observe the rituals. (ADSU, August 30, 1925)

Here is "loving kindness," and it should be noted that Dharmapala often headed his diary entries "may all be happy." It is clear, if one reads the diaries with sympathy, that he really longed to feel this loving kindness. Still, six years later Dharmapala could still bring himself to express such sentiments as "the imbecility shown by Jesus in Gethsemane is an indication of his cowardly nature." (ADSU: July 23, 1931)

So, Dharmapala was often angry. Also, often conflicted about individuals or communities. No matter, for instance, about the pale-faced aliens, they were the best one could hope for. They were "looking after" the Buddhist monuments:

> Rejoice and be glad that the British are here. They are better than the Japanese, or Chinese, or Tibetans, or Indians. May the British people become followers of our lord. (ADSU: April 13, 1933)

It is not too much to say, I think, that Dharmapala could not find long-term satisfaction in any institution or community. All of this is left out of the garden which was "a paradise for a child." We are sometimes presented by Dharmapala with a very fully constructed and culturally correct type of person—even the snakes are alive to the local cultural ideal. But, of course, this sort of history, as "total" as can be in the sense that twenty-two hundred years of unchallenged Buddhist faith seem unproblematically sedimented in the mind of one particular Sinhalese boy, yields a picture of some Ceylon where it would be unnecessary to advise children "to be brave, and to retaliate when they are given a blow."

If, on the other hand, much is left out of the garden, it is still a very full place, full of movement, ancestry, and the self-image of a man who has painfully manufactured—out of tradition, opportunity and accident, in a modern colonial and international world—a career of action and accomplishment. In this somewhat specialized essay I have highlighted the tendency of anthropologists to rely on some version of the cultural exemplification model for the life history. Dharmapala, in his "garden-paradise" voice, employed a mode of thought very similar to this. In his attempt to place himself within an unbroken stream of Buddhist tradition, Dharmapala depresses the particularities of his own biography and seems, for a moment, not to be, in Radin's phrase, "any definite personage," and thereby eligible, so to say, to be a number of different people.

BIBLIOGRAPHY

Amunugama, Sarath, 1985, "*Anagarika Dharmapala* (1864-1033) *and the Transformation of Sinhala Buddhist Organization in a Colonial Setting,*" in Social Science Information, Sage, London, Beverly Hills and New Delhi, 24, #4:697-730.

Angrosino, Michael V., 1976, "*The Use of Autobiography as Life History: the Case of Albert Gomes,*" in Ethos, Summer 1976, Vol. 4, #2, 133-154.

Arnold, Sir Edwin, 1896, *East and West, being papers reprinted from the "Daily Telegraph" and other sources*, London, Longmans, Green and Company.

Barnett, Yukiko Sumi 2004, "*India in Asia: Okawa Shumei's Pan-Asian Thought and His Idea of India in Early Twentieth-Century Japan,*" in Journal of the Oxford Historical Society: 1-6.

Barua, B.M., 1934, *Gaya and Buddha Gaya*, Calcutta, Indian Research Institute.

Beal, S., 1881, "*Indian Travels of Chinese Buddhists,*" in Indian Antiquary, Volume X.

Beglar, J., 1887, *Revised List of Ancient Monuments in Bengal*, Calcutta, Bengal Secretariat Press.

Bharati, A., 1970, "*Pilgrimage Sites and Indian Civilization,*" in Chapters in Indian Civilization, Editor, J. Elder, Dubuque, Iowa, Kendall and Hunt.

Bharati, A., 1963, "*Pilgrimage in the Indian Tradition,*" in History of Religions, Summer, Volume 3, #1:135-167.

Blavatsky, H.P., 1954, *Collected Writings*, Vol. VI, Blavatsky Writings Publication Fund, Los Angeles.

Boas, Franz, 1943, "*Recent Anthropology*," in Science, Vol. 98:311-14; 334-37.

Burney, Colonel H., 1836, "*Translation of an Inscription in the Burmese Language, discovered at Buddha Gaya in 1833*," in AR, Vol. XX:161-89.

Campbell, Bruce F., 1980, *Ancient Wisdom Revived: A History of the Theosophical Movement*, Berkeley, University of California Press

Chakravarti, C., 1956, "*The Cult of the Buddha among Brahmanic Hindus*," in Journal of the Bihar Research Institute, Buddha Jayanti Special Issue #1.

Chaudhuri, Sukomal, 1982, *Contemporary Buddhism in Bangladesh*, Calcutta, Atisha Memorial Publishing Society.

Clifford, James, 1989, *The Predicament of Culture*, Cambridge, Ma., Harvard University Press.

Cohn, Bernard, 1974, "*The Role of the Gosains in the Economy of Eighteenth and Nineteenth Century Upper India*," in Symposium on the Sacred Complex in India, editors, L.P. Vidyarthi and Makhan Jha, Ranchi, Bagla Press:88-95.

Cohn, Bernard, 1985. "*The Command of Language and the Language of Command*," in Subaltern Studies No. 4, Writings on South Asian History and Society, Edited by Ranajit Guha, Delhi: Oxford University Press, 1985. 276-329

Crooke, W., 1896, *Tribes and Castes of the North-Western Provinces and Oudh*, Volume II, Calcutta, Government Printing Office.

Cunningham, Alexander,1972 [1871], *Archaeological Survey of India Report, Volume I*, Delhi, Indological Book House.

Cunningham, Alexander, 1966 [1873] *Archaeological Survey of India Report, Volume III*, Delhi, Indological Book House.

Cunningham, Alexander, 1966 [1874] *Archaeological Survey of India Report, Volume VIII*, Delhi, Indological Book House.

Cunningham, Alexander, 1968 [1879] *Archaeological Survey of India Report, Volume I*, Delhi, Indological Book House.

Dharmapala, Anagarika, 1927, "*On the Eightfold Noble Path*," in Asia, Volume 27, #9.

Dharmapala, Anagarika, 1918, *Buddhism in Its Relationship to Hinduism*, Calcutta, Mahabodhi Society.

Dharmapala, Anagarika, 1917, *The Arya Dharma of Sakya Muni, Gautama Buddha*, or the *Ethics of Self-discipline*, Calcutta, Mahabodhi Society.

Dumont, L., 1966, *Homo Hierarchicus*, London, University of Chicago Press.

Farquhar, J.N., 1925, "*The Fighting Ascetics of India*," originally in The Bulletin of the John Rylands Library, Volume 9, No. 2, July 1925, reprinted for private circulation.

Fanon, Franz, 1968, *The Wretched of the Earth*, New York, Grove Press.

Geertz, Clifford, 1974, " '*From the Native's point of View*': On the Nature of Anthropological Understanding," in Bulletin of the American Academy, vol. 28 no. 1 (1974), pp. 26-45.

Giri, Swami Sadananda, 1976, *Society and Sannyasin*, Varanasi, published by the author.

Grierson, G.A., 1893, *Notes on the District of Gaya*, Calcutta, Bengal Secretrariat Press.

Griswold, Alexander B., 1965, "*The Holy Land Transported*," in Paranavitana Felicitation Volume, Colombo, M.D. Gunasena: 173-222.

Guruge, Ananda W.P., 1984, *From the Living Fountains of Buddhism*, Colombo, Ministry of Cultural Affairs.

Hamilton, Walter, 1828, *The East-India Gazetteer, Vol. I*, London, Parbur, Allen and co.

Hamilton-Buchanan, Francis, 1925, *Journal of Francis Buchanan* (afterwards Hamilton) kept during the Survey of the Districts of Patna and Gaya in 1811-1812), ed. and with notes and intro by V.H. Jackson, Patna, Government Printing - Bihar and Orissa.

Hamilton-Buchanan, Francis, 1937, *An Account of the Districts of Bihar and Patna in 1811-1812*, Bihar and Orissa Research Society, Calcutta, Calcutta Oriental Press.

Hobsbawm, Eric and Terence Ranger (eds) (1983) *The Invention of Tradition.* Cambridge: Cambridge University Press.

Imam, Abu, 1966, *Sir Alexander Cunningham and the Beginnings of Indian Archaeology*, Dacca, Asiatic Society of Pakistan.

Jacques, C., 1979, "*Gaya Mahatmya-Introduction*," in Purana, Volume 21, #2.

Jha, J.S. 1966, *Records of the Judge and Magistrate of Patna for the years* 1820-25, K.P. Jayaswal Research Institute, Patna.

Klostermaier, K., 1979, "*Hindu Views of Buddhism*," in Canadian Contributions to Buddhist Studies, Editor, R. Amore, Waterloo, Wilfred Laurie University Press.

Kluckhohn, Clyde, 1945, *The Use of Personal Documents in Anthropology*, SSRC, Bulletin 55.

Mandlebaum, David, 1973, "*The Study of Life History: Gandhi*," in Current Anthropology, Vol. 14, #3, June: 177- 206

Mackenzie, C., 1902, "*Extracts from the Journal of Colonel Mackenzie's Jain Pandit of his route from Calcutta to Gaya in 1820*," in Indian Antiquary, Volume 31, February:62-75.

Marcus, George E. and Michael M.J. Fischer,1986, *Anthropology as Cultural Critique*, Chicago, University of Chicago Press.

"Maitreya," 1925, *The Buddha-Mimamsa*, or the Buddha and His relation to the Religion of the Vedas, Calcutta, Thacker, Spink & Co.

Malalgoda, K., 1976, *Buddhism in Sinhalese Society,1750-1900*, Berkeley, University of California Press.

Markham, C.R., 1879, second edition, *Narratives of the Mission of George Bogle and the Journey of Thomas Manning to Lhasa*, London, Trubner Company.

Martin, Montgomery, 1838, *The History, Antiquities, Topography, and Statistics of Eastern India*, Volume 1, London, W.H. Allen.

Mitra, R., 1878, *Buddha Gaya*, Calcutta, Bengal Secretariat Press.

Mitra, Rajendralala, 1878, *Buddha Gaya*, The Hermitage of Sakya Muni, Calcutta, Bengal Secretariat Press.

Money, Alonzo, and Charles Hollings, 1886, *Correspondence Relating to the Special Services Rendered at Gaya in Bihar*, Bengal, East Indies, Florence, L'Arte Della Stampa.

Muller, F. Max, 1901, *Last Essays*, Second Series, London, Longmans, Green, and Co.

Narayan, S, 1980, "*The Sacred Complex at Rajgir*," in Aspects of Social Anthropology in India, edited by L.P. Vidyarthi, B.N. Sahay and P.K. Dutta, New Delhi, Classical Publications.

Obeyesekere, Gananath, 1976, "*Personal Identity and Cultural Crisis: The Case of Anagarika Dharmapala*," in The Biographical Process, Editors, Frank E. Reynolds and Donald Capps.

Obeyesekere, Gananath, 1975, "*Sinhalese-Buddhist Identity in Ceylon*," in Ethnic Identity, editors, G. DeVos and L. Romanucci-Ross, Chicago, University of Chicago Press.

Obeyesekere, Gananath, 1972, "*Religious Symbolism and Political Change in Ceylon*," in The Two Wheels of Dhamma, American Academy of Religion, No. 3, Chambersburg.

O'Flaherty, Wendy, 1976, *The Origins of Evil in Hindu Mythology,* Berkeley, University of California Press.

Okakura, Kakuzo, 1903, *The Ideals of the East*, New York, The Century Co..

Olivelle, Patrick, 1977, *Vasudevasrama Yatidharmaprakasa* - A Treatise on World Renunciation, Part 2, De Nobili Research Society, Vienna.

Olcott, Henry Steel, 1931 *Old Diary Leaves*, Madras, Adyar, Theosophical Publishing House.

Olcott, Henry Steel, 1883, *A collection of Lectures on Theosophy and Archaic Religions delivered in India and Ceylon*, Madras Theosophical Society, Madras.

Olcott, Henry Steel, 1882, *A Buddhist Catechism According to the Canon of the Southern Church*, Chicago, Open Court Publishing.

O'Malley, L.S.S., 1935, *Popular Hinduism*, Cambridge University Press, Cambridge.

O'Malley, L.S.S., 1965, *The Indian Civil Service, 1601-1930*, London, Frank Cass & Co.

Patil, D.R. 1963, *The Antiquarian Remains in Bihar*, Kashi Prasad Jayaswal Research Institute, Patna.

Petech, L., 1950, "*The Missions of Bogle and Turner according to the Tibetan Texts*," in T'oung Pao, Volume 39.

Prasad, Rajendra, 1957, *Autobiography*, Bombay, Asia Publishing House.

Prothero, Stephan, 1996, *The White Buddhist: The Asian Odyssey of Henry Steel Olcott*, Indiana University Press.

Radin, Paul, 1920, *The Autobiography of a Winnabago Indian*, Berkeley, University of California Press.

Reischauer, Edwin O., 1980, *The Japanese*, Harvard University Press, Cambridge.

Roerich, G., 1959, *Biography of Dharmasvamin*, Patna, Jayaswal Research Institute.

Ronaldshay, Earl, 1928, *The Life of Lord Curzon*, London, Ernest Benn, Ltd.

Roy Chaudhury, P.C., 1958, *Gaya Old Records*, Bihar, Patna, Secretariat Press.

Sapir, Edward, 1938, "*Foreward,*" *to Walter Dyk's Son of Old Man Hat*, New York, Harcourt, Brace and Co.

Shelley, Percy Bysshe, 1972, *The Complete Poetical Works of Percy Bysshe Shelley*, editor, Neville Rogers, Oxford, The Clarendon Press.

Sinnett, A.P., 1969, ninth Edition, [1881], *The Occult World*, London, Theosophical Publishing House.

Stadtner, D.M., 1991, "*A Fifteenth-century Royal Monument in Burma and the Seven Stations in Buddhist Art*" in Art Bulletin, Vol. 73 No. 1: 39-52.

Stenerson, Douglas C., 1991, "*Some impressions of the Buddha: Dreiser and Sir Edwin Arnold's the light of Asia,*" in Canadian Review of American Studies, No.3 Winter: 387-405.

Tagore, Surendranath, 1984, "*Some Reminiscences by Surendranath Tagore,*" *in Okakura Kakuzo: Collected English Writings*, editor Sunao Nakmura, Tokyo, Heibonsha Limited.

Tambiah, S.J., 1976, *World Conqueror and World Renouncer*, London and Ithaca, Cornell University Press.

Temple, Richard, 1877, *The Minutes of Sir Richard Temple, Lieutenant-Governor of Bengal*, Bombay, Government Central Press.

Tillet, Gregory, 1982, *The Elder Brother: A Biography of Charles Webster Leadbeater*, London, Routledge and Kegan Anthropology (Northern Illinois University).

Trevithick, Alan, 1999, "*British Achaeologists, Hindu Mahants, and Bumese Buddhists: The Mahabodhi Temple at Bodh Gaya, 1811-1877,*" in , in Modern Asian Studies (Cambridge), 33, 3: 635-656. .

Trevithick, Alan, 1990 "*Some Structural and Sequential Aspects of the British Imperial Assemblages at Delhi ", 1877-1911*, in Modern Asian Studies (Cambridge), July 1990: 561-578.

Trevithick, Alan, 1992, "*Anthropological 'Life Histories' and the 'Life History of Anagarika Dharmapala'* ," in Journal of Anthropology, (Northern Illinois), Vol. 7, #1-2:91-111.

Turner, V. W. (1969). *The ritual process: Structure and anti-structure*. Chicago: Aldine.

Turner, V., 1974, *Dramas, Fields and Metaphors: Symbolic Action in Human Society*, Ithaca, Cornell University Press.

Turner, E., and V. Turner, 1978, *Image and Pilgrimage in Christian Culture*, Oxford, Columbia University Press.

Vidyarthi, L.P., 1978,[1961] *The Sacred Complex in Hindu Gaya*, Concept Publishing, Delhi.

Vidyarthi, L.P., 1959, "*The Extensions of an Indian Priestly Caste," in Man in India*, Volume 39, January-March:28-35.

Vivekananda, Swami, 1926, *The Complete Works of Swami Vivekananda*, Almora, Advaita Ashrama.

Wallace, A.F.C., 1956, "*Revitalization Movements," in American Anthropologist*, Vol. 58, April: 264-281

Wright, Brooks, 1957, *Interpreter of Buddhisn to the West: Sir Edwin Arnold*, Bookman, New York.

INDEX